Contesting History

Contesting History
Narratives of Public History

JEREMY BLACK

B L O O M S B U R Y
LONDON • NEW DELHI • NEW YORK • SYDNEY

Bloomsbury Academic
An imprint of Bloomsbury Publishing Plc

50 Bedford Square	1385 Broadway
London	New York
WC1B 3DP	NY 10018
UK	USA

www.bloomsbury.com

Bloomsbury is a registered trade mark of Bloomsbury Publishing Plc

First published 2014

© Jeremy Black, 2014

Jeremy Black has asserted his right under the Copyright, Designs and Patents Act, 1988, to be identified as Author of this work.

British Library Cataloguing-in-Publication Data
A catalogue record for this book is available from the British Library.

ISBN: HB: 978-1-4725-1951-1
PB: 978-1-4725-1950-4
ePDF: 978-1-4725-1952-8
ePub: 978-1-4725-1953-5

Library of Congress Cataloging-in-Publication Data
A catalog record for this book is available from the Library of Congress.

Typeset by Fakenham Prepress Solutions, Fakenham, Norfolk NR21 8NN
Printed and bound in India

For
Mark and Rosemary Yallop

CONTENTS

PREFACE

History is the past and the accounts offered of the past. As such, history covers different experiences and perceptions and is, at once, both objective and subjective. Accounts offered of the past provide the subject of this book, but it deals with a particular type, or rather range, of these accounts. The focus is on the uses of history to construct narratives of state and national identity and purpose, and on the resulting contests.

Thus, there is concern here with instrumentality, with the uses of history in a particular perspective. That, of course, scarcely exhausts the subject of the uses and contesting of history, but this approach exemplifies the point that history proceeds through the accounts offered of the past. And so with this book. Others will want different interpretations of the subject, and there are first-rate books for them accordingly.[1] Here, although I touch on other topics, ranging from family narratives to the impact of film, my prime concern is the roles of state and nation, and this concern has strongly influenced the selection of case studies.

A focus on state and nation may appear somewhat dated in a discipline now greatly, and successfully, concerned with cultural approaches and, at the level of state and nation, with transnationalism. Transnationalism, a term now often used in book proposals, titles and sales literature,[2] is both a means of analysis and, like other historiographical and conceptual approaches, a value-system, if not ideology. Transnationalism presents the present and future in terms of international communities that are not contained within, or expressed in terms of, national states. Instead, there is an emphasis on universal values and institutions, expressed in and through human rights and international courts, as well as on the extent to which communications, culture, trade and, in particular, migration are making national criteria invalid.

Transnationalism is then read back into the past, a process also seen in Europe with calls for 'the Europeanization of memory', specifically of the Second World War.[3] On the global scale, David Cannadine, a leading American-based British historian and co-author of a recent book on teaching British history, has recently emphasized the need for the presentation of history 'not to assist in constructing the artifice of discrete, self-constrained, self-regarding, and mutually exclusive groups', but, instead, to focus on 'humanity's essential (but under-studied) unity'.[4] This is an approach that contrasts with the more traditional method of comparative history. The transnational emphasis thus links with important currents in academic work, notably toward transnational and world history, as well as the study of identities grounded on ethnicity, religion and gender. In turn, these interests affect both the historiography of present work and the way in which the historiography of earlier periods are assessed.[5]

Separately, the emphasis on this unity of humanity is certainly conducive to a left-liberal internationalist approach, notably in Europe, but also in the USA, an approach to world politics and history that is uneasy about many of the marked changes, recent, current and apparently imminent, in the global economic and political system. From this perspective, the 'end of history' that was depicted in the 1990s, in response to the close of the ideological strife of the Cold War,[6] can therefore, in the case of the subject of history, as well as of culture more generally, be descriptive of the apparent inroads of globalization and modernity. These allegedly constitute a rival to a more humane transnationalism. Globalization is presented as a universal neo-liberal capitalist order apparently threatening distinctive cultures, and the latter are viewed positively.

Conversely, such cultures can be treated in a more hostile light, and the 'end of history' can be prescriptive and proscriptive, as a demand that the oxygen of attention and support be removed from nationalist responses to globalization, responses grounded in history. From a cosmopolitan perspective, these responses are held to be the ideology of the xenophobic Right.

Whether considered attractive or unattractive, a sense and presentation of group-identity therefore is a key element in human society. Furthermore, tensions, indeed conflict, between such groups are a fundamental driver in human history. The practice of arguing that identities are imagined and constructed,[7] rather than inherent, has led to a tendency to underrate the significance of what is thus contextualized, as well as to underplay the extent to which identities and aspirations could reflect widespread grass-roots desires, as well as governmental manipulation. Indeed, as this book shows, the role of the 'history wars', disputes over interests and identity that link past and present, that are so important in the present world, cannot be readily understood outside the context of state and nation, each of which can be seen as more complex than agencies for and of governmental manipulation. That both state and nation have meanings that are fluid and contingent does not make them less significant. In fact, the opposite, for both state and nation can therefore adapt to changing circumstances.

Moreover, this is a work of individual scholarship and, as such, I offer my own perspective. I have spent my career addressing topics such as diplomatic, military and high political history that others, mistakenly, have not regarded as relevant or as intellectually at the cutting edge. The revenge of time, however, indicates that many of the assumptions of much scholarly work in recent decades, for example of the weakness or marginality of religion, have proved flawed. I do not feel any need to apologise for taking an unpopular approach. Instead, I offer this book in the view that an approach focused on states and nations offers an effective introduction to past and present, although, like all accounts, scarcely a complete one.

Such an approach certainly addresses the context within which educational policies are defined because, at this level, transnationalism is weak. The relationship between politics, educational policy and school curricula makes this clear. In Australia, for example, controversy in the 1990s surrounded the government-sponsored process of drafting a national curriculum for high schools, not least because, as John Howard, the conservative Prime Minister from 1996 to 2007, insisted, history had been central to the entire project of educating a nation of Australians.[8] Similarly, the content of the National Museum of Australia in Canberra proved highly contentious, and notably in the treatment, in the First Australians Gallery, of the Aborigines, the population displaced by Western colonists from 1788. Howard was angered by what critics referred to as 'black armband history', an emphasis on the hardship inflicted on the Aborigines.

In Britain, the contents of the historical section of the National Curriculum was to the fore as this book was being written, and thus offers an obvious case study. The appointment of Michael Gove as Secretary of State for Education in the Conservative-led coalition government established in 2010 led to a sharpening and refocusing of the debate about what should be taught in schools, and over how it should be taught. The debate became more controversial because it was located in the midst of a vexed and longstanding discussion about the nature of British national identity.

The teaching of history was presented as having public purpose in this context, and to an extent not shared by any other subject. Indeed, the distinctive nature of the subject as the sole one to be scrutinized by politicians led to some complaints by historians.[9] However, critics generally failed to acknowledge that the return for this scrutiny included the place and time devoted to history in the curriculum. The time devoted is not as much as it could have been: history as a school subject in England and Wales is compulsory to age 14, not, as has been suggested, 16.

Nevertheless, history has more curriculum time, and a bigger role, than economics or politics or sociology. Indeed, and not solely in Britain, the apparent role of teaching history in sustaining a sense of national identity ensured that it received a degree of governmental support that it would otherwise not have had. This continues to be the case. At the same time, this support brought governmental attention and political scrutiny, or what could be presented as political scrutiny.

And so with the discussion in Britain about changes to the National Curriculum, discussion that rose to a height in 2013. In part, the reforms proposed a more coherent account of the national past, with a chronological framework and progression that had hitherto been weak, if not lacking. That discussion, which was part of a pattern of longstanding contention on the issue,[10] saw strong, sometimes virulent, hostility: from professionals who disliked government interference and complained of a lack of expertise on the part of government,[11] and from those suspicious that the interference was designed to foster a nationalist and conservative agenda.[12]

There were similar debates about history in schools during the Conservative government of Margaret Thatcher (1979–90), with Kenneth Baker, Secretary of State for Education, taking a close interest in the subject. The history curriculum has also been widely debated elsewhere as a politico-educational issue, as with the Teaching American History programme in the USA.

Suspicions about a nationalist and conservative agenda had also been the response in Britain in the late 1990s and the late 2000s to proposals for a museum of national history, proposals supported by Baker. Thus, paranoia was brought in to play a major role, as so often in the case of 'history wars'. More cogently, there were concerns in the 2010s that the National Curriculum for history, as initially proposed, was simply too crowded and demanding for the time actually available to teachers.

For an instructive text, it is worth noting the letter from a number of historians (including myself) published in *The Times* of 27 February 2013. As an instance of the process by which history was 'used', or rather employed, as part of a public debate, the letter was organised and drafted by Chris Skidmore, a Conservative MP with history books to his credit. That this genesis was not apparent from the letter indicated the problems with letting texts stand on their own. The letter in *The Times* stated the case for the use of history to provide a social good. Instructive passages included:

> [...] history has a special role in developing in each and every individual a sense of their own identity as part of a historic community with worldwide links, interwoven with the ability to analyze and research the past that remains essential for a full understanding of modern society. It should be made possible for every pupil to take in the full narrative of our history throughout every century [...] to place history back at the centre of the national curriculum and make it part of the common culture of every future citizen.

Allowing for profound differences in political context and culture, the last has been an abiding aspect of the use of history across the centuries.

I was initially approached, in 2012, to write a second edition of my *Using History* (London, 2005), but, as I made clear from the outset of the project, this book is different in its organization and its coverage. In one respect, however, the book is similar. There is a deliberate attempt to offer numerous examples, notably from around the world in recent decades. All too often, the coverage of historical controversies in books of this type focuses on a small number of well-ventilated examples. In contrast, the intention here is to indicate the range of 'history wars' and their central role in political consciousness across the world.

At the same time, there will be the standard scholarly concern with context and analysis. It is all too easy to offer a political reading of public history that asserts a clear account of causation and fails to capture a situation of greater complexity. For example, the appearance, in 2009, as a searchable database, of *The Records of the Scottish Parliament*[13] can be readily linked to pressure for independence backed by the Scottish National Party, or at least for the separate identity for Scotland represented by the establishment of a new Scottish parliament after the Labour victory in the 1997 general election. In practice, however, although both parties supported the project, the initial funding was provided by the Conservative government in 1996, a government opposed to such a parliament, let alone to independence for Scotland.

As a reminder, at the same time, of variety in national projects, and thus of the danger of deploying only one example, the *Dictionary of Irish Biography*, launched in 2009, and a product of Ireland's earlier economic boom, was presented by the Prime Minister, Brian Cowen, as 'a powerful statement of our Irish nationality', one that freed the country from dependence on its British counterpart, the *Oxford Dictionary of National Biography*. Published, in the event, by a British press, the Dictionary faced the problem of reconciling Ireland as a geographical space with the more potent idea of the Irish as a people of ancestral descent, a nation.[14] Similar problems are encountered across the world.

A more potent contrast is that between the use of history as a positive response to the needs of the new, and, on the other hand, its employment as a negative response to change with the critique of the new framed in terms of tradition. Thus, this book addresses the recent focus upon public history, the presentation and representation of the past, to and by audiences, a practice centrally linked to the use and contesting of history.

I am most grateful to Frances Arnold for asking me to write this book and for helping me to clarify the objective, and to Emily Drewe for seeing the book through. I have also benefited greatly from the advice of Bill Gibson, Frédéric Saffroy, Harold Tanner and Neil York on earlier drafts, and of Helen Birkett, James Chapman, Robert Guyver, Levi Roach and Kaushik Roy on individual chapters. It is easy to glance over such comments, but I know the hard work such reading and commenting entails, and I am most grateful for it. I am also very grateful to those with whom I have discussed the topic, including Michael Axworthy, Brian Blouet, Hugo de Burgh, Mike Cailes, Tom Holland, Erik Jensen, Tony Stockwell and Robert Tombs.

In thinking about and working on this book, I have profited from the opportunity to travel widely, and to discuss the topic with many foreign academics and non-academics. In particular, I derived valuable information and ideas from visits in 2011–13 to Austria, Belgium, Belize, Brunei, Bulgaria, Canada, China, Colombia, Costa Rica, Cuba, France,

Georgia, Germany, Honduras, Hungary, India, Japan, Malaysia, Mexico, Nicaragua, the Philippines, Portugal, Qatar, Singapore, Slovakia, Sri Lanka, Turkey, Ukraine, and the USA.

I have also benefited from having advised the British Post Office on the treatment of history in stamps, from being a trustee in the unsuccessful attempt to establish a museum of British national history, from being asked in 2013 to offer 'constructive criticism' on the proposed new British national curriculum for history, and from the opportunity to lecture at George Mason, High Point and Mary Washington universities, the University of North Carolina at Chapel Hill, the Qatar Campus of Texas A and M University, and the College of William and Mary, to the University of Oxford Summer School, to Brigham Young's Oxford programme, to the Third Annual London Film and Media Conference, to the 2013 Chalke Valley History Festival, to the 2013 Green Mondays conference on the Next Industrial Revolution, to a 2013 conference held in Exeter on 'The Tory World: A Deep History of the Tory Party and its Views of Britain's World Role', and to the Foreign Policy Research Institute and the World Affairs Council in Philadelphia, New York and Wilmington. Teaching for the 'Grand Challenge' programme at Exeter in 2013 and for the University summer school proved instructive in helping shape ideas. Moreover, the chance to contribute to radio and television programmes on British, Georgian, Russian, German and Turkish history proved very helpful, as did advising for two episodes of 'Who Do You Think You Are?'.

Lastly, friendship as ever for me, has been very important during this project, both psychologically and materially, notably in offering company and hospitality. It therefore gives me great pleasure to dedicate this book to two good friends and fellow Devonians, Mark and Rosemary Yallop.

PROLOGUE: THE NATIONAL MUSEUM OF MALAYSIA

The National Museum of Malaysia, located in the country's largest city, the almost aggressively modern and fast-growing Kuala Lumpur, is an attractive and well-presented museum containing four galleries, each stacked with interesting exhibits. The museum also amply displays how history is employed to make points helpful to the process of national mythmaking. A caveat is in order before criticism appears the order of the day. First, in this respect, Malaysia is no different to many states, for example neighbouring Singapore, and is better than some. Exhibits in other museums can be similarly 'deconstructed', and the National Museum of Malaysia is less egregious than many. Secondly, there are problems, for every country, in providing a clear, accessible, coherent and short account of national history. Thirdly, the purpose of museum contents is not that of satisfying historians, but, rather, the general public and in a context complicated by the issues of post-colonialism.

The National Museum very much serves the case for Malaysia in two important respects: first, in the very issue of what to cover and, secondly, in terms of what is said to visitors. As far as the first is concerned, the key decision was that, in what became the capital of the new state, first Malaya, which gained independence from British rule in 1957, and, subsequently, from 1963, Malaysia, the museum should be national. It was constructed on the site of the museum of the local princely state, Selangor, which had offered a different perspective. Built in 1906, under Sultan Ala-ud-Din Sulayman Shah, the Selangor Museum was damaged by Allied bombing in 1945 at a time when Malaya, a British colony, was occupied by Japanese forces. The museum was later demolished to make way for the National Museum, which was opened in 1963 in accordance with the wishes of the Prime Minister, Abdul Rahman Putra al-Haj, that a national museum be founded.

The Director from 1958 to 1963 was Mervyn Sheppard, a former member of the Malayan Civil Service who had become a Malay, converting to Islam and adopting a Malay name. Sheppard was also the founding

Director of the National Archives. He wanted the design of the new museum to include the architecture of the royal Malays and succeeded in this goal thanks to support from the Prime Minister.[1]

In its coverage, the National Museum treats Malaysia as a unit, whereas, in practice, it is a creation only of 1963, gaining its present shape in 1965 when Singapore left the federation. As a result of the focus on Malaysia, rather than Malaya, parallels are noted between its constituent parts, Malaya, Sabah and Sarawak, whereas relationships between the two latter and the other parts of the island of Borneo-Brunei (also part of the north coast) and Kalimantan (Indonesian Borneo, the bulk of the nation), are seriously downplayed.

So also in the case of links between Malaya and neighbouring Thailand (earlier Siam). The relationship between them was less clear in practice than what is presented in the museum, where the links between Thailand and north-west Malaya are essentially presented in terms of Thai aggression and Malay nationalism. That element is a less than complete account, and certainly underplays other aspects of the Thai-Malay relationship.

Searching for an exemplary past, the National Museum focuses on one appropriate for the constitutional system, religious affiliation, political party, and public ideology, dominating modern Malaysia, and, more particularly, modern Malaya. The focus for this past is on the Malay sultanate of Melaka, a spelling used (although not in all exhibits) in preference to the Malacca more familiar to Europeans. Founded in about 1400, this sultanate is presented as both successful and impressive: 'This multiracial society was peaceful and harmonious', a reference to the public ideology of modern Malaysia, with its stress on good relations between Malays, Chinese, Indians, the indigenous peoples of Sabah and Sarawak, and others. Thus: 'The immigrant groups had no difficulty integrating with the local residents ... they accepted foreign influence into their culture when it was suitable and did not conflict with Islam.'

The last is a reference to the ideology of the current government, specifically its notion of conditional Westernization, but also a stress on Islam, the religion of the majority of Malay inhabitants, who make up about 55 per cent of the total population and dominate the Barisan Nasional, the governing coalition since independence. Moreover, the emphasis on racial harmony in Melaka implies that Malaysia's communal tensions are a consequence of British colonialism.

However, any stress on Islam leaves the Chinese and Indian population of Malaysia in a somewhat anomalous position, as they have long been since the affirmative action policies disadvantaging them that were adopted by the government in the early 1970s and pushed anew by Dato Seri Mahathir Bin Mohamad, the Prime Minister from 1981 to 2003 and a populist nationalist. This situation contrasts with the more successful policy of ethnic and religious inclusion in neighbouring Singapore. The National Museum of Singapore, formerly the Singapore History Museum, offers an account of Singapore that focuses on the different traditions melded in the city.

In the National Museum of Malaysia, Melaka is presented as a centre of intellectual development under Islam, as well as having an exemplary politics: 'The concepts of fairness, of equality of persons, and of discussion and consultation were practised in government and made Melaka prosperous and respected.' Although there is only limited information available on the regional position, it is suggested that, at its height, Melaka's power and influence covered nearly the whole of the Malay peninsula, as well as several states in Sumatra. In another glance at the modern situation, Melaka's links with China are presented as harmonious, which does, indeed, appear to have been the case for the fifteenth century, both politically and commercially, and is certainly a convenient claim in offering a modern prospectus that is not dominated by the West.

The impact of the West is presented in the museum in terms that emphasize the vitality of local resistance. That Melaka did not fall in 1511 to the first Portuguese assault, but only to latter attack, is stressed, as is the role of assistance from Johor and Aceh (the key regional powers) in the Dutch capture of Melaka from the Portuguese in 1641. This stress accords with the modern emphasis on Western imperial expansion being dependent on local co-operation, but that is not the reason why that approach is taken in the museum. Instead, the stress is on the continued strength of Malay powers. Johor is validated by reference to Melaka: 'The Johor Sultanate continued the exalted reign of the Malacca Sultanate.'

Resistance to imperialism also receives attention in the museum. Thus, for the seventeenth century, 'The Dutch occupation of Malacca and their monopoly of tin activities along the Straits of Malacca drew protests from the local population'; while, for the 1780s, there is a discussion of the mutual help of Johor and Selangor in resistance to the Dutch. The Pangkor Treaty of 1874 between the Raja of Perak and the British is discussed as follows:

However, James Birch [the first British Resident in Perak] did not honour several terms of the Treaty especially those dealing with the practices of the Malay People and Islam. Consequential to that, the Malays rebelled and murdered Birch on 2 November 1875. The assassination was the ultimate manifestation of anger by the Malay people in Perak as a result of the conspiracy and deceit by the British in lieu of the Treaty.

Maharaja Lela, who led the rising against Birch, was summarily tried and hanged. He is now a popular hero of Malay resistance, a contrast frequent in the history of former colonies. For example, Omar Mukhtar, the leader of Libyan resistance to Italian conquest, was captured, court martialled and executed in 1931, only, after independence in 1951, to become the national hero with streets named after him and his mausoleum prominent in Benghazi.

More generally in the museum, a pattern of resistance to Western power was depicted. For the nineteenth century, the language used looked toward more recent times:

> British intervention in the administration of the Malay States, the rule of James Brooke in Sarawak, and the North Borneo Company's management of Sabah all sparked reactions from the local populations. Freedom fighters emerged who defended the dignity and sovereignty of their individual lands.

In the case of the Malay princely state Kedah, this process was linked also to opposition to neighbouring Siam.

The last photograph in the section on resistance is of an elderly warrior photographed in 1969, a situation of continuity to the age of Malayan independence, which began in 1957. This is a photograph of Mat Kilau, who was one of the leaders of the rising against the British presence in Pahang in 1891–5. In 1969, a very old man emerged in Pahang, insisting he was Mat Kilau, a claim that was implausible. Today 'Warrior Country' is a tourist attraction where trekkers can follow the 'Mat Kilau Trail' along the Tembeling River. A similar emphasis on the longevity of opposition to the imperial power, in this case France and then the USA, can be found in Hanoi's Museum of Vietnamese Revolution. The longevity of opposition to oppressors, Thai, Burmese, French, Japanese and American, is also the theme of the National Museum in Vientiane, the capital of Laos.

The treatment of the twentieth century in the National Museum of Malaysia scarcely emphasizes Malaysia's role in the British Empire. The First World War, in which Malaysia was an important support for the imperial economy, is ignored. For the Second World War, the few photographs displayed include the visit of the Malay rulers to Singapore in April 1942, during Japanese occupation, as well as one of Japanese officers with the Sultan of Kedah, a close relative of the first Prime Minister of Malaysia. The emphasis therefore is on accommodation, not resistance.

In Singapore, the emphasis in museums is on the Asian Civilisations Museum, the most impressive of the museums under the care of the National Heritage Board. Although part of this museum occupies the Empress Palace Building, designed in the 1860s to house government offices and named in honour of Queen Victoria, British imperial rule has only a small impact on the museum. Instead, the latter aims to reconnect Singapore with its cultures of origin, notably in East and South Asia. Much of Singapore's population is of Chinese or Indian origin. In contrast, Japan, Korea, and northern and central Asia are greatly downplayed in this museum.

National history museums vary in character. Hanoi's National Museum of Vietnamese History provides a clear defence of Communism and independence with its accounts of royal weakness and of French imperial cruelty. Tendentious, but then Britain does not have a museum of national history. The dinosaurs in the Natural History Museum in London offer a safer topic, not least because evolution, although controversial in some countries, is a less contentious issue in Britain than national history. Nor, for example, does Malta have a museum of national history.

Cultural artefacts also serve to make points about identity, links and achievement in museums such as Hong Kong's Museum of Art and Doha's Museum of Islamic Art. The latter, opened in 2008, seeks to demonstrate the quality and range of Islamic art, and the central place of the Islamic world as a civilizational space. Designed by I. M. Pei, who was inspired by the ablutions fountain of the ninth-century mosque of Ahmad Ibn Tulun in Cairo,[2] the very expensive museum also asserts Qatar's role as a proponent of Islamic culture and the Islamic world, and, in doing so, seeks to win both international and domestic credibility for the Emir, his dynasty, and the autocratic government system.

More generally, interest in folk-art has proved particularly significant in trying to demonstrate a distinctive ethnically grounded cultural identity, an identity that served to give a historical resonance to nationalism. This emphasis on indigenous cultural nationalism can be seen in museums and artistic patronage.[3]

What is illustrated in this prologue is the theme of this book, that of history being used to serve interests and agendas, and with these interests and agendas largely set by states. The historical self-image of states and nations is the subject of much of this study. The manner in which this self-image has changed over time is a necessary part of this story. Let us turn to this broader theme.

CHAPTER ONE

Introduction

It is an irony of the present age, the modern condition, that history appears far stronger as a force than had been widely anticipated. This chapter begins by considering the weight of history in the modern age, before assessing key contexts and mediums for the formulation and propagation of historical views. The social and cultural range of this phenomenon will be evaluated.

A Changing World

The 'death of the past', the 'end of history', and related phrases and concepts, were all frequently promulgated, promoted and discussed in the twentieth century, and particularly in its closing decades. And under-standably so. The end of the Cold War, with the collapse of the Soviet Union in 1991, prompted much talk of the 'end of history'.[1] Moreover, the 'end of history' in the 1990s was also seen in the decline, or even fragmentation, of the nation, in the face of globalization and associated transnational perspectives.

There was also a significant broader context. The human condition is different to the situation across most of the past, and increasingly so. People live in new environments, physical, social, economic, cultural and political, and their imagination and sense of identity has had to adapt, or at least respond, accordingly, even if the response often was and frequently remains a hostile reaction. Whereas, prior to the twentieth century, most of the world's population lived on, or close to, the land, in agrarian societies, now an increasing percentage live in urban environments where agriculture is of minor consequence. Linked to this, but also separate, long-established social and cultural patterns, and cultural assumptions and practices, have been challenged, and been either transformed or overthrown.

This was, and is, change on a scale never seen before, not least because the world's population was, and is, greater than ever before. Indeed, it reached 7.2 billion in 2013, and, given growth rates, is currently predicted to rise to 9.6 billion by mid-century and to 10.85 billion by the end of the century, based on a medium fertility assumption.[2]

Moreover, the geographical, social and economic changes of the last century have been more insistent in terms of their impact than those over the previous millennium. This is a bald statement, but one that captures a transformation of life-experiences, lifestyles, life-expectations, and the human condition, all of which have an impact on the historical imagination and on our perspective on the past.

That far more people live in cities is particularly significant as they represent a very different environment to agrarian society, not least as many have become increasingly cosmopolitan, indeed transnational, in recent years. The United Nations suggests that, by 2030, the figure of those living in cities will be over five billion, compared to over half the world's population of seven billion in 2011. There are projections, for 2050, of three-quarters of the population being in cities, with most of the increase taking place in the cities in Asia and Africa, where the fastest rates of increase are occurring.

The experience of the natural rhythms of life is weaker in urban society, compared to its rural counterpart. Furthermore, the process of rapid urbanization has proved highly disorientating. Cities are potent *lieux de mémoire* (places of memory), both reflecting past experience and with their past being experienced in terms of the rush of the present, including fiction, film, and rebuilding.[3] The reception of 'texts' of the past, such as photographs, helps some of these experiences to resonate, while others fall silent.

The Call for the Future

What place then does history, an imaginative engagement with the past, have for a humanity where change is taking place at an unprecedented rate, and linked to this is making most of the past apparently redundant history? That, indeed, was a question frequently asked over the last century. Educational reformers, then (and now), many of whom pressed for a focus on more recent history, history that was supposedly more relevant, were themselves only a pale imitation of a more pronounced and widespread call, for both the embrace of the future and the understanding of the present, rather than for dwelling on the past.

This call could be found across the political spectrum, a situation that remains the case. It was seen with radicals on the Left, rejecting what were presented as redundant *ancien régimes*, including, allegedly, in educational content and method. This call also came from conservative modernizers, enthusiastic for strengthening the state and nation via reform, and keen to argue that the past could only be valid in the perspective of the present, and could only be made valuable if much was discarded.

Deploying the Past

And yet, despite this focus on the future and the present, and on the recent past as leading toward the future, in practice the present age is greatly suffused with references to the past, much of it the 'deep history' of the influence of the distant past. Moreover, history is deployed in order to provide understanding of the present, or, at least, apparent understanding, although, generally, in terms of the values of the present. This situation was very much seen after the Cold War, for all the talk of the 'end of history' then.

The bitterness of ethnic and religious divisions in the conflicts of the 1990s in the former Yugoslavia, notably in Bosnia and Kosovo, and the major role of historical identities and references in these divisions, for example in Serb nationalism, appeared to show that history certainly had not ended, and that the past was very relevant. The (Christian) Serbs made frequent reference to oppressive rule by the (Muslim) Ottoman Turks when explaining their stance over Bosnia and Kosovo, in each of which there was a large Muslim population. Religious hostility was given an historical background and dynamic, not least by referring to the consequences of Ottoman victory over the Serbs in Kosovo in 1399. Serbian nationalism exemplified the ethnic construction of the nation state as opposed to the civic ideal where citizenship provides equality before the law. The latter offers a far greater potential for trust between parties.[4]

Furthermore, in opposition to the thesis of the 'end of history', the idea of a 'clash of civilizations', advanced by Samuel P. Huntington, enjoyed considerable traction, at least in the USA, in the 2000s. In this perspective, civilizations were grounded in historically specific and engendered cultures. The idea of a 'clash of civilizations' served to provide an alleged historical setting for the American-declared 'War on Terror', by linking the clash between Islamic fundamentalism and Westernization from 2001 to a longer-term religious opposition between Islam and Christendom.

So also with the tendency to ground the assessment of American power in an historical context. The dominant American role in international relations in the 1990s and 2000s led to much discussion of America as a modern empire, and to the drawing of parallels, and contrasts, with older empires, notably Ancient Rome and the British Empire. China today is presented by some as acquiring an empire through economic control of, for example, mines in Africa. As an aspect of this process, there was a literature comparing strategy across the ages.[5]

Much of this literature in practice is highly ahistorical, in that it compares what are not really similar. Writers underplay, or indeed ignore, both the specific cultural contexts within which policies were defined, and the particular ideological and linguistic connotations of the terms used. The definition of the past in terms of the present can be seen, for example, in the attempt to ascribe to Rome or Byzantium a 'grand strategy' that is similar in character to that of a modern state. There are also comparisons at the functional level, as in the argument that the overreach of the empire of Spain under Philip II (r. 1556–98) and his successors prefigured that of modern America;[6] which, however, is very much a comparison between highly different examples. So also with that of imperial Britain facing numerous threats in the 1930s with America in the 2000s; although, in that case as opposed to the point involving Spain, comparisons could be deployed with more value, and also had a greater current resonance.

Even when the past is rejected in the modern age, it is with frequent reference to history as a new beginning. Thus, in March 2013, when Italy's radical Five Star Movement took their seats in Parliament for the first time, after winning a quarter of the popular vote in the elections the previous month, its leader, Beppe Grillo, blogged 'History is beginning'. The movement is an explicitly new political force that is based on an opposition to existing political practices.

Moreover, but very differently, an understanding of history offers change, and those who support or experience it, a grounding in continuity. For example, after total defeat in the Second World War (1939–45), history became a means by which the nation, as idea and practice, was kept strong in German and Japanese intellectual and popular culture. History also served to explain how national identity had been transformed and tested by war, defeat and occupation, but had still survived.[7]

In addition, across the world, historical animosities give life to national, religious, ethnic and social animosities, or at least to senses of different identities. These animosities and senses express, but can also oppose, or qualify, the master narratives that 'interpret a given community's historical and cultural experiences in order to support shared identity, understandings and collective aspirations'.[8] In this context, the recovered memory of the past is important in setting collective goals, although politics and polemic both play a major role in this process of understanding and expressing this memory. Normative assumptions thus take on meaning both in history and as a result of history.

This situation was, and is, a continuing process. For example, in international relations, what would now be termed strategic culture, namely a conceptualisation of long-term interests, was (and is) of great significance in defining supposedly inherent interests, and in providing a belief in the necessity to be aware of lasting enmities and to give force and effect to a sense of the possible in the present. The fears of Margaret Thatcher (1925–2013), British Prime Minister (1979–90), about German reunification, which occurred in 1990, looked back to the anxieties and experience of her youth during the Second World War when, in 1940–1, Britain had seemed highly vulnerable to German attack.

In turn, the latter helped provide her with a vocabulary for her concerns in 1989–90 about how the fall of the Communist bloc might make a West Germany, now joined by East Germany, more powerful and threatening, as well as more dominant in a European Union that therefore became more of a challenge for Britain. Thatcher, who sought the advice of academics on the point, saw German policy in terms of a menacing historical continuum,[9] and not with reference to a new start in 1945, prefiguring another new start in 1990. Francois Mitterrand of France came to different conclusions, although also afraid of German reunification.

Thatcher drew on a kind of embedded exceptionalism of Britain standing alone protecting and realigning what was presented as the Free World. Winston Churchill, Prime Minister from 1940 to 1945 and from 1951 to 1955, had this sense too and also located it in an historical continuum. Laurence Olivier's depiction of Admiral Nelson defending Britain against Napoleon was one of his favourite films during the Second World War.

This book addresses the contrast between the situation mentioned earlier in the chapter, the denial of history, and that considered here, a discussion of its role. The choice of words is significant, for 'discussion' is more pertinent than 'understanding'. The latter suggests a degree of agreement and a maturity of analysis that are not in fact generally the case. Historians can supply a kind of stability to political debate by encouraging the avoidance of anachronism and by showing the respect for evidence that challenges anecdotalism.

Contrasting Examples from South Asia

The role of references to the past is ever-present in politics, even if politicians do so in order to claim the future. Two very different examples from neighbouring states in South Asia in early 2013 exemplify this point. On 2 March 2013, Arun Jaitley, a senior member of the main Indian opposition party, the Bharatiya Janata Party (BJP), told the party's national council meeting at New Delhi that the slow growth of the Indian economy in the 1950s and 1960s was not a 'Hindu rate of growth' – in other words, what he and his listeners saw as the supposedly inherent product of Indian culture. Instead, Arun Jaitley argued, this slow growth was the result of the misguided socialist planning of the Congress government under Pandit Nehru, Prime Minister from 1947 to 1964, and should therefore be called 'the Nehru rate of growth'. Congress is the rival of the BJP.

This claim provided an historical context for his colleague, Prakash Javdekar, to contrast the rate of growth under the BJP government in

1998–2004 with the lower growth and higher inflation rates under the subsequent Congress-led UPA government.[10] Thus, history was deployed in the cause of the forthcoming 2014 elections, but drawing, in this case, on a different vocabulary to the sectarian Hinduism more commonly associated with the BJP's use of the past.[11] At the same time, this episode represented an attempt to justify what was presented as the Hindu position and to claim it for BJP ideology and purpose.

A very different echo of the past occurred in the neighbouring state of Bangladesh in early 2013. Despite its title, its International Crimes Tribunal is a domestic law court, trying those accused of atrocities in the successful, but bloody, war of independence from Pakistan, the origin episode[12] of the state in 1971. This tribunal, however, turned out not to offer the reconciliation generally sought from such tribunals. Instead, it sentenced to death Delwar Hossain Sayeedi, a leader of the Jamaat-e-Islami, the country's largest Islamic party, for pro-Pakistani crimes during this war. That verdict led to murderous and sectarian violence from the Islami Chatra Shibir, Jamaat's student wing. Clearly, politics played a part in both trial and response, not least, in the latter, manoeuvring between Jamaat and its former coalition partner, the Bangladesh Nationalist Party, also currently in opposition.

Moreover, as a sign of the varied current politics of the past, alongside opposition violence against the verdict have come public demands for the punishment of the indicted war criminals. In a sign of the ready reference of history that is very frequent in the politics of accusation, the prosecution likened one of the accused, Ghulan Azam, the head of the Jamaat in 1971, to Hitler. This comparison was designed for an international as much as a domestic audience. Similarly, in June 2013, Recep Tayyip Erdogan, the authoritarian Prime Minister of Turkey, was depicted as Hitler in posters produced by protesters in Istanbul. This use of Hitler represented a form of transnationalism.

History and Political Culture

In most states, the process of contesting the national past is less bloody than in modern Bangladesh, but can still be of great consequence for political culture. For example, in the USA, the National Standards Controversy in the 1990s over the teaching of history[13] is now largely muted. Nevertheless, the extent to which history plays a key role in America's vexed 'culture wars' is readily apparent. Although some commentators suggest that this contention is less than was the case in the 1990s, and that the National Standards controversy was really only a blip, other indications are of a deeper-rooted problem over presenting the national past and thus defining the national exceptionalism that is dear to most Americans.[14]

This problem reflects the number of potential national narratives and their incompatible nature. This number, in part, arises from the diversity of sectional narratives, notably the strong Southern white narrative which can smack of an insular self-congratulation.[15] In turn, these narratives have distinctive local aspects and voices.[16] Academics can present the more general situation as an aspect of Postmodernism, an intellectual analysis, which, in challenging the idea of a dominant view, validates an infinity of micro-narratives. However, the suggestion in this book is of a more limited number of coherent narratives reflecting would-be nations or visions of nations or attitudes that contribute to such an end.

As this book will show, the role of the state in using history has a long genesis. Indeed, rulership and the use of history are linked processes. At the same time, the situation is not one that has been uniform in intensity. Instead, a more 'modern' statist form of history developed from the nineteenth century, as bureaucratic governments employed an ideology of nationalism to provide both coherence to states and content to new education systems. Nationalism became the stuff of politics, providing identity, and indeed a modern form of religion in which the state worshipped itself and its community.[17]

The current state of nationalism, however, is less clear. It has become much less potent in Europe, as a result of the Second World War, the Cold War, and the aspirations and practice of the European Union. However, as this book will indicate, the situation is different across most of the rest of the world. Nationalism remains significant in many states, although there are also examples of collaborative transnational history-writing, for example in South Korea and the Balkans.

The Family

State and nation are not the sole level of activity. The prime context for the formulation and propagation of historical views is, of course, the family. History is the sense of the past – both what occurred, and how we understand and describe it. As such, history overlaps with experience, indeed, is the ordering of experience, whether personal or collective, about the past. The focus of this is the family, because it is within a family context that individuals acquire their initial experiences and learn to express them, where the educational process begins, where values are inculcated, and where social norms and assumptions are most readily assimilated. The most formative years are those of childhood and youth, and it is then that the family context is most significant.

This argument is not made in order to deny other influences in childhood and youth. Nor is it the case that all children and all the young go through a family context. Rates of family breakdown and institutional care vary both geographically and through time, and, in many societies, the young have had to be self-reliant and to begin work early. Furthermore, there have been instructive studies on cultural aspects of childhood and youth that are not family-based, for example the values expressed in children's comics[18] and children's television.

Accepting these significant caveats, nevertheless there is a centrality for the family that requires consideration. The family is (and was) scarcely a sphere free of contention, whether between parents, between parents and children, between children, or involving more extensive family networks such as grandparents. Yet, the family also entailed discussions between members in which the past, and not just of the family, was (and is) expounded and explained, and values, preferences and prejudices were (and are) expressed, indeed inculcated.

The family past was the key issue, and it is interesting to note in the 2000s and 2010s the widespread engagement with family genealogy and history, notably in Britain and the USA, but also more widely. Indeed, any concern with using history needs first to consider the extent to which genealogy has served to explore and affirm identity, fixing it in, and across, time. This process can be seen in both religious and secular contexts.

In the 2000s and 2010s, the nature of genealogy was different to that of a century earlier, being both democratized and employing a range of mediums. The digitization of records, the spread of personal computers, self-help manuals, and websites such as 'Genes Reunited', helped people research their own family histories. Television programmes served to engage public interest, providing a vicarious family history in the shape of the celebrities who were discussed; with a different form of 'reality television' offered by placing families or groups in re-enacted settings of the past, such as *The 1900s House* (1999) or *The Trench* (2003), the last a use of the First World War for entertainment. In programmes such as Britain's *Who Do You think You Are?*, celebrities and others were apparently made close by the television camera, and then their family history and historical experience were pursued. In both Britain and the USA, there was a stress on the hybrid nature of many family backgrounds, and on the significance of the family as the product of difference, whether social or ethnic or both.

Viewing figures for such programmes were very high, although there were instructive national contrasts which, in part, reflect the willingness to probe family pasts in light of the difficult nature of recent history. To discover that your grandfather was in the Burma police service was less problematic for a British family (Britain was the colonial power in modern Myanmar from 1885 to 1942 and 1945 to 1948) than the realization that a German grandfather might have been an active member of the Nazi party, or than a Chinese family finding that in theirs was a small landowner murdered by the Chinese Communists in the bloody social revolution of the 1950s.

Democratization has recently played a central role across the world in the engagement with family genealogy and history. In place of an interest in the family history and heritage of élite families, notably royalty and aristocracy (although the former is still on display at royal weddings), have come both an eagerness to study the families of all and a willingness to engage with what would have been generally excluded from the family record in the past, namely crime, illegitimacy and inter-racial relationships. This contrast is notable in the case of Australia. Whereas crime, transportation to the convict settlements (the origins of the British colonial presence there from 1788), and illegitimacy had each been stigmas that had been concealed or ignored, in recent decades there has been a delight there in discovering a 'colourful past'.

This change can be welcomed as an appropriate response, in a democratic age, to the ambiguities, compromises and circumstances of the past, as well as dealing with the more specific issue of trying to explain the reality and memory of the family past. The contrast with the widespread, longstanding emphasis on purity of blood and lineage, for example in the early-modern Iberian world created by Portuguese and Spanish imperialism, is readily apparent. In part, this contrast reflects very differing views across time on participation in a national community and on the nature of the latter. In particular, the ethnic, indeed racial, definition of nationhood has become less pronounced in most (but not all) states.

Thus, the modern nature of family history arises as a potent instance of obtaining a history to suit the present. Moreover, such family history provides a social history that is democratic and popular in content and tone. The latter approach is opposed to analyses of social history based on the discussion of social groups defined and considered in accordance with intellectual strategies. Marxist analyses provide a prime example of such discussion.

Yet, the account of a 'colourful past' can be highly misleading, not least in underplaying the misery and tedium of what today are held up as interesting. Such a situation involves not only presenting a misleading account of the past, but also, by extension, of the present. In the context of an apparently attractive past, the present can seem to be a matter of failure or of falling off.

This is an example of the broader process of obtaining a history that suits the present, in so far as there is often a willingness to criticise the latter by reference to a supposedly more acceptable past. In that sense, history becomes a sphere for travel in search of a frame of reference, rather like the imaginary travelogues (in space, not time), notably to or from Persia (Iran), China, Abyssinia (Ethiopia) and distant oceans, used by eighteenth-century European writers, such as Montesquieu, Lyttelton, Voltaire, Johnson and Swift, in order to criticise, or at least throw light on, their own societies.

The family as history is now a prime medium through which the past is experienced, understood and interpreted. For example, the First World War (1914–18 for most participants) becomes, in this perspective, not a case of strategy and politics, but of the life and fate of great-grandfathers. As a result, the emphasis, in considering the war, is on individual suffering and total casualties, rather than on why the war was fought, or on the strategic, institutional and economic dimensions of the conflict. The plans announced by the British government in June 2013 for the commemoration of the First World War do not command much confidence on this head, but, anyway, already have led to considerable controversy.[19] The emphasis on the individual perspective was also seen in the success of the ITV series *The World at War* (1973–4), which owed much to the accounts of how the Second World War was experienced by people worldwide.[20]

The focus on ancestors captures a key psychological reason for history, that of the link between the generations as a way both to defy mortality and to provide continuity, a reason that also provides a central means of history. Edward Nares (1762–1841), a Church of England clergyman who, in 1813, thanks to personal connections, became Regius Professor of Modern History at Oxford, began his manuscript autobiography:

> Since life is above all things precarious and God only knows how long I may live, and as I have at present children so young that though it should please God to spare their lives, I may not live to see them come to maturity; and as it is reasonable to think that when they grow up they will be anxious to know who they are descended from; and yet many have none to tell them. For these reasons, and no other, I have resolved to put together such particulars of my life and connections as may satisfy their enquiries and serve to inform them who and what their father was, as far as such knowledge can be honestly and correctly communicated by frail man.[21]

So also with the family as the interpreter of history, for these and other stories are developed in that context. This point is also true of issues that are at once both more particular and broader. The history of the locality is understood thus first as the history of 'our house' or where we lived/live. The history of religious groupings is approached as 'we are Catholics or Hindus, and not Protestants or Muslims …' etc.

History, therefore, is constructed for many from the individual, in the sense of the particular family, to the general, in the sense of other families. Moreover, the general, in the different form of political, social, economic and other pressures, is experienced by families through their memories and the way in which they are recorded and discussed. The experience of the global economic Depression of the 1930s, or of Western colonialization, are prime examples. Correspondingly, although diaries, correspondence and, more recently, visual material are significant, the oral approach provides the prime means and method of history in this perspective; it is the way in which families transmit and comment on memories. Related to this focus have come changes in history as an intellectual pursuit and in the related methodology. Alongside public history, memory and memorializing are now key themes in academic history and in schools.[22]

Memory and Reconciliation

History as memory encompasses both the memory of personal experience, or direct memory, and memory that does not immediately rest on this personal experience. Each is affected by subsequent currents of opinion, the latter far more than the former. As direct memory lessens, so the collective historical experience changes. Moreover, memories and oral records, like songs and, indeed, written accounts, are 'renewed' or changed in the light of what subsequently happens. Each thereby acts as a link between present and past.[23]

Again, this situation is not identical across the world, which is an important aspect of the role of reading history in constructing identity and meaning. In particular, in societies that are, or have been, totalitarian, anxieties about expressing views in public, combined with the often ambivalent role that present and past members of families have taken in support of the state (or evading it), further force a focus on the private space of the family. There is a greater degree of safety in this space, as well as the need to produce an account of what has, and is, happening. Eastern Europe and Russia during the Communist period provide prime examples. To remember publicly those who had been killed or deported was dangerous. The same is true of China today.

In response, individuals and families ranged in their strategy and tactics, from forgetting and self-repression, to defining and redefining belonging.[24] These processes were complicated by the experiences of the generation to which the individuals and families belonged.[25] At the same time, the strength of private memories might be such as to create a collective memory very different to that of the state. This was seen in Latvia, where the large-scale Soviet deportations in June 1941 were treated as attempted genocide in this memory during the period of resumed Soviet control from 1944 to the collapse of the Soviet Union – an approach very different to that of the Soviet state.

The fall of the Eastern Bloc in 1989–91, in turn, was followed by a rejection of the recent past, in part illuminated by new knowledge about the crimes and flaws of Communist rule. There was a varied memorialization of Communist brutality. In Tallinn, the capital of Estonia, the KGB headquarters, now a police building, bears a plaque noting its role as 'the headquarters of the organ of repression of the Soviet occupation'. In Prague, the Museum of Communism includes a mock-up of an interrogation room of the period. Different memories arise from the treatment of ethnic Russians stranded within the Baltic States (Estonia, Latvia, Lithuania) after the end of the Cold War, many of whom feel excluded from the civic society of these countries. In turn, not all ethnic Russians are excluded, while strategies and tactics of accommodation take place in a very different context to the situation under Soviet rule.

East Germany was subject to a range of recollection. At the level of the state, there were two commissions of enquiry by the *Bundestag* [Parliament] in the 1990s, followed, in 2005–6, by the Sabrow Commission which considered how East Germany should be remembered. There was the establishment of a documentation centre, of a Berlin Wall Memorial, and a number of other memorials. East Germany also became the subject of literature, film and memories. On the part of some, there was a regret, at least in part, about the old order passing.[26] Nostalgia, in the shape, for East Germany, of *Ostalgie*, a theme probed in the popular German film *Good Bye Lenin!* (2003), was linked to an idealization of the Communist past that also offered a glimpse of an alternative future.[27] With its comic plot device of a pretence that the Communist era had not in fact ended, the film itself indicated how the present can be made to overlap with the past in order to fulfil personal needs for continuity and meaning.

At the same time, there was the requirement, across the board in East Germany, for a negotiation of the 'double past', of the Nazi and Communist regimes. This was the case at specific sites used by both regimes, for example concentration camps, notably Sachsenhausen, and, more generally, in terms of the memorial strategies of government at different levels, as well as of cultural works and of personal experiences.[28] Individuals also faced this challenge, including, in 2013, Angela Merkel, the German Chancellor, when her (somewhat minor) role in support of the Communist regime attracted discussion. In turn, this issue directed attention to the nature of the regime. A similar task faced other Eastern European states that collaborated with Hitler and were then ruled by Communist regimes: Romania, Bulgaria, Slovakia, Hungary and Croatia.

The Family and the State

Alongside variations across the world, the family is scarcely unchanging and uncontested as an historical entity or 'space'. Indeed, the historiographical significance of feminism in part rests on its importance for enriching and/ or complicating classic accounts of family.[29] Across time, the extent to which the extended family has acted as a social security system has changed greatly in particular societies. When it did/does so act, then news of the extended family was/is necessary.

A focus on individual and family suggests a very different pattern of development in the uses of history to that offered by a focus on entities and forces that appear to have greater authority and power, notably, but not only, the state and the role of economic pressures. The focus on individual and family is appropriate in so far as psychological dimensions are concerned, but also captures the extent to which these other entities and forces are in many ways mediated through far more specific experiences and understandings.

There are also significant linkages between the individual/family and these forces. Conscription into the armed forces provides a prime instance. The demand by the state for military service pressed hard on individuals and their families, and indicated both the major dependence of individual family narratives on the state and the transformative, frequently traumatic, character of being citizens. This demand was linked to realities and ideologies of state service, ideologies that involved historical narratives about the role of government in repelling threats to the nation.

Religion

There was also a pronounced linkage in many religions between the family and the processes of religious education and observance. Each of these processes tended to be historicized, in that doctrine and practice were grounded in the origin myths and historical development of particular religions. The family is often the key site of religious education, while, at the same time, religions provide meaning to the accounts of individual families. This gaining and fixing of meaning was enhanced by belief in Providence, and also by widespread interest in the idea of life after death, for example in purgatory and in ghosts.[30]

Myths and accounts of development helped provide a distinctiveness for individual religions. The atoning sacrifice of Jesus Christ as the root redemption in Christianity was an historical episode that offered a separate promise and a distinctive identity. Given the longevity of most religions, this process of separateness from the outset is not at the forefront of scrutiny. However, with more recent religions, such as Mormonism, it is very clear that an historical origin-myth and an account of distinctive development served the goals of strengthening a sense of separate identity. And so also with the modern history of long-established religions such as Judaism and Islam.

Mention of these religions again serves to demonstrate the theme of variety. In the case of Judaism, religion serves to integrate the state of Israel and its Jewish population, notably recent immigrants, while simultaneously creating issues of exclusion for the large number of Christians and Muslims who live in Israel. No other state has this religion as its established faith, which helps define Israel as different and distinctive, as well as providing a focus for the transnationalism offered by the Jewish diaspora.

At the same time, the role of the Jewish religious narrative in the foundation account of the state of Israel is controversial, both for Israelis and for foreign commentators. In 2009, this situation got the new American President, Barack Obama, into difficulties with much Israeli opinion when, in Cairo, in what was presented as his address to the Islamic world, he rejected the 'legitimacy' of continued Israeli settlement construction in the occupied (Palestinian) territories. Instead of stopping in Israel on his way home from Cairo, Obama visited the Buchenwald concentration camp in Germany. This focus on the Holocaust (the Nazi slaughter of the Jews) led many Israelis to fear that Obama did not appreciate their nation's Biblical roots. Whereas Israelis present modern Israel as the rebirth of the ancient Israel of the Bible, and thus as the Jewish homeland, Palestinians argue that Israel's roots are far more recent and essentially derive from Western guilt about the Jews after the Holocaust.

Thus, history is present and in dispute, not only in terms of events but also with respect to timeline, each conveying a different source and degree of justification. Competing claims for victimhood are significant factors in the struggle for control over historical knowledge; memorialization of the Holocaust obviously clashes with Palestinian concern about the Naqba, their fate and flight into exile in 1948–9.

In March 2013, on his first presidential visit to Israel, Obama sought to confront the issue, by endorsing the Israeli account. At the welcoming ceremony, he declared:

> More than 3,000 years ago, the Jewish people prayed here, tended the land here, prayed to God here. And after centuries of exile and persecution, unparalleled in the history of man, the founding of the Jewish state of Israel was a rebirth, a redemption unlike any in history.

History thus was again a source of explanation, verification and justification. This was not an account that left much room for the Palestinians. Obama also visited not only the Holocaust memorial at Yad Vashem, a key destination for official visitors, but also, at the Israeli national cemetery at Mount Herzl, the grave of the prominent Zionist Theodor Herzl (1860–1904), whose activities preceded the Holocaust. In 1896, in *Der Judenstaat*, Herzl advocated a Jewish state in Palestine and, the following year, he founded the World Zionist Organization.

The sites visited and remarks made provided a way of using history symbolically to locate political position, and notably in comparison with other visitors. Thus, in 1964, visiting the Holy Land, a designation of Israel and Jordan that described his response but was also a political gesture, Pope Paul VI (r. 1963–78) did not go to Yad Vashem nor refer to Israel, and also defended the controversial stance of Pope Pius XII (r. 1939–58) during the Holocaust: Pius XII, under whom Paul had served in the Vatican diplomatic service, was criticized for not publicly opposing the persecution of the Jews.

Many foreign leaders have refused to lay a wreath at Herzl's tomb. In 2013, with reference to Obama, Michael Oren, Israel's ambassador to the USA, told *Haaretz*, a leading Israeli newspaper, that 'everything in this trip is rife with significance and symbolism [...] poignantly meaningful to people in the Middle East. By laying a wreath at Herzl's grave [...] Obama was reaffirming Zionism and the idea of a Jewish state'.

In contrast to the focus in (most) Judaism on the state of Israel, Islam involves a high degree of transnationalism. This Islamic transnationalism extends to rival accounts of the world of Islam, notably those of Sunnis and Shi'ites, rivalry which has led to competition between and within countries. Political tensions have been greatly affected by this competition.

Moreover, this competition has resulted in sectarian pressures that helped make some Islamic states weak, if not apparently redundant, unless they acted as standard-bearers for Islam. Thus, after the Islamic Revolution of 1979, Iran acquired a particular historicized destiny as the self-appointed leader of international Shi'ism, while this role also helped provide the new regime with a justification for its autocratic and brutal rule, including the violent suppression of democratic protests after rigged 2009 presidential elections. Religion proved particularly amenable to this role, as it offered meaning, purpose, destiny and cohesion. The elections of 2013 did not see comparable brutality, but the candidates offered to the people had first to be selected by the religious establishment, and this process dramatically limited the choice.

At the same time, the Iranian regime can be seen as operating politically, rather than simply religiously, so that the Iranian interpretation of history pivots upon the political needs of the Islamic republic, and not on a religious interpretation of history as such.[31] This point serves as a reminder of the need for a careful analysis of policy and political culture.

Despite the potential distinction between religious goals and political means, secular narratives of identity and development across much of the Islamic world were challenged by the role of Islam. Even if the unit in question was that of the individual country, there were significant contrasts between secular and Islamic accounts. The Muslim Brotherhood provided a very different account of Egyptian history and Egypt's destiny to that offered by secularists defending the republican system in power there from 1952. This clash was present in the army-led overthrow of the Muslim Brotherhood government of Egypt in June 2013.

More generally, the use of history is probably most pronounced in the case of religion, as belief is historicized in doctrine. Furthermore, the emphasis on, and in, religious legitimism looks back, in its interpretation of orthodoxy in terms of the past, rather than being focused on any notion of present consent. This focus on the past, moreover, can lead to a rejection of the application of historical analysis to religion, unless in prescribed exegetical forms. Thus, with Islam, there is widespread strong opposition to the treatment of the Koran as a text subject to analysis – a method employed, in contrast, in Christian Biblical analysis from the nineteenth century, notably in Germany.

At the same time, individual religions with a strong historicist dimension can, within them, have very different views of the past. For example, the Wahhabi sect of Islam, long – and still – very powerful in Saudi Arabia, is hostile to whatever apparently encourages *shirq*, the sin of idolatry. This approach has led to hostility to the preservation of historical Islamic sites, including the archaeological, historical and cultural heritage of Mecca and Medina. The expansion of mosques there has recently resulted in the deliberate destruction of monuments relating to early Islamic history. Fundamentalist Islamic views also led to the destruction of sites and material judged heretical in Mali in 2012, notably in Timbuktu, including the archives in the library.

So the world shall be his foot-stool, and the soul of time his slave:/ Our God is marching on!

Julia War Howe, the author of 'Mine Eyes Have Seen The Glory of the Coming of the Lord', the *Battle Hymn of the Republic* (1861), the marching song of Union troops during the American Civil War (1861–5), was in no doubt that time was subordinate to God. This view, one central to religious doctrine, encouraged an authoritarian stance. Indeed, the pattern of religious activity for most of history was of authoritarian cults punishing heterodoxy and linked to government – a pattern in which the presentation of history was supposed to serve clear ideological interests. Many of the intellectuals in these societies were part of the religious establishment or linked to it. They did not provide equal service to the religious ideology in question, but their attitudes were framed by their background.

The tendency to refer to past orthodoxy is lessened for religions in which the emphasis is on individual belief, and this belief is seen as presenting a measure of justification, for both believer and religion. Such a practice of religion is particularly pronounced in the USA, and again for historical reasons, namely the absence, from the winning of independence, of a state church. In this context, the prime emphasis is not on traditional religious allegiances, as political and social stigmas against changing churches are (relatively) limited in the USA, a situation that has become more pronounced in recent decades. Moreover, the stress there, notably in the evangelical Churches, is on individual commitment. The latter is not an approach requiring historical meaning. This point was grasped across the world in the twentieth century by secular ideologies that, at least in theory, were interested in the loyalty and commitment of the individual, rather than the background of the individual's family.

Parts of the world, notably Western Europe, have seen a marked decline over the last century, and notably the last half-century, in religious activity and observance and in religiosity. Thus, in Britain, national days of prayer ended in the 1950s as part of a more general decline in religious observance.[32] Moreover, the legislative context has changed in many countries. There have been repeated defeats for religious traditionalists over abortion, contraception, homosexuality, the age of sexual consent, Sunday trading and pornography.

However, religious responses to the past may become more significant as the percentage (as well as number) of the world's population that is religious increases. Differential birth rates between religious believers, notably strong believers, and others suggests that this process will become of greater significance, not least among Muslims, Christians and Jews. Moreover, the population of India, where there is a high rate of religiosity, is set to pass that of China, where organized religion is weaker.

Although authority is inherent in religious belief and practice, with their orthodoxies and traditions, religious groups have also helped in many countries to create a pluralistic and tolerant society. Moreover, traditionalists have had to accept women priests and bishops in some churches.

A Range of Historical Uses

There is a continuum, rather than a stark divide, between religious and secular narratives and analyses. Many of the latter, indeed, have a providential, or at least privileging, purpose or effect, often very much by design. This was true both of the 'Whig Interpretation of History' and of the Marxist approach. The first was a progressive account, strongly linked to the advantages of a Protestant succession to the Crown over the absolutist tendencies of a Catholicising dynasty, which was highly influential in Britain in the nineteenth and early twentieth centuries. The Marxist approach was powerful in the twentieth century, and not only in Communist states. Similarly, many Americans, notably from the mid-nineteenth century, regarded themselves as an elect or privileged nation of exceptional character and purpose.[33] This attitude proved more potent than the anti-version, born of revisionism and often fuelled by concepts of metaphysical guilt.

As is already apparent, the purposes and mediums of history range widely. Indeed, history involves the ordering and presentation of memory and experience, and what is passed as both.[34] Therefore, by its nature, history covers the human condition. To discuss, first, individuals and families, and, then, religions suggests a widely contrasting dichotomy in the means of history and in the interplay of forces moulding and recording experience. At the same time, however, there is a wide range of intervening and intermediary spheres for activity, institutions and practices, each of which involved and involves uses of history. These uses therefore emerge as on a continuum in the case of character, context and scale.

The idea of intermediary activity itself is problematic, as it might seem to imply that such activity is less significant. This approach is encouraged by the general focus, as in this book, on a process of invented tradition stemming from the hegemonies of governmental authority, élite power and ideological dominance, including that of religion.[35] However, there is also much initiative at the level of those who are not at these heights. In part, these activities give instrumental force to the policies of the powerful, and many of those who act at intermediary levels are in practice organized, or at least given status, by state authority. Nevertheless, intermediaries are still able to influence, if not appropriate, distort and thwart, these policies.[36]

Key instances of intermediary activity between the individual and the existential (religious), and between the individual and the state, include the pressure from economic entities. Indeed, from the perspective of both employees and employers, especially the former, the world of work involves competing narratives. The perspective of employees, propagated, and thus appropriated, by trade unions, generally entails accounts of righteous struggle against oppression, with a clear and pointed conclusion coming from this history – as is generally the case with most public history. The death in 2013 of Margaret Thatcher, British Prime Minister from 1979 to 1990, led to the repetition by many, as historical account, of the partisan narrative of oppression deployed by striking coal miners in 1984–5. This narrative ignored the extent to which the strike itself had bitterly divided the miners, while more pits were closed under previous Labour governments, and there were deeper concerns about the effect of wage claims on inflation and over who was actually running the country.

The emphasis in the case of trade unions is on the need for unity and the lasting value of struggle and common purpose. Teleology plays a major role in this account. In contrast, history from employers generally involves a narrative directed not against employees, but rather the form of the company history. Again, the theme is one of virtuous struggle. A very different group of intermediaries are teachers who commonly have their own views about the uses of history and politicization.

Conclusions

The uses of history thus are a matter of objective as well as method. The two can combine to lead to a degree of didacticism, and certainly not to a willingness to qualify arguments or to criticise methods. This represents a key conclusion: the uses of history are a matter of style as much as content, the two mutually dependent. In the use of history by governments, the employment of style and content can tend to be self-serving, in the sense that there is little, even no, willingness to question conclusions and methods. Instead, the theme is clarity. In that perspective, history can be highly useful to governments and others, as well as highly critical.

Genre plays a role in the question and type of clarity. For example, much of what is written about the past displays the abrupt certainty demonstrated by most (although not all) of the monuments constructed to commemorate the past, and thus to claim it.[37] This appropriation of historical place to the purpose of the state, as aspect of the more general evolution of *lieux de mémoire*, was particularly common in the totalitarian regimes of the twentieth century which had the resources and determination to build and rebuild, and tended not to be concerned about the legal rights of property-owners. In Italy in the 1920s and 1930s, Benito Mussolini, the Fascist dictator, presented the 'Third Rome' he was constructing as a successor to Classical and medieval Rome. This concept inserted Fascism into the narrative of the city and the wider world it had reached, providing a symbolic setting for Mussolini's ideas of the new man and the new Italy.[38]

In a different political context, the proliferation of monuments is a marked feature of recent decades, and one that is particularly noticeable in cities that have changed political identity, such as Berlin, where first Nazism (1933–45) and then Communism (in East Berlin from 1945 to 1989) left legacies that had to be confronted. The intention in Berlin, once it again became Germany's capital after the fall of the Iron Curtain, is very different to that of Mussolini or Hitler, as is the stylistic language, and there is a degree of (self-)critical appraisal; but there is also a common element of conviction in this memorialization.

So also with anniversaries, which are often inherently controversial as they record major political events. This was especially so when they were celebrated in an imperial context, for example Bastille Day in Algeria,[39] as some of the colonial population rejected the process. This process was also seen with the anniversaries of Soviet Communism celebrated in unwillingly incorporated territories, such as Estonia, Latvia and Ukraine. In contrast, national days linked to the struggle for independence scarcely invite discussion as to whether gaining independence was anything other than a total good.

More generally, anniversaries record history but, in doing so, reflect the political power of the present. In North Korea, 15 April, the birthday of Kim Il Sung (1912–94), the founder of both state and ruling dynasty, is celebrated, but will not be when the regime falls. The national celebration in Hungary of the anniversary of the unsuccessful 1956 revolution against Soviet control only became possible after the end of Communist rule in 1989. Prior to that, the commemoration of the 1848–9 rebellion against Austrian (Habsburg) rule, a rebellion in part suppressed by Russian forces, was an issue of great sensitivity. The Communist regime sought to lay claim to the legacy of the nationalist rebellion, but also presented Communism as an advance on its goals.

In the case of education, the capacity of a narrative to generate questions is one of the big issues in the teaching and learning of history. As a consequence, history, as a subject, has a substantive as well as a syntactic knowledge base. The major normative values of academe, at least of modern academe in the West (a very important qualification), are very different to the certainty of assertion characteristic of public history. History as a subject can be explained from the Western perspective, in the words of Richard Evans, Regius Professor of History at Cambridge, as 'a critical academic discipline whose aims include precisely the interrogation

of memory and the myths it generates'.[40] There is, indeed, an impressive
scholarly literature on this field, one that has grown rapidly over the
last two decades, notably, but not only, in Britain and the USA. Indeed,
the cultural location of this literature suggests that this means of interrogation, this use of history, is especially appropriate for liberal, tolerant
societies.

However, there are readily apparent differences between the Western
countries in this academic (and public) willingness to interrogate the past;
although the extent to which the contrasts underlying these differences
should be seen in cultural or political terms, and as long-term or contingent,
is open to discussion. On the global scale, the contrasts between countries
are more notable. In addition, across the world, the academic values
asserted and defined by Evans have only limited purchase in the public use
of the past, a theme we will consider in the next chapter.

CHAPTER TWO

The State, the Private Sector, and Academe

> Iulia, my daughter – I think I told this story for her and her generation, the people born in the third millennium, people for whom the times of Nicolae Ceauşescu are on the same level of fantasy as those of Vlad the Impaler.

In the Acknowledgements section of *Kill the General*,[1] his novel on recent Romanian history, Bogdan Hrib (1966–) noted the way in which the past is swallowed up and flattened, with its significance drained away by distance. Ceauşescu, dictator from 1965, was overthrown in a revolution in 1989, while Vlad the Impaler was a notoriously cruel medieval ruler. For the young, these both become mythical figures, although Ceauşescu in fact played a key role in defining a path for a modern Romania that the Romanians have reacted against, both in 1989 and subsequently. This reaction, in turn, has framed the current political situation there.

Fiction and History

Beginning this chapter with a novel that seeks to bridge the divide between the Ceauşescu era and the present reminds us of the varied voices that explain the past. Hrib's novel covers the narrator's childhood, and then moves between 1985 and 2010, including an account of the 1989 revolution. In repeatedly moving between past and (then) present, the novel captures both memory and the impact of the past, in a manner that is denied Hrib's daughter for the period before her experience of life.

Novels, and other fictional forms, might seem distant from the subjects of historiography and public history, but they capture the way in which many people understand a past beyond their personal experience. Indeed, the success of historical novels is a notable feature of the 2010s, and not solely in Britain where Hilary Mantel's prize-winning novels on the circle of Henry VIII in the 1530s have led to an increase in discussion of how the past is experienced and presented. Historical novels have long been important as a popular approach to the past, and questions relating to their veracity and impact are long-standing, preceding those linked to cinema. This case is relevant anew because Mantel deliberately juxtaposed the historical imagination of the novelist to the approach of the academic historian,[2] arguing that the former provided more appropriate guidance to the mental world of the past. For her and Hrib, the state was the key level of activity, affecting the individuals in her plots. Although Mantel preferred the approach of the novelist, she seems to have taken G. R. Elton's thesis of the greatness and significance of Henry's leading minister, Thomas Cromwell, rather unquestionably. Thus, there is, at least in this case, a certain amount of academic sub-strategy even if the imagination takes over at a certain stage.

This interest in historical novels has proved a significant way in which the public has engaged with the past, and, indeed, has done so to an important extent since the nineteenth century: there are earlier historical novels. Historical dramas had played a comparable role from the sixteenth century, and in the case of Bible stories from the outset of the commemoration of Jesus' life.

There are significant parallels between historical and fictional writing. In 2010, Trevor Dean summed the situation up by focusing on the text:

> Though in content and positioning, in readability and temporal construction, history and fiction share common narrative modes, history marks its difference by referentiality and historiography [...] By these means, historians succeed in concealing the elements of their writing that they share with the writers of fiction.[3]

In short, historians adopt techniques to appear impartial. In practice, given that appearing in print or on the visual media means that historians necessarily adopt literary and rhetorical forms focused on a choice and use of narrative strategies, there is a considerable crossover with other forms of persuasion and of narrative. This can lead to an overlap between history and fiction as related rhetorical techniques,[4] although its extent can be debated. There is certainly an overlap in what Adrian Jones terms 'vivid history', an attempt to evoke a past, rather than to present it in formal arguments about outcomes and processes.[5] Thus, Birgit Vanderbecke's novella *Das Muschelessen* (*The Mussel Feast*, 1990) presents, in a family, the tyrannical nature of the East German state, and reveals the psychological nature of its rule and fall. There are also academic historical works that adopt such an approach. In eighteenth-century Britain, novelists, most prominently Henry Fielding, presented themselves as having the authority of the historian.[6]

More generally, in overlapping, or at least coinciding, with fiction, history thus contributed (and conformed) to memory, with the differing types of narrative providing memory aids that could be complementary as well as clashing.[7] The situation, however, varies by country. For example, the emphasis on lucidity in scholarly writing in national traditions differs very greatly, in part as a consequence of the differing role of publishers in framing and financing books and, thus, establishing the reputations of authors.

At the same time, there are significant cultural and procedural differences between academic historical and fictional writing. In particular, the latter focuses on the perspective of the individual novelist and seeks a distinctive voice accordingly, one that rests not only on style, but also on a particular imagination. In contrast, despite frequent claims to be original and definitive, academic work responds to the existing scholarship and interacts with it in an accretionary fashion.

History and the Public

The location of this debate about historical fiction is far from constant. Compared to the more self-consciously new 1960s and 1970s, historical experience today plays an increasingly appreciable role in national popular cultures, challenged, as they are, by the rise of globalization.[8] As a result, public discussion of historical matters has become more heated. Such contention is unsurprising given that historical work, whether by academics, popularizers, governments or individual memory, asserts the causality and significance of what occurs, and thereby enables individuals and societies to establish and locate themselves in time, to advance their views, and to defend their personal integrity.

In addition, the themes outlined in the Introduction direct attention to two relationships. The first is that between, on the one hand, the state, government, officials and their accounts of history, and, on the other, the range of groups that interact with the state. The second relationship is between the public accounts of history, understood, for the purpose of this book, as the discussion of history by, and for, the public, and those of the academic world. As this chapter will show, each of these relationships have been, and are, dynamic and, also, vary across the world. Combined, the relationships are also instructive about the world of history, indicating how, frequently, this world entails a mismatch between different approaches, if not a case of those employing particular approaches failing to communicate and, notably, to use the same language.

The particular twist here is that, like others in the genre, this book is written by an academic, employs academic language and concepts, and seeks to explain the subject for educational purposes. These are worthy purposes, and it is scarcely surprising that critical exegesis plays a key role in the academic approach. However, there is also a misleading tendency in this approach for this subject. At the risk of being accused of *trahaison des clercs*, betraying the values of my profession, there is a danger that the academic approach sometimes – indeed, often – adopts an unhelpful judgemental position. Such a position is instructively critical about the habitual use and misuse of the past, notably in terms of the supposed 'lessons of history'; but, at the same time, the critical voice and, even more, the judgemental position frequently do not engage with the potency and success of methods that are totally different to the academic approach.

It is not that much public history largely ignores the academic approach, but, rather, that it is essentially oblivious to the existence of such an approach. Again, the contrast varies across the world. Thus, in Germany, there is more of a public interest in academic debates than there is in the USA. Similarly, there is much more of an interest in Australia than in New Zealand.

Truth and Reconciliation

Differences in the degree of awareness of academic work are an aspect of a more general variety in the nature of engagement with the past. To take a specific instance of this engagement, one very much focused on the state, the treatment of 'truth and reconciliation' projects makes this point clear: they have different meanings in Sri Lanka in the 2010s, and Northern Ireland in the 2000s and 2010s. In the case of Sri Lanka, the focus on supporting the state, in the sense of the current government, is much clearer than in Northern Ireland, where there is a much greater willingness to criticise government.

Indeed, with respect to Sri Lanka, the condemnation of the process by which the Tamil Tigers' insurrectionary separatist movement was brutally suppressed, with heavy casualties, in 2009 comes essentially from abroad, notably from Europe and the USA. 'Truth and reconciliation' thereby is played out not only locally, but also across the international stage. Although Western opinion in this debate is significant, the views of Asian powers are more important now than over the last half-millennium. China, an important ally of Sri Lanka today, is not concerned about the criticism, while the opinion of neighbouring India is affected by geopolitical factors and by the ethnic politics of southern India, notably the large Tamil population.

Chronological contexts also reveal very different meanings for 'truth and reconciliation' projects. In 1979, the pro-Vietnamese People's Republic of Kampuchea, newly established by a successful Vietnamese invasion, condemned the murderous leaders of the previous Khmer Rouge regime

(r. 1975–9) in Cambodia to death for genocide. These leaders had fled from the capital, Phnom Penh, in 1979, but, supported by China, the opponent of the Soviet-backed Vietnamese, then Khmer Rouge, continued to resist the government of Kampuchea. This trial was very different in character and context to the later joint United Nations-Cambodian tribunal that, in the 2000s and 2010s, tried Khmer Rouge leaders for war crimes and crimes against humanity. Nevertheless, alongside this variety between states and contexts, readers would be well advised throughout this book to remember that there is a particular contrast in this subject between academic and non-academic approaches. The latter tend to be more open to the treatment of history as a live political issue.

Public Commemoration

Chronological contexts also affect the success of public commemoration. Carefully stage-managed accounts of national history have become less effective, as the public increasingly has access to a range of media and stimuli, notably international radio and television broadcasts, and, subsequently, the internet and social media. Political factors also play a role, especially in states with totalitarian regimes, which are best placed to retain such commemoration, as with Vietnam. In Hanoi, on National Day, Ho Chi Minh's Declaration of Independence from French colonial rule in 1945 is celebrated, while his embalmed body can be revered at his mausoleum, and there is also his house as well as a museum devoted to him.

In contrast, democratic countries with liberal values see frequent criticism of governmental presentations of the past. Thus, in Britain in 2013, the posthumous commemoration of Margaret Thatcher's life was accompanied, alongside much praise, by a degree of bitter criticism of her policies when Prime Minister in 1979–90 that would not have been seen in public discussion in many other countries. This criticism encouraged contention, not only about those years but also about how best to commemorate the lives of past leaders. It is likely that there will be considerable controversy when Tony Blair eventually dies, and notably over Britain's role in the invasion of Iraq in 2003.

World History and States

The state and the nation are the central players in the public history discussed in this book. This point is made abundantly clear by the consequences of large-scale decolonization in the twentieth century, a major change in the context and content of public history considered in Chapter Eight. Not only did that process create new independent states organizing their own histories, but, also, a linked and powerful demand to include their history and perspective in global history.

This development is particularly seen with Africa and, as Michael Brett pointed out in 2013, 'the choice of African history as a subject is itself a value judgment, of its worth as well as its possibility; it is part of the post-colonial consensus that aims to place the continent on a footing of equality with the rest of the world'.[9] Claims that Ancient Egypt was a 'black' civilization, the African character of which had been ignored in subsequent scholarship, and claims that this civilization was responsible for much otherwise attributed to Classical Greece, were advanced from the mid-1920s, and, more strongly, the mid-1950s, as part of an assertion of African importance and in order to strengthen the African-American pedigree. The claims were unfounded,[10] but reflect the more general extent to which the use of history in part involves the attempt to offer differing accounts of the relative value, or, at least, interest, of different parts of the world.

Returning to states, both individual and aggregate, there is the danger that selecting an approach to history focused on the state becomes self-fulfilling by making the state appear the key theme.[11] Indeed, this approach is a prime instance of a more general conceptual, methodological and historiographical flaw with categorization, making the unit of analysis disproportionately important. In the case of modern states, there is also the role of those states that did not survive, states that frequently complicate public attitudes today, not least by creating an alternative public history for commemoration and consideration.[12]

However, the thesis advanced in this book is that the role of state and nation in the public discussion of history, notably in education and commemoration, as well as frequently distinctive national features, such as language, ensure that the focus on the state is appropriate. Moreover, states have proved key historical actors as well as vital intermediaries and contexts for transnational processes.[13]

Technology and History

As a reminder of a contrasting perspective, and of a changing situation, the interplay between the verbal and the visual as means of presenting the past is altering rapidly as a consequence of new technology. Moreover, the interplay between the verbal and the visual is an important aspect of the relationship between public and private. This relationship provides both overlap and contrast: in the Western model, and notably in the modern age of heavily financed capitalism, the private sector has proved better able to respond to the opportunities of new technology than the state. At times, this context has created a structural tension between the opportunities of the private sector and the requirements of the state, one that, in totalitarian regimes such as modern China and Iran, has encouraged the policing of the internet. The freedom to access sources is a given in liberal democracies, but not in totalitarian regimes.

Cinema

Over the last century, film and then the internet provided opportunities to depict the past – opportunities that, in the West, were largely taken by private interests. There was, however, a separate use of film in totalitarian societies, some examples of which are discussed in Chapter Eight. Totalitarian regimes proved adept at using film for their own benefit in depicting history to support their ideologies. This was seen in particular with Nazi Germany and the Soviet Union, but was also the case with other dictatorships, such as Fascist Italy. This use of film could be intensive.

In the Soviet Union, the focus was on retelling the recent history of the Bolshevik revolution of 1917, with films such as *Strike, Battleship Potemkin, The End of St Petersburg* and *Lenin in October*. Thus, very recent history was given the ideological treatment. Subsequently, Russian history was harvested for useful subjects, particularly Stenka Razin and Pugachev, peasant rebels against the tsars. Moreover, from the late 1930s, there was a focus on tsars who could serve to demonstrate the need for transformative efforts against foreign threats, notably Peter the Great and Ivan the Terrible.[14] Thus, Russian history was interpreted in the light of the present. These rulers appear as progenitors of the modern leader in the shape of Joseph Stalin, the dictator from 1924 to 1953.

Had the Communist system prevailed in the Cold War, or even survived it, then this element of history in film would presumably have remained common. However, there were serious weaknesses in the Communist media world, not least a lack of flexibility, a didacticism that lent itself to mediocrity, and a stylistic approach that took scant account of public taste.[15]

Heavily influenced by Joseph Goebbels's Propaganda Ministry, Nazi Germany had its own filmic account, as with the propaganda 'documentary' film *Der ewige Jude* (*The Eternal Jew*, 1940). However, there was still a commercial imperative. *Der ewige Jude* is notorious as a piece of anti-Semitic propaganda, but it was not a box-office success and the evidence suggests that audiences were put off by its virulent hate propaganda. In contrast, the no less anti-Semitic *Jew Suss* (1940) was a popular success that couched its propaganda in the form of an historical narrative in which a fiendish Jewish moneylender covets and terrorizes a virtuous Aryan maiden.[16]

In the case of film, notwithstanding government imperatives, however, the search for entertainment and profit[17] was a key element in Anglo-American cinema, including the treatment of history. This emphasis was seen both in the topics covered and in the approach taken. There is a massive and rapidly developing literature on film history, and there is no intention here to summarize it.[18] Nevertheless, several points emerge. The use of history in film is to provide stories, but also to reflect public engagement with the past and, in particular, with what are seen as key episodes from the past. Here the past is moulded by the search for profit, while being presented in terms of tropes and topics that are at once timeless (heroism, war) and yet also heavily dependent on particular conjunctures.

The latter can be seen in the topics covered. For example, large-scale American participation in warfare in South Asia in the 2000s and 2010s led to interest in coverage of this and related topics, such as the Tehran hostage crisis of 1979–80 that was the subject of *Argo* (2012). Like *Charlie Wilson's War* (2007), an account of American intervention in the 1980s, in support of the Islamic opposition to the Soviet occupation of Afghanistan from 1979 to 1988, *Argo* provided an attractive story of American success and good intentions that offered a benign glow for more troubled times.

There are also important differences across time in the topics of more distant history that are covered. To a certain extent, there is a broader pattern of capitalist globalization, with those markets most subject to the impact of Hollywood, notably the anglophone ones, finding their history downplayed or presented negatively to meet the suppositions of American viewers. The latter has proved the case for Britain, most egregiously with the inaccurate as well as hostile treatment of medieval Britain in *Braveheart* (1995), and also with the inaccurate as well as hostile depiction of British forces in the American War of Independence in *The Patriot* (2000).[19] This pattern can also be seen with lighter adventure stories intended for the young, such as the *Pirates of the Caribbean* series in which the villains are uniformly British officials; the first, *Dead Man's Chest*, appeared in 2006.

More significantly, the tone adopted is subject to historical change. The positive British engagement with both empire and war, seen in British (and indeed American) films of the 1930s, 1950s and early 1960s, was replaced by darker, and more problematic, if not critical, accounts that cut across the previous practice of referring back for exemplary conduct, as with *Fire Over England* (1937), a film that suggested parallels between the Armada crisis of 1588 and the threatening contemporary situation. The historical imagination and perspective at play and offered in *The Charge of the Light Brigade* (1936), a heroic account of a disastrous mistake in 1854, and in *Zulu* (1964), a depiction of the heroic and successful defence of Rorke's Drift in 1879, were not those of *Oh! What a Lovely War* (1969), a highly critical account of the First World War. These films provided very different accounts of war and of Britain's historical role.

In the case of Australia, Peter Weir's iconic film *Gallipoli* (1981) offered a political dimension to disenchantment, one directed against the imperial link with Britain. In this deeply distorted account, the British contribution to the campaign was downgraded and misrepresented. The impression offered was of British inefficiency, cowardice and dilatoriness leading to the sacrifice of the Anzac troops.[20]

As an instance of the extent to which 'history wars' extend to cinema, albeit with many variations in the attitude of governments, *Argo* was condemned by Iranian officials as promoting Iranophobia. There was talk in March 2013 of an Iranian lawsuit against Hollywood directors and producers, and in Tehran a 'Hoax of Hollywood' conference was held that was attended by Seyed Mohammad Hosseini, the Minister for Culture and Islamic Guidance. *Argo* has not been screened in public in Iran, although pirate DVDs are readily available there on the black market. The conference statement condemned *Argo* as a 'violation of international cultural norms' and presented the award in the USA of the Oscar for Best Picture to the film, an award that was made by Michelle Obama, as a 'propaganda attack against our nation and all of humanity'.

Other films that offended the Iranian government include *300* (2007), an account of the heroic Greek resistance to a major Persian invading force at Thermopylae in 480 BCE. The film was described by Mahmoud Ahmadinejad, the Prime Minister, as 'insulting to Iran'. This response reflected the extent to which modern Iran (like modern Greece and Italy) seeks to lay claim to the legacy of greatness in Antiquity. More recent films also caused controversy, including *Not Without My Daughter* (1991), a film about an American woman fleeing Iran, and *The Wrestler* (2008), which featured a fighter called the Ayatollah, and was thus accused of perpetuating hostile stereotypes.

In the case of China and Japan, the key episode at issue in disputes over visual representation in film and on television is the Nanjing massacre of 1937. This episode, and current treatments of it, remain highly sensitive in both countries (see pp. 187–91).[21]

In contrast, most states are able to handle presentations on film with fewer difficulties. For example, the majority of French commentators are not outraged by British treatments of Napoleonic-era campaigns, as in the *Sharpe* (1993–8, 2006, 2009) and *Hornblower* (1998–2003) television series. The extent to which, in these and other British programmes, there is often a negative portrayal of some British characters, as a counterpoint to the British heroes, lessens the degree to which national rivalry takes centre-stage.

A different form of criticism of the past is that offered by modern German accounts of the Nazi period. Films such as *Der Untergang* (*Downfall*, 2004)[22] and television series such as *Unsere Mütter, unsere Väter* (*Our Mothers, Our Fathers*, 2013) dwell on this appalling period. On the whole, the tone is critical, although visual media can lend itself to the 'Stockholm Syndrome', making the protagonist a subject of sympathetic concern. This is a problem with *Unsere Mütter, unsere Väter*, as the willingness of German soldiers to commit atrocities is excused by being blamed on compulsion. The series has caused complaints in Poland as the depiction of the Poles suggests a degree of anti-Semitism. This issue touches a wider Polish sensitivity, not least as charges of anti-Semitism affect the international impact of the Polish self-portrayal as (undeserved) victims of the Second World War and the Cold War.

The issue of accuracy in television and film is not solely a matter of 'history wars', and the related extenuation and attribution of blame. *Downton Abbey*, a highly popular television story about the English aristocracy in the early 1910s that was broadcast from 2010, is fictional and depicts an imaginary family. *Downton Abbey* also presented what was claimed to be an accurate account of such a family, was filmed in a real stately home, and included mention of real people, such as the then Chancellor of the Exchequer, David Lloyd George, and episodes, notably the sinking of the ocean liner the *Titanic* in 1912, which began the story, and British entry into the First World War, which closed the first series. Moreover, partly because such a programme operates on the popular drama boundary between the educated and the entertained, the viewing public considers the series as an accurate account. Indeed, this belief led to complaints if there were inaccuracies in period detail,[23] while also giving rise to many conversations about the plausibility of aspects of the plot, for example social relations between servants and masters, and the sexual activities of particular characters.[24] Such British series can be compared to American programmes on the Civil War or China's series on the life of Mao Zedong's son who died in the Korean War.

There is also the impact of programmes that are deliberately untrue, notably comic accounts of the past. The four *Blackadder* television series, shown in Britain in 1983–9, and *Blackadder Back and Forth*, a one-off special produced for the Millennium celebrations in 2000, had a considerable impact.[25] In part, this impact rested on making the past ridiculous. At the same time, the last series, on the First World War, had particular resonance because it matched the popular belief in the deadly futility of the conflict, a belief in fact that fails to take note of its outcome in the shape of Allied victory.[26]

The tendency in the arts, if successful, to accord with, rather than challenge, public views on history can be seen also with popular historical writing. The latter frequently relates to the public mood, not least in terms of topics that are believed of consequence. Thus, Robert Hutchinson in *Elizabeth's Spy Master* (2006), his popular biography of Francis Walsingham (c. 1532–90), presented the Secretary of State (1573–90) as a great patriotic defender 'of this island state', alongside Nelson, Wellington and Churchill. Hutchinson established a modern context at the outset:

Walsingham would not have felt uncomfortable with the draconian Prevention of Terrorism Acts that have passed onto Western nations' statute books in recent years. Indeed, he would have been thwarted and handicapped by the modern notion of the importance of human rights and the restrictions on harsh methods of questioning imposed by Western societies. In the 1585 *Act for the Surety of the Queen's Person*, he and Burghley produced a startling example of counter-terrorist legislation.[27]

Leaving aside the views of those who sympathize with Elizabeth I's rival, Mary, Queen of Scots, who was Walsingham's principal target, as well as Catholics, the subject of repressive action, what is striking in this comparison is the attempt to debate the past in terms of the present, in order to make the book comprehensible and to help it sell. This approach is historiographically dangerous and leads to an anachronistic presentism. However, there are indeed parallels between the different kinds of suspicions that involve politico-religious groups willing to use assassination and even more murder to overthrow the status quo.

Despite the major role of the American film industry, it would be misleading to represent as being opposed state (governmental) and private (film and other media) in the account of the treatment of the past as if there was no overlap. In the specific case of Hollywood, there is not only concern about the views of the American public but also direct governmental intervention, especially in the provision of advice, for example in films linked to Intelligence activities. Thus, *Argo* in part reflected a more widespread attempt to present a positive account of American policy. There was no reference in the film either to prior American intervention in Iranian politics from the 1950s in support of the Shah's regime, or to the relationship (still unclear) between the hostage crisis and the electoral struggle for the presidency in 1980 between Jimmy Carter and Ronald Reagan. Selective contextualization can make for a successful film but poor history.

More generally, across the world, there is considerable overlap between state and public in the treatment of history, not least with the frequently close integration of state and private in cultural activity and relevant economic policy. This point appears more apparent in some cultures than others, for example China, rather than the liberal Anglo-American tradition with its constitutional limitations, political freedoms, notably of expression, and free market economics. The links between government and Hollywood that have existed, and still do exist, pall in comparison to the situation across much of the world. There is the chicken-and-egg question of what came first, with a strong state in the case of China a product of a particular culture, but also a cause of it.

Public History

Thus, the different contexts of state power and national assumptions are important in the processes surrounding the democratization of history, the

ability of so many to express opinions on the past, that has become so significant in recent decades. Currently, this democratization is greatly assisted
by the spread of the internet and of social media. Across the world, and
within individual states, this democratization has a varied public impact and
resonance. Linked to this point, public history can be variously defined by
the subject matter, by the approach, and in the shape of its different practi-
tioners; but also has a different character and content across the world.[28]
Thus, contrasting roles for public and private are seen in particular countries
and across time, as in the establishment of museums and the creation and
preservation of national monuments, such as the supposed replica of George
Washington's house at Mount Vernon.[29] In many states, there was no role
for the private sector comparable to that in this American case.

The role of non-Western cultures and states has traditionally been underplayed in accounts of historiography because these accounts tend to be
written in terms of liberal Western traditions. Moreover, generally they are
written by academics working in university institutions that, particularly
over the last seventy years, have been moulded according to these traditions. In this book, the focus will rather be on the statist tradition. The
approach taken in the following chapters will be chronological, indicating
how history, notably as a process of the identification of state and nation,
has been experienced and changed over the centuries.

CHAPTER THREE

The Public Life of the Past to 1400

Societies were suffused by the past for most of human history. This situation can be discussed and explained in both material and ideological terms, and each, indeed, was of importance. This chapter begins by considering both aspects before assessing key elements in the use of the past as well as certain important developments.

The Conditions of Existence

A leading element that encouraged the dominance of the past in human imagination was provided by the material circumstances of human existence. In particular, despite social mobility in the Church and administration, and through younger sons taking new lands, there was only a limited sense of the improvability of life, because there appeared only minimal prospects for such improvement. Such a sense of improvability is the view that leads towards a concept of progress in human time and of the future as progress. However, the perfectibility of man seemed possible only through miraculous means, notably divine intervention bringing salvation and immortality, and improvability therefore appeared to have only a limited prospect.

Indeed, the conditions of human existence were set by the largely unchanging rhythms of natural life. These rhythms were seasonal in their basis, and thus recurrent, the past providing the model and the basis for comparison. The seasonal rhythms were not unchanging, but were interrupted by calamities, such as animal and human diseases, or extremes of weather that humans could do little or, more commonly, nothing to mitigate, let alone solve.[1]

Historians need to be wary of determinist accounts, an approach in which the past can be used to offer a clear causation and a misleading validation. Nevertheless, in the material circumstances described in the last paragraph, there was doubt, anxiety, and a clinging to the beliefs and rituals of the past. These beliefs and rituals appeared to offer both propriation to God (or the gods), and consolation and meaning to humanity. Life was hard, the nature of work was grinding, the amount of food and fuel available generally limited, and, despite opportunities for enjoyment, most people had only limited leisure and energy to think about their position or to do much to improve it. As the means of education were restricted in these societies, there was also scant literacy.

This situation affected the nature of recovered memory and the ways in which accumulated experience could be passed on. Partly as a result of limited education, most people did not have the opportunity to receive or articulate views, other than in very local contexts, namely those of family, household and neighbourhood. Oral history was the key element here. It had a characteristic element of storytelling, an element that is retained in the present. Oral history also looks back for rhetorical and stylistic models, a characteristic also seen with much writing about history until comparatively recently.

Moreover, through their values and stories, local communities not only constructed their own history, but also influenced the impact of the history received from external agencies – history here understood both as the events of the past and as how the past was explained: two linked, but different, aspects of experience.

Despite this role for local communities, the general pattern of receiving knowledge was hierarchical by modern standards. This hierarchical structure was notably so with religion due to the intercessionary activity of the priesthood and its central part in education.

Alongside material factors came ideological counterparts that focused on reference to the past, and reverence for it, each of which was far greater in scale than the general modern situation. The most pronounced feature was ancestor worship, whether explicit, as in China, or implicit, as more commonly in monotheistic (one god) religions. In the latter case, the prestige of lineage as a social norm represented a variant on ancestor worship. Key elements for prestigious lineage were its length, exalted social status, and signs of divine fortune. These were factors that spanned societies across the globe, and were seen in different social milieux. At the pinnacle of society, there were accounts that linked ruling dynasties to gods and providential intervention, as well as rituals and ceremonies that sustained and reflected these links.

Dynastic Accounts

The most potent instance were the emperors of China. The importance of this position was shown by the extent to which new dynasties that conquered China, including those that were not Chinese in their origins, sought to incorporate the imperial tradition. This process continued until the last successful invading dynasty, the Manchu, which took power in 1644 and reigned until 1912. The Chinese sense of time focused on the past and the legitimacy it offered. Alongside a developed practice of record-keeping, there was a fascination with legendary times, with recording them, and with establishing descent from them, a fascination linked to issues of dynastic continuity and legitimacy. Longevity and continuity were characteristics regarded with approval, and this situation was reflected in the respect devoted to history and in its conceptualization and presentation.

These characteristics were not unique to China, but were given a particular form there. In China, histories were submitted for imperial approval, a practice for which a process of bureaucratization occurred. During the Tang dynasty (618–907), much thought was given to the development of a formal system of historical compilation, while, in the late tenth century, Emperor T'ai-tsung (r. 976–97) established the History Office and initiated the *Four Great Compendia of the Song Dynasty*.

As with the histories produced in the West in this period, although in a different context, functional considerations played a role alongside ideological counterparts in encouraging the appearance of historical works and in framing their contents. Dynastic histories were greatly concerned with the lessons that history could teach to present generations, potent models from the past providing an opportunity for change based on looking back. At the same time, the sensitivity of validation by the past led in China to strict censorship of the unofficial writing of histories and political memoirs,[2] a process that prefigured that of the Communist regimes of the twentieth century.

As far as the dissemination of a uniform view was concerned, there was nothing comparable in Western Europe, in part because of the divided nature of power. In particular, opposition between the Papacy and the (Holy Roman) Emperors, notably from the eleventh century, ensured that rival accounts, unwelcome to the other authority, were produced, with writers enjoying a measure of support accordingly. In contrast, in Byzantium (the Eastern Roman Empire based in Constantinople), the Emperor dominated the Orthodox Church.

Dynastic aggrandisement was not solely a matter for China, but was the case for dynasties elsewhere, including with new ones. History was employed to manufacture a legitimacy that testified to the more general process of sanction in terms of the past within a widespread context of sacral kingship. In fifteenth-century Melaka (Malacca, in modern Malaysia), the new rulers in fact stemmed from the royal line of the rajas of Srivijaya in Palembang, Sumatra; but, in contrast, seeking a more exalted pedigree, the Malay Annals stressed their remote ancestry and deployed myths and legends in order to connect the new rulers to great figures, and thus to demonstrate their rightness to rule.

So also with the Great and Lesser Annals in Sri Lanka. These were chronicles written from about 500 CE on palm leaves by Buddhist monks. In these *Annals*, the descent of rulers was traced to Vijaya, the legendary founding father of the Sinhalese in the fifth century BCE. At Polonnaruwa in Sri Lanka, the one-time capital of the most powerful state on the island, the Gal Pota (Stone Book), a block of stone assuming the shape of an ola book (book written on palm leaves), survives. It carries a large inscription providing information on the lineage of King Nissankamalla, a ruler of the twelfth century, as well as on his invasion of southern India and his building of a temple at Ramesvaram.

Lineage and the doings of mythical forbears were factors in the historical writing of the Classical West, as well as subsequently during the medieval and early modern periods. Current rulers in the medieval West and elsewhere saw themselves as being endorsed when they commemorated prominent figures from the past, both ancestors and epic leaders such as Hector of Troy and Alexander the Great. In France, the twelfth-century choirs of the churches of St Denis and St Remi included tomb effigies of such rulers.

In England, the Norman and Angevin kings sought to appropriate parts of the Anglo-Saxon past, notably with the cult of Edward the Confessor (r. 1042–66). This cult was an aspect of demonstrating legitimacy through continuity, for, far from being a conquering usurper, William I, 'the Conqueror' (r. 1066–87), the first of the Norman dynasty on the throne of England, was presented as the rightful heir of Edward. Harold (r. 1066), who succeeded Edward, only to be defeated at Hastings by William, was thereby seen as the usurper. *Domesday Book* (1086) lists tenure in Edward's then William's reigns, consciously omitting Harold. Honouring the cult of Anglo-Saxon saints proved an important part of establishing continuity on the part of Danish (Canute and his sons, r. 1016–42) and Norman conquerors in the eleventh century, and then later with the Angevin dynasty; although there was also suspicion of some saints.

In the Classical West, the use of history included offering appropriate support for the public accounts and rituals that were central to state myths, and, linked to that, providing an exemplary narrative for rulers and people.[3] Royal courts and religious institutions, many of which enjoyed royal patronage, were particularly significant milieux for the production and use of historical accounts. In royal settings, histories tended to proclaim monarchical and dynastic prestige and glory, and to support territorial expansion. For example, under Antiochus III, the Great (r. 223–187 BCE), of the Selucid Empire, a Hellenistic empire in the Middle East, Court historians produced precedents for his conquests, and extolled Antiochus' predecessors. This process was linked to his ancestor cult and to the settling of the epithets of the predecessors.[4]

Hellenistic rulers were particularly keen to demonstrate their link to Alexander the Great of Macedon (r. 336–323 BCE), who had created the first Hellenistic Empire by overthrowing his Persian rival in 331 BCE and had won great glory by doing so. This link established legitimacy and prestige, and was also important in the rivalry between these rulers, for example those of the Selucid and Ptolemaic dynasties, and in defining them as different to non-Hellenistic 'barbarians'.

Similarly, medieval German Emperors sought to demonstrate their descent from Charlemagne, who, in 800, revived the Western Roman Empire, being crowned in Rome. Linked to this, they also tried to show their descent from the Ottonians, the powerful Emperors of the tenth century. Barbarossa, the Emperor Frederick, had Charlemagne canonized by his antipope in 1165. The legacy of Charlemagne also led to a degree of competition with the French monarchy, who could claim similar descent. Descent was a matter of proving legitimate succession and of establishing the talisman of success. It was also significant in societies that made much of blood-right.

In addition, the legacy of the great Mongol conqueror Chinggis Khan (c. 1155–1227) was to be claimed by Central Asian rulers from the thirteenth century on. Links demonstrated legitimacy and prestige, and also offered a type of potency. For dynastic reasons, it was easier for some rulers to find a close link with Chingiz than for others, for example for Babur, the founder, in 1526, of the Mughal Empire in India, rather than for Timur the Lame (Tamerlaine), who died in 1405. Yet, the importance of this mandate of the past ensured that links with Timur, in turn, were asserted. That Babur, in the early sixteenth century, was keen to highlight his links with a ruler three centuries earlier demonstrated the importance of continuity and, in particular, the value of the distant past and the degree to which it was more significant than the recent past.

Dynasticism was a profoundly conservative means of legitimation and one that continued into more recent centuries. Even when meritocratic monarchs emerged – those who, like Nadir Shah in Persia in the 1730s and Napoleon in France in 1799, gained power through their own efforts – they themselves sought to establish a dynastic legitimation for their families and thus to ground their position. Having crowned himself Emperor in 1804, Napoleon divorced his first wife, Josephine, a commoner, in order to marry Marie Louise, the daughter of the Emperor Francis I of Austria, formerly the Holy Roman Emperor Francis II. Thus, the legitimacy of the past was joined to a new legitimacy based on power.

That both of these instances date from the period 1730–1815 indicates the extent to which this process was not one only seen in distant time. Furthermore, modern republican dynasties suggest the continued resonance of the dynastic practice. This is seen with the Assads in Syria, rulers in two generation, and with the family of Kim-Il Sung in North Korea, rulers in three generations. Members of the latter family have hitherto been the effective head of state throughout the history of that state. However, the context and ideology of dynasticism are now very different to the situation in the eighteenth century.

Oracles and Prophecy

Looking back as a means of legitimation was/is not only the case with
dynasticism. It was/is also seen with the weight of religious practice and
teaching. However, in this case, there was also the validation offered by the
new, notably in terms of providential events, but, in addition, through the
truths supposedly provided by oracles and prophets. One of the major uses
of Greek and Roman history thus became the lessons it offered of respecting
oracles.[5] To do so was the accepted way of reasoning at the time, with
oracles providing the basis for appropriate choices, and thus events. In turn,
ignoring oracles provided a way to explain failure. Ancient Chinese beliefs,
most prominently advanced by Confucius, made similar points. Under
the Han dynasty (206 BCE–9 CE, 25–220 CE), one of the Court astrolo-
ger's duties was record-keeping. Indeed Sima Qian (145?–86 BCE), who
inherited the position from his father, also inherited an unfinished project
he brought to fruition: writing a history of Chinese civilization from the
earliest known recorded times to his own era. His completed *Records of the
Grand Historian* stands as the model for all subsequent officially sanctioned
Chinese historical writing.[6]

Oracles were also involved in the Christian tradition, both because the
old Roman sibyls, such as the Tiburtine Sibyl, were Christianized, and also
in the shape of saints and their relics. Prophesying played a major role in the
chronicles of a number of cultures, for example those of the ninth century
Abbasid caliphate based in modern Iraq, then the leading Islamic state.
Prophecy there was also linked to the presentation of history in terms of
parables, with the emphasis in both on morality.[7]

More generally, in both time and place, history was located in a
continuum of past, present and future. Thus, historical writing, reading
omens, and astrology were all linked. Providentialism and storytelling
were key elements in the interlinked accounts of past, present and future.
Prophecy and astrology as guides to the future drew part of their credibility from similar explanations of the past. At the same time, prophecies
were revised in order to take note of a changing present.[8] The interlinked
accounts of past, present and future serve as a reminder that history, as a
process of change and explanation, was not seen as distinctive, in its effects
or even causes, to the past and restricted to it.

This is a key point in evaluating the use of history. History certainly
in the Classical period, that of ancient Greece and Rome, but also more
generally, both geographically and chronologically, was not a particular
account of the past, because the sense of the past as different was limited.
As a result, the past was ever-present, which helped ensure that history
had a purpose, notably for moral guidance or by providing instruction by
example.[9] Because the past was present, the sense of the past as different,
because past, was, by modern standards, limited.

This situation affected the utility of history as a category, process and means of explanation. This was because the presence of the past and, certainly, the lack of a strong sense of development through time, helped determine the significance attached to time, the understanding of change, and the possibility of fixing accounts of cause and effect to particular chronological contexts. Moreover, there were not fixed forms characteristic only of historical writings. Instead, common stylistic and rhetorical forms and devices were seen in writing and speaking about past, present and future.[10]

Myth

In turn, the role of providentialism and storytelling, the two frequently linked by the use of oracles, underlined the mythical character of historical exposition and its dependence both on otherworldly agencies, operating beyond, in and on the human sphere, and on priestly intermediaries. Use of the term myth presupposes a clear contrast with history. In practice, the construction and exposition of each represented exercises of imagination as well as utility, a situation that is still pertinent. To modern eyes, myth overlaps more with fiction, but the extent to which ready distinctions can be drawn is unclear as myth and history overlap and feed on each other, both employing imagination.[11] The role of storytelling in each is emphasized in the narrative approach. Powerful oral traditions contributed to this approach.

An emphasis on ancestry linked to religious foundation myths was widely seen. In the Pacific island of New Caledonia, society was organized into clans with reference to mythical ancestors. An impressive instance is provided by New Zealand, where tribal historical narratives continue to play a role in Maori culture. Arriving from Polynesia about 800 years ago, Maori mythology focused on the demigod Māui, under whom the islands of New Zealand allegedly originated. The landing places of the canoes were of more particular note, as genealogies were traced back to those who came on the canoes. The assertion of a relationship to Māui was also important, as part of a process in which tribal success over other tribes involved conflict between gods, leading to the spiritual union of conquerors with the land they had conquered. Oral traditions in New Zealand provided a record of ancestors and bound their descendants to the land, linking places and people. Tribal histories related the past to spiritual conflict, with warfare on land related to that between gods. Similar patterns can be seen elsewhere, for example in early Buddhism.

Across the world, although myth is still very much in evidence in the modern age, there is an unwillingness to embrace the approach explicitly, and, instead, the myth in question is sometimes presented as public history. Thus, the transformation and representation of myth in different contexts is an important theme that is in the background to this book.

The context of history relates to the form as well as the content of the understanding of time. Astrology, for example, plays a role in modern culture, notably with horoscopes. Moreover, some leaders over the last century had links with astrologers, particularly Hitler. Nevertheless, oracles and astrology as a basis for government policy would now be regarded as peculiar. As Iran since the revolution of 1978–9, however, shows, religious arguments can still play an explicit role in the discussion of policy.

Sacred and Human Time

The interactions of sacred and human time and action played a major role in human assumptions for most of the past, and thus shaped experience. The need to understand the role of the sacred helped explain the centrality in history of astronomical and astrological observation and record-keeping, and of calendrical systems. In contrast, the development of history in the modern sense, of a narrative and analysis of change in human society (as opposed to an account of divine intervention), rested in part on an understanding of the significance of time, and, specifically, the separation of present from past. Such a separation created the past as a subject and one that did not describe and determine the present.[12]

However, the separation of past from present did not have particular weight for societies that put an emphasis on cyclical theories of time, and thus on a return, in the future, to the present, nor for societies that, whether or not in a cyclical context, had a strong desire to recreate the past. The cyclical emphasis was especially the case for peoples who focused on the rhythms of the seasons that dominated agriculture, fishing and forestry, which were the activities that determined most livelihoods. Even industry and trade were affected. The water and wind energy crucial for power were transformed by the seasons, as were the interplay of winds and currents, the melting of snows, and the beginning of the growth of grass, all of which were important for trade routes, and thus for production and consumption. The role of cyclical theories and natural rhythms was shown in the derivation of the word revolution, which originally carried with it the meaning of return to the starting point, as with the movement of the heavenly spheres.

Alongside the materialist account, indeed explanation, of cyclical views, the varied interpretation of time[13] was also a consequence of the diverse nature of creation and revival myths, and of ecclesiological accounts of time and of divine intervention.[14] Allowing for this variety, the interaction of human and sacred space was a central theme and context for history, and one that did not generally encourage a sense of major development through human time. This interaction involved events, notably the works of divine Providence, the actions of prophets, and the activities of priests, or the malign doings of diabolical forces and their earthly intermediaries such as witches. News of these told, and retold, familiar tales and superstitions as part of religious worldviews that linked past, present and future within a prospectus of essential stability or at least a prospectus determined by this religious worldview.

Christian History

Origin stories were particularly important for religions, but so also were the affirmation, sanctions, parameters and prohibitions that past practice and judgement brought to doctrine, liturgy, organization and rights. Thus, in Christendom (as in Judaism), there was a continual process of referring back, notably to earlier religious figures and their writings, and to the Councils of the early Church. Referring back continued when the apparently 'new' was offered, as with the Protestant Reformation of the sixteenth century. The Reformation was anchored on a reading of the Bible and Primitive Christianity, and an attempt to remove the subsequent accretions of Catholicism.

For Christians, the Gospels provided historical evidence for the life and teaching of Christ. However, in place of the basic historical background in the Gospels of a real Jesus, a cosmic Christ developed through systematic theology. Experience was replaced by a non-historical religious discourse matching an ordered religious life. Moreover, rules helped define unacceptable practice. The Church Councils established rules on theology and liturgy. In addition, computus, the process of the calculation of time, notably the date of Easter, the key date in the Christian year, depended not only on mathematical knowledge but also on an understanding of past practice.

A discussion of early heresies was an important part of St Augustine's influential *City of God* (412–27 CE). As an example of changing values and of the consequently altering history of reference and discussion, this aspect of the work does not currently attract attention. Instead, the discussion, in Book Nineteen of the work, of the parallel between Alexander the Great and a band of brigands is most commonly cited. In many respects, this part and past is unrepresentative of the content of *City of God*.

Alongside heresies, and overlapping with them in the process of legitimation through definition, Christianity took dissimilar paths in its early years, with Ethiopian Orthodoxy, for example, very different to Catholicism. A similar process can be seen with both Buddhism and Hinduism. Each of these paths had their own narratives that were grounded in an historical account that provided legitimacy, authentication and distinctiveness. Tracing the origins of approved current practices, for example in liturgy or organization, back, in the Christian case, to the early

Church, provided a way to demonstrate appropriate conduct, and thus to require support.

Within these paths, individual ecclesiastical foundations, notably archbishoprics, bishoprics, churches and monastic orders, competed to construct, record and assert individual histories that justified their claims. These claims made specific the wider creation in which human agents acted and were acted upon, and in which knowledge, based on an experience of the past and an understanding of the present, was used to seek truth about the future.

For example, Herman the Archdeacon, a monk at the wealthy abbey at Bury St Edmunds in England in the 1090s CE, implied an interplay between chaotic world forces, to which God usually permitted directing power, and, on the other hand, merciful divine regulation that occurred, particularly in 'ages of mercy'. Thus, a central task of the chronicler, at once historian and hagiographer, was to provide information on this divine intervention, notably via the miraculous career of the local saint, king and martyr, St Edmund, who had been killed by heathen Danish invaders, but who had survived through his sainthood. Information and intervention therefore served to display the continuing potency and, thus, power and relevance of the saint,[15] a process made more necessary by rivalries between particular cults. New saints meant new miracles and new hagiographers, as in the cult of Thomas Becket at Canterbury, and, in turn, miracle stories were collected in a branch of historical works.[16]

Time, sacred and human, and place were linked by the chroniclers[17], in a process that looked toward the histories of peoples that were to follow with the proto-nationalism discussed later in this chapter. The attempt to emphasize collective piety and to minimize paganism was an aspect of this link of time and place, and also in the positive discussion of peoples that can be discussed in these terms. Conversion accounts and relics played an important role in this history.

So also with other religions, for example Buddhism. The remnants of the Buddha's body were given to kings and then placed in temples, providing a clear endorsement. As a result, the history of the individual remnants was important. Thus, the sacred tooth of the Buddha, which arrived in Anuradhapura, the capital of the leading Sri Lankan state, in the fourth century BCE, passed from dynasty to dynasty in Sri Lanka, the role of guardianship confirming the legitimacy of kings. When Elizabeth II visited Ceylon (Sri Lanka) as its Queen in 1954, she paid respect to the tooth. As such, she fulfilled the role of her predecessors in Ceylon, traced out in the idea that there was a seamless succession of rulers backed to Vijaya, the legendary founding father of the Sinhalese in the fifth century BCE.

In medieval Christendom, information on martyrs and relics was also of interest to bishops as it helped strengthen their claims to metropolitan status. Information about the ongoing miracle-working powers of relics thus also entailed a retrospective rewriting of saints' legends as new priorities were added. Local histories often sought to join the account of the locality and its particular historical rights, rites and magic, with national and universal history, the first detailing the support offered by rulers, the second signs of the central events of Christian revelation.

That histories were written by those with clerical education, interests and careers underlined this approach.[18] As formal education was very much under the control of the clergy, and largely for them, it was not surprising that their concerns dominated what was written.

New foundations, such as the archbishopric of Hamburg and the abbeys of the Cistercian monastic order, in turn sought the validation of new saints' lives, lives that were also helpful in competition between sees. In his *Vita Anskarii* (life of St Ansgar), the key figure in the mission to northern Germany, Rimbert, offered an instance of the way in which successive bishops, notably Ansgar (d. 865), emphasized hagiography to gain status and papal privileges, first in obtaining episcopal and then archepiscopal status, the latter confirmed by Pope Formosus in 893.[19] Cistercian validation was exemplified by the lives produced by the Cistercian hagiographer Jocelin of Furness, who flourished from 1175 to 1214. *Vita Waldevi* was the life of a near-contemporary Cistercian abbot, Waltheof, Abbot of Melrose. The *Vita Waldevi* appears to have been commissioned as the first step in an application for canonization. The project was part of the Cistercian construction of a golden age.

In Christendom, as in other religions, including Islam and Buddhism, historical writing was thus often joined with relics, providing an affirmation of value, identity and need. By describing and defining religious activity, history served to provide religious identity through time and space, but also to assert the specificity of particular interests. Moreover, alongside similarities between cultures, came differences, if not contrasts, with the past presented and used in distinctive fashions. These included differing meanings of language and symbol, notably particular conventions of rhetoric and narrative techniques. Myths were employed to capture essential relationships, as in India.[20]

To that end, epics could be altered to take note of changing circumstances. Thus, the *Mahābhārata* (*c.* 400 CE), the world's longest epic poem, in its various redactions, saw the addition, or substitution, of contemporary peoples, kings and regions. A similar process occurred with the sacred Hindu texts known as the *Purānas*, which transmitted traditional knowledge.[21] The role of myths in Indian consciousness has encouraged the idea that ancient and medieval India had an ahistorical culture, but this view has been challenged, and it has been argued, in contrast, that a linear view of time was deployed there.[22]

These general comments on the historical imagination and use of history in CE 1–1500 are also relevant for more modest levels of activity and identity. Community as a whole rested on an awareness of, and belief in, continuity, and to a degree that was more insistent than in the modern world, where stress, instead, is more commonly on current consent and future prospects. In the past, freedoms and liberties were particular, rather than general, and that emphasis led to a strong focus on the processes and records by which these privileges had been gained, preserved and expressed. As authority as a whole was often imperial in its origins and pretensions, so it was necessary to explain why this authority was lessened or delegated in the case of particular jurisdictions, such as city councils or trading organizations or manufacturing guilds.

History, therefore, established particular rights. Historical research contributed to dynastic interests, both by establishing claims to privileges, notably precedence and territory, and by defining succession laws, as with the Salic Law in France. Legitimacy rested not on the consent of the people, but on the weight of rights which were proved by ancestry and descent. This situation was true across society, from the ruler to the peasant. Moreover, the culture of chivalry ensured that there was a relevant material culture. Questions of lineage also encompassed heraldry, with assertion and disputes being waged via coats of arms.

The strength of a historicist culture does not mean that the latter is not subject to change. Indeed, this change was both significant and created a need for explanation. In practice, this need was often met by denying that change had occurred. A key method to do so was by incorporating the consequences of change into this very historicist culture. In the space available, it is only possible to focus on one culture, Western Christendom, but many of the points made for it are also valid for other cultures. For example, proselytism, generally by means of conquest, created, both for Islam and for Christianity, the need to offer new histories, both of that process and for the regions thus converted. The building, naming, dedication and operation of new churches and mosques was an aspect of this process – not least as these buildings recorded the history of their foundations and marked the process of proselytism.

Christendom had created a need for history when the historical moment, the end of history, the apocalyptic conclusion, receded from being imminent, while time before this conclusion both became longer, and had to be narrated and organized. A use of history as demonstrating and foretelling the prophesied move toward the Second Coming of Christ and the Last Judgment remained significant, but was now less urgent as the central theme. At the same time, the use of history for providential purposes remained highly significant, as, indeed, it has done, both in the West and elsewhere, to the present. This providentialism was seen at play for nations, communities and individuals, as with sacred winds that helped save both Japan (in the thirteenth century) and England (in 1588) from invasion. Winston Churchill, British Prime Minister from 1940 to 1945, and others employed providential language at the time of the Second World War.

The Church took the key role in narrating and organizing time, and this situation remained the case for centuries, not least because, in Christendom, as elsewhere, so many of those who were educated were clerics. Moreover, religious institutions had the means to create and preserve historical (and non-historical) accounts. Cults of sainthood, notably relics and pilgrimages, helped ground religious practices of narrating and explaining time in popular support.

A focus on origins and ancestry affected much of the understanding and writing of history, with the authority of earlier accounts encouraging an emphasis on new work largely as a continuation of them, while also favouring what is somewhat unfairly seen as 'scissors-and-paste' treatments of the past. There was also a large-scale fabrication of historical sources, such as papal decretals and the Donation of Constantine (awarding of rights to the Papacy by the Emperor Constantine, the first Roman emperor to promote Christianity), or the eleventh-century claim that St Martial was one of the Apostles, in order to establish and enhance particular claims.[23] At the same time, a religious worldview and an interest in origins were scarcely incompatible with scholarly values such as independent judgement, impartiality and critical acumen.[24]

Although there were earlier analogues such as Roman annals, medieval European chronicles were an innovation rather than a continuation of earlier traditions. These chronicles began in forms such as Easter annals, king-lists, and chronological lists of benefactors, many of which were compiled by monasteries to help them date documents. These lists could begin at fairly arbitrary points, and, at least, not at any clear point of origin in the sense of origin myths. Most of the 'great' canonical medieval chronicles, for example Orderic Vitalis (1075–c. 1142), the Anglo-Norman author of the *Historia Ecclesiastica*, were mainly interested in their own time or a generation or two before, an approach that certainly reflects their significance for later historians.

In some chronicles, origin stories were clearly important and they were told as memorable tales over which a certain amount of care had been taken, but they were not necessarily the reason for the writing of the history. For example, the *Decem libri historiarum* (it only appears as *Historia Francorum* in later interpolated manuscripts) of Gregory, Bishop of Tours (c. 538–94) provided an account of the Creation, the origins of Christianity, the story of St Martin (the beginnings of Gregory's see of Tours in France), and the origins of the ruling Merovingian dynasty then ruling much of France. However, Gregory had achieved all that by the end of Book Two, and the remainder is an ever more detailed narrative of events of his own time or the generation just before.

Roughly the same could be said of the *Historia Ecclesiastica Gentis Anglorum* (*Ecclesiastical History of the English People*, 731) by the Venerable Bede, a Northumbrian monk who provided very carefully crafted origin stories of how Christianity came to England, but whose real preoccupation was the confrontation of the Celtic and English churches in the period within a century of his own time. Bede says most about the generation before his, and is surprisingly silent on his own lifetime, which is generally interpreted as implicit criticism. His *De Temporibus* (*On Time*) was intended to challenge millenarian predictions.[25]

Despite works such as that of Bede, who presented the English as one Christian people, national identities were 'not widely prominent' in Europe in 1000.[26] At the same time, the Church was affected by the reality and rise of state accounts of powers and rights. The clash of Church-state relations was played out for centuries, and historical references played a major part in this clash. The imperial pretensions of rulers conflicted with the ecclesiology of the Papacy. Past claims, examples and privileges were deployed, and, if necessary, forged, accordingly. And so also with the arts. The Church proved adroit at using the arts to record its historical credentials and claims, as with paintings representing the Donation of Constantine or clashes between saints and emperors, notably the Emperor Theodosius being confronted by St Ambrose, Bishop of Milan, in 389 and 390. At the second confrontation, the Emperor was forced to perform public penance for ordering a massacre.

New events were historicized in terms of respective interests, as with the conflict between Pope Gregory VII and Henry IV, King of Germany in 1076–7, a clash that included the excommunication of Henry in 1076 and the latter's short-term reconciliation with Gregory after a meeting at Canossa. Chroniclers on both sides left highly partisan accounts of the dispute, despite the evidence known about what was really at stake. In turn, these incompatible views encouraged a second excommunication, in 1080, followed, in 1084, by Henry capturing Rome, installing an antipope, and having himself proclaimed Emperor.

Over the following centuries, distinctive national histories emerged and developed. Compared to universal history, these national histories offered a different account of origins, an account that was a more central concern than is the case today in public history. Medieval writers sought to trace the origins, and thus rights and character, of nations, states, dynasties and cities, with the key themes being longevity, legitimacy and links to Classical civilizations.[27] Thus, Geoffrey of Monmouth, in his *Historia Regum Britanniae* (*History of the Kings of Britain*, 1136), linked these kings to the house of Priam, who had ruled Troy. He had Aeneas of Troy's grandson, Brutus, found Britain and London. Geoffrey, indeed, had Brutus call London 'New Troy', and this account of a Trojan origin of London was repeated by William fitz Stephen in about 1173 and by Matthew Paris in about 1252.

Geoffrey also provided details of the story of Gog and Magog, two legendary giants who allegedly acted as guardians of London. All sorts of pre-Roman Celtic and ancient Greek and Roman mythological references and traditions were jumbled up to produce these figures, almost certainly derived ultimately from folk tales which had transformed real historical warriors incrementally into larger and more supernaturally powerful beings. Alongside the link back to Troy, there were fictional Welsh geneal-ogies which seemed to trace people back to the Bible.

The interest in urban foundation legends led to links back to Classical myths and literary works providing stories, themes or templates. Civic rituals of remembrance inscribed these stories into the annual cycle of communities, helping to create a common identity with specific values.[28]

The history of emperors and, even more, kings (as with those of later republican polities) reflected themes of national distinctiveness, not least with the emphases on origins and war. Such histories also, however, highlighted the universal ecclesiology as a result of the stress on the signifi-cance of a particular code of behaviour, as for example in the *Genealogia Regum Anglorum* (1153–4) by the Cistercian monk Aelred of Rievaulx (1109–66). In some respects, this idea of a king portrayed a semi-sacral figure whose ability and willingness to heed divine injunctions matched the Classical importance of heeding omens, although Christian commentators probably put a greater emphasis than Classical forbears on the purity of royal motivation. Divine Providence was a key theme and means.

Dynastic chroniclers therefore are often seen as Providential in orientation, although reference to God frequently seems to be a matter of apotropaic duty, intended to avert bad luck by reminding readers of the need to acknowledge God. Moreover, by the thirteenth and fourteenth centuries, there was a large number of non-monastic chronicles. Many writers pursued events with a relative lack of theological adornment and do not seem to have been inspired by a drive to 'justify the ways of God to men'. That was certainly not the central theme in the Icelandic sagas, which were as much family histories as they were literature. Indeed, many of these ancestor stories, for example *Egil's Saga*, had an amoral quality. Family histories on mainland Europe, such as the *Deeds of the Counts of Barcelona*, also lacked a religious drive.

Proto-Nationalism

If the Papacy proved particularly effective in the early thirteenth century, notably under Innocent III (r. 1198–1216), its relative power and authority was compromised by subsequent divisions, notably a schism that left two rival popes and competing sources of validation. At the same time, the assertiveness of individual rulers who sought greater power over the Church in their dominions was an aspect of a proto-nationalism that was linked to ideas of distinctive character as well as rights, and that drew on a conviction that nations had a continuity that conveyed these rights.

Alongside the significance for medieval Catholic Europe of what can be described as transnationalism,[29] notably in religion and culture, this proto-nationalism was seen widely across Catholic Europe from the fourteenth century, but with many significant antecedents. The dynastic theme remained significant, but also broadened out with a greater emphasis on place and people. As in the Islamic world, there was a determined attempt to assert links with earlier dynasties. The heroism of particular rulers, such as Alfred of Wessex, underlined the value of such descent. The praise of earlier monarchs in dynastic histories served to provide an exemplary background for the description of current rulers. The latter, in turn, could take a major role in supporting appropriate accounts of the past. Discontinuities, in contrast, were explained by Providence, as when the Carolingians claimed that their Merovingian predecessors had been ineffectual rulers, and hence replaced by Providence.

The anonymous *Gesta Principum Polonorum* (*The Deeds of the Princes of the Poles*), another early twelfth-century work, provided an account of the mythical foundation of the dynasty and information on Boleslaw the Brave (r. 992–1025), the ancestor and namesake of the author's likely patron, Boleslaw III (r. 1102–38). This account of dynastic history provided an exemplary background for the description of Boleslaw III's reign.[30] Alfonso X of Castile (r. 1252–84) sponsored official history as an aspect of a more general engagement with culture as a means for national identity, as well as of celebrating his victories over the Moors in southern Spain. Aside from supporting a general history of Spain written in Castilian, Alfonso also tried to make Castilian the official language of law and administration, and had the Old Testament translated. Alfonso's reign began a process of developing official history, written in the vernacular, as a political tool.[31] In 1165, Emperor Frederick I Barbarossa had his antipope Paschal III canonize Charlemagne, while in the mid-fifteenth century, Henry VI of England supported the canonization of Alfred, King of Wessex.

A focus on ancestors enhanced the position of ethnic and social groups as well as ruling dynasties. Myths centred on the migration of people at the time of the collapse of the (Western) Roman Empire in the fifth century proved a key way to locate the history of nations.[32] In Hungary, chronicle literature came to identify the population with the Scythians of antiquity and with the Huns who had conquered the region in the fifth century. This descent was linked with a passage from the historian and encyclopedist Isidore of Seville (c. 560–636), who claimed that the Hungarians had drawn up a covenant giving elected representatives the right to make laws and administer justice. This idea, repeated in medieval chronicles, supposedly substantiated aristocratic rights. Peasants were excluded from the inheritance.[33] In Germany, the idea of Germanness took shape in part after the tenth-century Saxon emperors began to take armies into Italy. Legends about earlier migrant bands of soldiers, for example Trojans, played an important role in accounts of particular German 'descent groups'.[34]

Opposition to rulers deemed foreign played an important part in encouraging proto-nationalist identity and history.[35] Examples included Scotland (against the kings of England), Flanders (against the kings of France), the Swiss cantons (against the Habsburgs), Germany, in part as a result of the clash between Emperor Ludwig IV (r. 1314–47) and the Papacy,[36] and the Hussites of Bohemia (against Emperor Sigismund [r. 1410–37] and the German princes). John Barbour's poem the *Brus*, composed in Scots in 1375, was an anti-English national epic centring on Robert Bruce and the 'freedom' of Scotland, which had been secured by Bruce's victory over Edward II of England at Bannockburn in 1314. In turn, such works served to discredit those who looked to England at the time of their composition. Ancestry myths were therefore brought into the present and recent-present of an experience shared by a people who lived in a specific territory. Aggressive feelings of national identity were also seen between England and France in the Hundred Years' War, while fourteenth-century England also saw such sentiments directed against Scotland.[37]

The use of the vernacular was an aspect of proto-nationalism and this affected the writing of history. In addition to the continued use of cosmopolitan languages, notably a powerful Latinity, as well as French in England,[38] there was a turn toward historical records in the native language which was appropriate given the increased use of documents in administration and law.[39] Symbols of collective identity developed, including national saints, such as St George in England.[40] Efforts made to canonize figures central to local cults, such as St Brigitta and St Nikolaus of Linköping in Sweden, were aspects of a national assertion within the international order of Catholicism,[41] although there was also a more far-flung pattern of devotion across Christendom, for example of St George.[42]

Conclusions

Well prior to the Protestant Reformation of the sixteenth century, and notably from the thirteenth and fourteenth centuries, the monastic tradition of historical writing generally lacked vigour and was superseded by the rise of vernacular works not produced in a monastic context and intended for individual reading. In England, the tradition of chronicle-writing at St Albans, the major English centre for the thirteenth and fourteenth centuries, came to a close in the 1420s and was followed by a speedy collapse of the genre in England. Writing in the vernacular became common from the mid-thirteenth century, with texts such as the *Histoire Ancienne* and the *Grandes Chroniques de France* appearing in considerable quantities. The latter included translations of Latin chronicles.

In addition, instead of a stress on the Christian viewpoint of universal history, came history as the humanistic narration of politics, both of the Classical world and also of the kingdoms and cities of the modern world, the latter encouraging a newly strong notion of heritage. Thus, far from the medieval period being a relatively static one, after which, and in reaction to which, change occurred with the Renaissance, there were significant developments in it. These included, in the later Middle Ages, a rising popular opinion related to a developing sense of national identity, as in England and France, and a manuscript boom that included inexpensive formats, such as tracts, as well as more expensive illuminated manuscripts.

The rise of lay literacy was a significant element, as history therefore became a commodity produced in multiple copies of manuscripts for a growing audience. The control over the understanding of the past offered by fewer copies held essentially in Church and Court contexts was replaced by developing communities of readers, each able to respond individually to the work in question.[43] Politically, these communities were in part defined by the developing governmental structures of the periods, including the administration of the law.[44] Alongside the Church, which had the most sophisticated such structure, there was a strengthening of state structures that was important to the process of self-identification.

CHAPTER FOUR

Historicizing New Beginnings, 1400–1650

The Renaissance

The revival of knowledge of, and interest in, Classical literature, which played a major role in the Renaissance, provided not only information on the Ancient world that helped foster further interest, but also models for considering more recent times and for understanding the current situation. Thus, Spanish historiography on the conquest of the New World owed much to the ideas offered by Classical works which, notably with Roman expansion, provided a suitable pedigree as well as reference point.[1] The role of Classical literature also helps explain why Egypt and, far more, Mesopotamia largely dropped from the cultural, intellectual and political radar of a Western civilization that was to be focused on Greece and Rome.

Alongside themes of continuity, the humanistic learning and tendencies of the Renaissance were linked to a self-consciously critical reading of sources, which was an important aspect of the process by which supposedly timeless values, such as Roman law, were presented as grounded in particular historical conjunctures.[2] The return to original sources, as well as a close concern with the accuracy of original texts, was also shown in debates over how best to read and translate the Bible.

In turn, when the authority and, therefore, impact of the Classics was challenged in the seventeenth century, notably in the 'Ancients' versus 'Moderns' debate, this debate included questions of historical method, such as the discussion of the use of rhetorical devices in historical narratives. This discussion was part of the ongoing dispute about sources, as such devices were frequently seen as fictional.[3]

It was not only in the West that a critical attitude towards historical materials was adopted. In China, from the early sixteenth century, differences between documentary materials and stories transmitted by hearsay were emphasized by historians such as Wang Shih-chen (1526–90). This process was linked to a greater emphasis on primary documents, and thus more writing on state affairs which was the great source of such documentation. Rising interest in history was related to a significant increase in literacy in China.[4]

Alongside proto-nationalism as a cause of change in historical content and form, there was a transformation of the Western understanding of time in the later Middle Ages, as thinkers, who were later to be grouped together in the Renaissance, sought to reach beyond an allegedly decrepit and degenerate present in order to grasp the reality of a more virtuous past. This classification of time presented a distinction that was not present in Christian thought, with its emphasis on a fallen mankind awaiting redemption through a Second Coming of Christ. Instead, history could be inserted into the account in order to distinguish between a dark age and an earlier antiquity that offered the possibility of a renewal, both now and for the future. Francesco Petrarch (1304–74), the first of the major Italian humanists, was an important figure in this development, one that helped make history useful by providing texts, ideas and practices for emulation. In 1345, Petrarch discovered Cicero's *Letters to Atticus*, part of the process of discovering rare and lost Classical texts and of drawing attention to them.[5]

History, therefore, was reshaped and given greater purpose and use in the West. Making time instrumental in this fashion, however, left open the question of how it could and should be used and contested for the future. Indeed, the frequent reference to Classical texts by Renaissance writers in the fifteenth and early sixteenth centuries saw a careful selection of texts in order to prove the views of the author. Contrasting the approaches taken by Erasmus and Machiavelli, two key writers of the early sixteenth century, on the justice of war provides a good instance of this process. And so also with the choice of Biblical texts. This selective use of history for present purposes was matched by the choice of the account of the past in order to locate or discuss innovations in the Western world, notably the results of the voyages of exploration to the Indian Ocean and to the 'New World' of, what was termed by the Europeans, North and South America.

Proto-Nationalism and the Reformation

The proto-nationalism ranged against supra-national authority in the later medieval West discussed in the last chapter easily translates into an account in which the Protestant Reformation of the early sixteenth century is linked to, and greatly accelerates, the growth of a national consciousness that was (and is) readily historicized in terms of a new narrative and analysis. There is considerable value in this approach, and it is certainly demonstrated in those states that, in embracing Protestantism, provided a new history of resistance to what was now presented as foreign authority and rule.

In Germany, a link was discerned between successful resistance in the early first century CE (AD) to the armies of imperial Rome, the imperial Rome that had executed Jesus (a theme far stronger then than now), and Martin Luther's crucial role in launching the Reformation from 1517 with the defiance of papal authority. Arminius, the central figure in the destruction of three Roman legions in the Teutoburger Wald in AD (CE) 9, attracted considerable attention, and was the protagonist in a work by Ulrich von Hutten, a key figure among the Imperial Free Knights, who became acquainted with Luther. There was a similar process in searching for antecedents for opposition to papal authority in Protestant states from England and Scotland to Sweden.

Secularism was not a theme in this proto-nationalism. Instead, much of the latter focused on the extent to which a pure early Church had been subverted by the efforts of the Papacy. This was an important aspect of the larger significance attached to 'sacred history', that on the Church.[6]

Thus, in the British Isles there was a stress on early conversion to Christianity prior to the imposition of papal authority, notably by the Synod of Whitby of 664. Linked to this, the historicity, and therefore legitimacy, of the Church of England became a matter of debate between Protestant and Catholic writers, with Archbishop Matthew Parker of Canterbury emphasizing antiquity in his *De Antiquitate Britannicae Ecclesiae* (1572). Catholics, in contrast, stressed the conversion of Britain by St Augustine. Sent by Pope Gregory I from Rome in 596, he had converted Aethelbert, King of Kent, the leading English ruler of the period. The thesis of early conversion, prior to papal action, proved useful to Protestants in both England and Scotland keen to demonstrate longevity and continuity. However, in Ireland, where this thesis was also pertinent, the argument lacked traction for political reasons: Catholicism there was associated with opposition to English rule.

A different rivalry was offered by martyrology. In place of Catholic saints, the Protestants recorded their own martyrs, notably in John Foxe's *Acts and Monuments of Matters Most Special and Memorable, Happening in the Church, with an Universal History of the Same*, popularly known as the *Book of Martyrs* and first published in 1563. The history of this work reflected the overlap of history and myth. In response to public interest in the account of Protestant suffering and fortitude, the *Book of Martyrs* was elaborated in successive editions, bolstering the Protestant heroism in a way that conformed to public wish and governmental requirements. Foxe's work depicted the Catholic alternative to Elizabeth I (r. 1558–1603) as wicked and provided an account of England as a kingdom in the forefront of the advance towards Christian truth.[7] After an order of Convocation (the clerical parliament of the established Church) of 1571, cathedral churches acquired copies of Foxe's *Book of Martyrs* and many parish churches chose to do likewise. The publication of the Bible in the vernacular was also significant for the development of languages, both established literary ones, which gained new authority and standardization, and others not hitherto committed to print, such as Slovenian.

The Reformation became an aspect of a politicized interrogation of history, both political and religious. This interrogation was a matter of policy but also of assessments and reassessments of individual and collective memory. Changes in meaning were aspects of these reassessments of memory, reassessments that transformed, but did not destroy, earlier understandings. These transformations included the re-imagination of the existing sacred geography of particular localities and countries, a sacred geography that reflected and sustained historical assessments.[8] Religious buildings and their contents were similarly re-imagined and treated accordingly, with destruction, appropriation and restoration all part of the process.[9] In the short term, there was also a process of recording and explaining the very process of Reformation in a form of instant history, as with Johann Sleidan's *Commentaries on Religion and the State of Emperor Charles V* (1555).[10]

In contrast to Protestant countries, in Catholic states the Counter-, or Catholic, Reformation sharpened a universalism based on the authority and mission of the Papacy and on new religious orders, although there could be a stress on particular practices and a distinctive ecclesiastical history, most clearly in Venice. The Jesuit Order, the leading instance of the new orders, took a particular interest in education and used history, in written and visual forms, not only to propagate an account of the order and its missions, but also to provide a wider ecclesiological narrative and analysis. The newness of the order, established in 1540, ensured that this history, which was very much intended to deploy scholarship to the cause of the useful, focused on the recent. There was no parallel in this case with that of long-established religious orders and institutions, for example the Benedictine Order, providing accounts of privileges and concerns going back many centuries.

The Papacy also deployed history in the service of its cause, and notably that of leadership of a Catholic Church under acute challenge. Thus, canonizations offered symbolic support to the Papacy and made important political points. The canonization in 1606 of Gregory VII, the Pope (r. 1073–85) who had resisted Henry IV in the Investiture Crisis, underlined the need for Popes to be resolute and drew attention to the unreliability, from the Catholic perspective, of the then Emperor, Rudolf II. Ignatius Loyola, the founder of the Jesuits, was canonized in 1662.

The emphasis, both contemporary and, even more, subsequent, on the new in the use of history in the sixteenth century, in this case in support of the new causes of Reformation and Counter-Reformation, was, and is, part of a long-established process. This process, this emphasis on the new, also spans the proto-nationalism of the late medieval age, the regalist historians of the late seventeenth century European *ancien régime*, the Enlightenment historians of the eighteenth century, the history of nineteenth-century state education, and so on, into an assessment of the use of history, in the twentieth century and more recently, in terms of new issues, concerns and methods. In each case, the use of history was, and is, presented in terms of responding to new challenges and opportunities. This theme indeed will be found in this book, not least because it helps explain the distinctiveness and interest of particular periods and issues – for example, the impact of decolonization in the late twentieth century on the historical consciousness in many countries such as India, and of the end of apartheid in South Africa where the first democratic election took place in 1994.[11]

However, at the same time, it is necessary to remember the role of abiding concerns in the use of history. These concerns include the identity of family, community and group, all of which continued to provide the building blocks of countries, and with a considerable impact alongside that of the state, or central government. Any judgement of the nature of relative impact has to take note of the destructive wars which were the consequence of government action. Moreover, the impact of local identities, as of the material circumstances of life, does not preclude national identities as well. Nevertheless, it is the role of the local and traditional in the understanding and use of history that is underplayed. Furthermore, in considering this role, it is necessary to understand that local and traditional were not necessarily conservative and static. Instead, these themes had a capacity for adaptability, change, indeed dynamism, that is instructive and generally underestimated.

If the emphasis in this book is on the state, other levels of using history, especially the transnational and the local, were also significant. In practice, much of this significance relates to alternatives, indeed frequently responses, to the state and its use of history. However, often that was not the prime frame of reference. For example, much of the use of history by individual religions was in rivalry with other religions, rather than with the state. From a different perspective, this rivalry with other religions was fought out in terms of relations, both positive and negative, with states and their governments. This was notably so in the West in the early-modern period, particularly the sixteenth and early seventeenth centuries, the period of the Wars of Religion.

Partly as a result of the prominence of these factors, the history of using history relates to a considerable extent to the history of religion. This may be an approach uncomfortable in the dominant secular character of modern academic culture. Moreover, it is an approach that appears dated if history – notably, but not only, Western history – is perceived in terms of a move away from religion. From the perspective of the 2010s, however, such a teleology appears problematic rather than secure. Instead, there is a need to address the significance of uses of religious history and of religious uses of history, a different issue but not for many of the devout. Furthermore, the nuances and variations of these uses require more consideration than in the classic account of receding religiosity and diminished significance.

The Protestant Reformation thus emerges of importance in this book not because it led to a decline in the religious use of history, but, rather, because it introduced a very different context for this use within Western Christendom, a context of religious division and greater state power. So also, in the new, near-contemporary, context arising in the world of Islam, with the conquest of Persia (Iran) by the Safavids, leaders of a millenarian Shi'ite movement, in the 1500s, and the subsequent rapid outbreak, from 1512, of large-scale warfare with the Ottoman Turks. The latter were Sunnis who saw themselves as the defenders, indeed guardians, of Islamic orthodoxy, and notably after they took over the guardianship of the Holy Places of Mecca and Medina in 1517, following Sultan Selim I's conquest of the Egyptian-based Mamluk empire in 1516–17. Selim assumed the title of Servant of the Two Noble Sanctuaries.

Sacred time was a key element, as Isma'il, the leader of the Safavids who proclaimed himself Shah in 1501, was seen by many as the reincarnation of Iman Ali, the Prophet Muhamad's adopted son and son-in-law and the founder of Shi'ite Islam, or as the hidden Iman, a millenarian figure. Control over shrines, notably Karbala, Kayir, Najaf and Samarra, was another aspect of this Shi'ite grasp of sacred time, while, conversely, Sunni shrines were desecrated. Moreover, the Christian community in Baghdad was destroyed by the Safavid conquerors. This history is downplayed in the account of Islamic history currently offered in the West, as the emphasis, instead, is on Muslim tolerance. Such an emphasis accords with current political strategies, notably that of the incorporation of Muslim immigrants.

As with Western Christendom, it was necessary for the Safavids and the Ottomans both to make sense of the recent past and to present an exemplary earlier history. The determination to claim superior status in the Islamic world was very important in this process, as was the need to annex earlier traditions and patterns of authority and power. The imperial theme that this superior status represented put particular requirements on the use of history, as it was necessary to demonstrate the providential inevitability of primacy. There was not the room for compromise about rectitude offered by any theory of equal and interdependent sovereign states. The same points about status extended to other Islamic empires, notably the Mughal Empire in India created following Babur's victory over the Lodi sultanate of Delhi at the battle of First Panipat in 1526 and also the Sa'adian Empire of Morocco.

The religious dimension to history was understandably to the fore in the West in the sixteenth and early seventeenth centuries, which was a period in which confessional strife was important in itself and provided a language to help explain political division and disputes between and within states. Themes of the debilitating consequences of internal dissidence, long a staple in the presentation of history, gained new prominence in this context. This theme was also seen in the arts, notably in the stylization of discord. Theatre offered important examples of the dangers of division. This thesis was repeatedly present in Shakespeare's history plays, notably those on the fifteenth century: the *Henry IV*, *Henry V*, *Henry VI* and *Richard III* plays.

In opposition to this stress on the need for order and obedience, historical and Biblical examples, as well as Classical arguments, in favour of tyrannicide, served to substantiate the claims about bad kingship that were deployed with particular alacrity, notably by Protestants, as these arguments served to justify resistance to authority. The French Wars of Religion, and the Dutch Revolt against rule by Philip II of Spain, provided prime instances of this process, but the overthrow of monarchs also took place in Scotland, Sweden, England and the Habsburg lands. The image of Judith with the head of Holofernes, one oft-repeated on canvas, provided a Biblical instance of exemplary resistance to evil power and there were Classical counterparts.

In turn, Catholics made use of historical arguments for resistance, including the validation offered by a Papal bull deposing Elizabeth I. A similar mixture of historical and present arguments was pushed to the fore elsewhere by Catholics arguing in favour of rebellion, for example against Henry III and Henry IV of France, who were assassinated in 1589 and 1610 respectively.

In such a context, history provided a battleground of examples that could be used to justify action, not least by undermining pressures for political cohesion and for observing the law. The Thirty Years' War in Germany (1618–48) proved particularly significant in this context as competing levels of rulership vied in this conflict. The historical arguments deployed in favour of imperial authority, that of the Holy Roman Emperor, competed with those used for territorial rulers such as the Elector of Saxony.

Then, and more generally, history was pillaged to support, and to challenge, territorial and dynastic claims. Legitimacy rested on the weight of rights, which were proved by ancestry and descent. Recent events had to be interpreted accordingly. Although different in their structure and content from their Chinese counterparts, in large part because they were less formulaic, Western dynastic histories fulfilled similar functions. Moreover, history served as a key aspect of the representation of authority that was so important to the culture and practice of politics.

Thus, historical research contributed to dynastic interests, both by establishing claims to privileges, notably precedence and territory, and by defining succession laws, as in France where the Salic Law was rescued from a fraudulent account, leading to a new presentation of male rights based on a supposed law of nature.[12] In 1529, Landgrave Philip of Hesse, a leading princely supporter of Lutheranism, created, at the University of Marburg, the first academic chair in history in Germany.[13] Antonius Corvinus, a writer in the circle of Philip of Hesse, identified him as a new Charlemagne. This was an aspect of the argument that the territorial German princes, especially Philip, were the true heirs of the Roman emperors, whose position had been reborn in Charlemagne in 800.[14] This argument challenged the claims more commonly made on behalf of the Holy Roman Emperor, in this case Charles V.

Art served the same end of asserting an identity through historical reference, as with the commissioning in 1660 of Rembrandt by the Amsterdam city authorities to paint the *Conspiracy of Claudius Civilis* for the new town hall. Providing a pedigree for the successful Dutch revolt against Philip II of Spain in the sixteenth century, Civilis had led resistance to the Romans in 69 CE in part of what became the Dutch Republic that was recorded by the Roman historian Tacitus. Similarly, Tacitus recorded opposition to the Romans in Caledonia (Scotland), providing it with a history. Paintings demonstrated the importance of symbolic images in historiography, an importance that was further strengthened by their reproduction as engravings.

The Classics were a key source of historical ideas and references. The value of the Classical world for reflection, the reflection which led to his book *The Prince* (1513), was captured by Niccolò Machiavelli (1469–1527), when writing from exile in 1513 to his friend, the Florentine ambassador to the Papacy. Referring to his reading, he wrote:

> I step inside the venerable courts of the ancients, where, solicitously received by them [...] I am unashamed to converse with them and to question them about the motives for their actions, and they, out of their human kindness, answer me. And for four hours at a time I feel no boredom, I forget all my troubles, I do not dread poverty, and I am not terrified by death.[15]

In *The Prince*, Machiavelli stated that

> As for intellectual training, the prince must read history, studying the actions of eminent men to see how they conducted themselves during war and to discover the reasons for their victories or their defeats, so that he can avoid the latter and imitate the former. Above all, he must read history so that he can do what eminent men have done before him: taken as their model some historical figure who has been praised and honoured; and always kept his deeds and actions before them.[16]

The grandeur and triumphs of the past became a key site and source of inspiration, although not without controversy. In his *The Education of a Christian Prince* (1516), Desiderius Erasmus (1466–1536), a prominent Humanist, urged caution in drawing examples from the past, a caution he generally encouraged, because he argued that tales of conflict encouraged more war. Thus, Achilles, Alexander the Great and Julius Caesar were, Erasmus claimed, dangerous topics for young boys. In contrast, Guillaume Budé (1467–1540), another Humanist, a scholar who served the rulers of France in diplomatic posts and as royal librarian, was far more positive about Alexander in his *De L'Institution du Prince* (*The Institution of the Prince*, 1519). The significance of honour in élite culture encouraged the reference back, both to ancestors and to models of behaviour.[17]

The ceremonial entries of rulers celebrated valour and success[18], as did their artistic patronage. The additions to his ancestral seat at Gonzaga commissioned by Francesco II, Marquis of Mantua (r. 1484–1519), were decorated with scenes from family military history, while the palace of San Sebastiano he built provided an opportunity for the display of what he saw as an apt comparison, *The Triumphs of Caesar*, painted by Andrea Mantegna from 1482 to 1492. As an affirmation of the present for the future, Francesco presented as a victory his performance at the battle of Fornovo (1495), where he had fought bravely and captured many prisoners, albeit failing to block the French march north in Italy. Mantegna's painting the *Madonna della Vittoria* was produced accordingly.[19]

In addition to establishing appropriate models, history was part of the world of politics, alongside news, each being employed to articulate topical grievances and to advance remedies.[20] History, indeed, complemented the news, as it established the frame of reference for successive crises, both in individual states and on a wider scale. Moreover, the enmities of the present were given added value and weight by depicting an historical pedigree. For example, in Venice, where a fire destroyed much of the Ducal Palace in 1577, the redecoration of the large *Sala del Maggior Consiglio* included paintings showing Venice's role in the Fourth Crusade (1204), and naval battles with the Ottomans in the 1470s, as well as the great naval victory over them recently won at Lepanto in 1571. Destiny in the shape of defending Western Christendom emerged clearly.

Another aspect of claiming, and thus contesting, the past, and the very processes of historical change and exposition, was seen in the determination of rulers to preserve and record their heritage. If there was no equivalent in Europe to the Chinese History Office, nevertheless the situation was different to that in the fifteenth century. Archives were founded, notably at Simancas in Spain, created by the Emperor Charles V (Charles I of Spain) in 1545, and in Florence, established by Cosimo de Medici, Grand Duke of Tuscany, in 1569. This interest in the historical record was, in part, a by-product of a growing secular use of bureaucratic means of government, but also reflected an awareness of the uses and interest of the past. In a similar vein, Pope Urban VIII (1623–44) separated the papal archive from the library. Alongside bureaucratic benefits, notably establishing legal rights, and demonstrating due process, honour politics remained a reason for retaining and using archives. This process was shared by landowners, with muniment rooms serving to link back to illustrious forbears.[21]

The historical record also played a major role in fiction. Thus, the leading English chronicle, Raphael Holinshed's *Chronicles of England, Scotland and Ireland* (1577, with a larger second edition in 1587), became not only significant for ideas of English nationhood[22] but also the major source for

Shakespeare's later history plays. In turn, the latter served as a prime basis for the public understanding of the past, notably serving the Tudor idea that their accession in 1485 had restored England to harmony, by overcoming a Richard III depicted as homicidal, by Holinshed, Shakespeare, and others. Holinshed was also a source for Shakespeare's plays *King Lear*, *Macbeth* and *Cymbeline*. A different approach in justifying the Tudors was taken by Polydore Vergil (1470–1555), an Italian in papal service who entered that of the English Crown, providing a pro-Tudor account of the fifteenth century in his *Anglicae Historiae* published in 1534 and subsequently required reading in English schools.

Printing

Printing served to disseminate works of, and about, the past. The first book printed in English was Raoul Lefevre's *Recuyell of the Histories of Troy* (c. 1473), which reflected the continued interest in a story that brought together Ancient Greece with the origins of Rome. In Hungary, the first printed book, Andreas Hess' *Chronica Hungarorum* (1473), traced the history of the Hungarians from Noah in the Old Testament to the present, a familiar tale, although, with 400 copies printed, one that could reach many readers. Johannes Thuróczy's chronicle of the Hungarians followed in 1488. These accounts were used to argue for aristocratic rights and elective government, a history framed both by present purposes, in order to elect and restrict monarchs, and by the tradition of Hungarian chroniclers.[23]

More generally, books and the printed word served both to provide interesting stories and as instruments to help in the use of history for expounding religious, political and cultural policies to audiences at once individual and collective. These two factors were linked, as in the account of the overcoming of Visigothic (Christian) Spain by Muslim invaders in 711 – an account of rape, revenge and betrayal, in which a rape by the last Visigothic king played a central role. This conduct contrasted with the image presented of the monarchs of modern Spain, and thus related success against the Moors to morality, as well as providing a story that was attractive to writers and readers.[24]

Printing was a medium, rather than a message: printing could serve both the interests of authority and pressure for its overthrow; it could repeat familiar accounts and also challenge them. Although the intention of individual works varied, the impact of publication was to increase their ability to reach a wide audience, those who could read – although the extent of illiteracy necessarily ensured that this was not a mass audience. History readily lent itself to the new entrepreneurial world of print, while, in turn, the general authority of print helped ensure its use as the medium for history, as for news. This authority owed much to the development of the printing of bibles in the vernacular during the Reformation. The Bible offered sacred history, and its appearance in print and in the vernacular made it more accessible, at least to the literate, and enhanced the reputation of other works to appear in print.[25]

Alongside historical accounts, there was a rise in Europe in time-based forms of publication, such as astrological charts, almanacs, serialized news pamphlets and newspapers. The focus on profit and commercial opportunity was significant in the world of print and provided a powerful strand in the development both of works reporting news and of history as a branch of literature. There was a degree of overlap between historical literature and works reporting news in their shared sense of location in time. Becoming history, news was placed in a sequence, while location in a sequence contributed to a sense of its enduring character.

Historical works helped explain the developing social spheres of Europe, notably major cities. John Stow's *Survey of London* (1598) discussed past and present together, proving a milestone work in the recording and study of London's past. Stow's *Survey* formed the basis of later histories of London and was a work that contributed greatly to the pride and self-identification of the city. London's theatres also saw the production of Shakespeare's plays. These plays provided a vivid account of national history, one that served political interests as an aspect of a wider historical culture that encouraged a sense of distinctive national development and was used accordingly.[26]

Conclusion

Rising interest in history as a printed product was related to a significant increase in literacy in both the West and China. The use of history was therefore an aspect of broader social change, while also helping explain this change to contemporaries in terms of ideas of development. Political and religious benefit was sought by explaining this relationship of past and present in accordance with particular arguments. The Reformation forced the pace of engaging with, and claiming, the past.

CHAPTER FIVE

'Ancien Régime' and 'Enlightenment', 1650–1775

The mid-seventeenth century brought a crisis of political control and social order across much of the world. As an instance of the way in which the past is reconsidered and rewritten in terms of the changing priorities of the present, the role of climate change in causing this crisis has recently been emphasized. Newly prominent as an issue of transformation in the present world, this topic is then pursued in history even if the comparison is problematic. At the present day, the central issue is that of global warming, whereas in the sixteenth and seventeenth centuries, in contrast, it was that of the 'Little Ice Age'. At the same time, in order to use history to offer a parallel, it can be argued that the key problem, then as now, was the disruption caused by climate change.[1]

The mid-seventeenth century crisis was followed by a widespread attempt, notably from the 1660s, to restore order and to revive authority. Efforts to build up élite cohesion played an important role in this process, as in China, India and Christian Europe. These efforts included a major display of state-sponsored historical activity. If the focus of this activity was very much on rulers, and with a stress on the dynastic rather than the national dimension, their guardianship of religious orthodoxy proved an important theme, both in the Islamic world and in the West. Alongside dynastic legitimism, and glory through defeating foreign opponents, this theme provided a set of issues and priorities that was at once traditional and still pertinent.

Dynasticism, War and History

Moreover, it proved useful for monarchs to refer back in order to establish continuity and also, by comparison, to underline individual and dynastic success. The paintings, frescoes, tapestries and statues that decorated palaces made these references clear. Louis XIV of France (r. 1643–1715) was taking part in a more general process when he commemorated his own successes while also drawing attention to those of his predecessors. Panegyrists were commissioned to extol his glories. References were both to distant history and to more recent examples. Louis was much influenced by the example of his grandfather, Henry IV (r. 1594–1610), a successful warrior, notably against Spain, which Louis also successfully fought, but, in addition, he looked across French history for former instances of exemplary greatness. In the royal palace of Seville, where Louis' younger grandson, Philip V of Spain (r. 1700–46), spent much time, there was an extensive and dramatic set of tapestries depicting Charles I of Spain (the Emperor Charles V) campaigning against the Moors of North Africa in the early sixteenth century. Philip sent an expedition that reconquered the city of Oran in modern Algeria in 1732.

More distant references were also offered to Classical rulers who were seen as exemplary. In the coronation sermon for William III (r. 1689–1702) after he replaced his uncle and father-in-law James II (and VII of Scotland), Gilbert Burnet invoked the Emperor Hadrian's reign of virtue which helped to restore order to Rome after the depravity and tyranny of Caligula and Nero.

What is underplayed in most historiography on the eighteenth century is the bulk of the use of history then, namely to sustain and extol existing authorities, at all levels, and whether secular or religious. One of the greatest historical works of the eighteenth century, accordingly, was the account of the victorious campaigns of the Qianlong Emperor of China (r. 1736–96), the *Yuzhi Shiquan Ji* (*In commemoration of the ten complete military victories*), composed in 1792. This depiction of recent Chinese history provided a picture of dramatic and consistent success, and celestial favour, an account in keeping with long-established patterns of Chinese historiography. And so also with the emphasis on warfare, which would not have surprised the Pharaoh Rameses II (or Adolf Hitler), and also with the tendency to offer a misleading gloss on campaigns. Alongside the clear triumphs – notably the conquest of Xinjiang in 1755–7, the Qianlong Emperor's major military achievement and one that ended a challenge that went back to the 1680s – came failures presented as successes. The latter process was particularly the case with the campaigns on the southern frontiers of China. There, war with Burma (Myanmar) in 1765–70 ended in serious defeat, and with Tongking (Vietnam) in 1788–9 in failure, while campaigning against Nepal in 1791 proved more difficult than was recorded.[2]

Given the need for success as a guarantor of prestige, and the value of prestige as a support for power and authority, this approach was not surprising. It was also seen in the West with the practice of presenting and celebrating checks, whether defeats or draws, as victories, for example with *Te Deums* – religious services giving thanks to God for victory.

The Qianlong Emperor's use of history was also apparent in other writings on a grand scale, for example the Four Treasuries project. He sought to compile all the worthwhile literature in China into one collection, the *Complete Library of the Four Treasuries*. This led, between 1773 and 1782, to the compilation of a list of 10,680 titles, of which 3,595 were copied in their entirety, each categorized as classics, history, philosophy or belles lettres. The Emperor ordered the hundreds of scholars who worked on the project to censor texts that made critical references to non-Han northern peoples, notably Manchus, but also Mongols and Khitans. The accompanying search for material judged seditious led to the destruction of about 2,400 unwanted works.[3]

The concern with dynastic reputation in China ensured that history was used so as to validate the particular historical vocabulary of individual dynasties and thus establish a creditable lineage. The Manchu dynasty, which ruled from 1644 to 1912, looked back to earlier steppe dynasties that conquered all or part of China, such as the Khitans (also referred to as the Liao), a people from Mongolia who established the Liao Empire in Manchuria in the tenth century, and, subsequently, the Mongols. This similarity affected the treatment of their history during the Manchu period. So also, in contrast, with the Ming dynasty, which the Manchu had replaced after a long struggle. Moreover, resistance and rebellions were a significant problem for Manchu rulers, notably into the 1680s, but also thereafter. Approaches favourable to the Ming were downplayed, and it received limited attention. Claiming continuity with the past to establish the legitimacy of continuity therefore did not involve giving all of the past equal weight.[4]

The Chinese pattern of using history to define and assert success, and thus demonstrate legitimacy, was more generally seen across the world. Indeed, this pattern defined much of public history, and the recent vogue for public history as an historiographical subject in part revives this pattern, albeit in a very different context and employing a contrasting vocabulary.

Using history to assert success, and thus demonstrate legitimacy, was also the practice in the Islamic world in the eighteenth century, as well as in India, and in South-East Asia with the expanding states there, especially Burma (Myanmar) and Siam (Thailand). In the Ottoman Empire, official Court chroniclers, such as Mustafa Naima Efendi (1655–1716) and Ahmet Ásim Efendi (1755–1819), focused on the achievements of rulers. More generally, inscriptions and illustrations proved potent forms of this history centring on success, as did oral records, notably in the form of sung tales.

For much of the world in this period, such records are often patchy, in large part due to subsequent conquest by imperial powers, and the rewriting of the past (and destruction of records) by the victors. The absence of a culture of print was also relevant. Tribal organizations generally lacked (and lack) the historical legacy of more developed states, or, at least, a comparable range of legacy in terms of artefacts. Nevertheless, these records of war and lineage can be seen, for example, in the tales that were (and still are) very important in the Maori culture of New Zealand.

And so also within Europe. Rather than presenting a form of baton-passing teleology, with the self-consciously progressive historians of Britain and France, such as William Robertson (1721–93), as the model, and the use of history in other countries either emulating or falling away from this model, it is more pertinent to note the continued practice of traditional forms of history and for long-established goals. To call this practice Chinese-style would be unhelpful, as there is no direct linkage or parallel. Nevertheless, the phrase captures the extent to which the state, presented as the ruler, his dynasty and his religion, was the central pantheon of historical concern and usage in Europe, as in China.

Thus, in Europe, there was the full panoply of ceremonial prints, paintings and statues, the endless references back to past heroes, and the emphasis on triumph over foreign challenges. In Savoy-Piedmont, from the decorations in the royal palace in Turin to the celebratory church of *Superga* overlooking the city, there was frequent reference back to Victor Amadeus II's victory over a French force besieging the capital, Turin, in 1706. The Austrian role in this victory was downplayed.

There and elsewhere, history served as a key cause and means of the representation of authority and power that was so important to the culture and practice of politics.[5] Moreover, history served to demonstrate the success of authority. Accordingly, works of art and related panegyrics were commissioned by the dynasty and élite supporters and put on display for their pleasure and for the edification of all. In practice, the audience was substantially the social élite and those members of the public who lived in capitals or were literate. The bulk of the peasantry knew little of such a presentation of news or history, unless it had a religious dimension.

The past was both a frame of reference and the source of ideas and evidence. In England (which after the Union of 1707 was joined with Scotland to become Britain), enmity towards Spain and France encouraged looking back at earlier relations with these powers. The domestic political context, however, was very different to that in Louis XIV's France, because the parliamentary system in Britain provided both opportunity and, to a major extent, need for adversarial politics. These politics required a vocabulary of ideas and references, a vocabulary that repeatedly drew on history for its evidence and resonance. In Parliament and print, the victories against Spain won under Elizabeth I (r. 1558–1603) provided a reproach to a failure to show comparable response and win similar success, in the 1620s, 1720s and 1730s.[6] Moreover, an apparent willingness to accept foreign attacks on British merchant shipping was condemned by linking it to past episodes of weakness. Thus, *Fog's Weekly Journal*, the foremost Tory newspaper[7], in its issue of 30 November 1734, referred to the unsuccessful reign of Richard II, who was overthrown in 1399: 'on the seas the merchant ships were frequently taken and plundered by the French and other nations'. Three years later, William Havard's play *King Charles the First* offered similar criticisms. Elizabeth also served as a model in other respects, for example in avoiding domestic division,[8] or in not having a standing army,[9] or in being robust against Catholics.[10]

The past was a continual frame of reference for British parliamentarians and newspapers. Thus, in criticising, in its issue of 5 April 1729, the Anglo-French alliance of 1716–31, the *Craftsman*, the leading opposition newspaper,[11] looked back to the example of the ministry of George, 1st Duke of Buckingham under Charles I in 1625–8. The paper complained that French influence then had left the navy useless and English trade vulnerable. Opposition writers were to be accused of presenting Sir Robert Walpole, the leading minister from 1721 to 1742, as reviving the 'power of the French Mayors of the Palace, which at last annihilated that of the Sovereign',[12] a reference to the distant Merovingian dynasty of the seventh century.

New developments were interpreted by British commentators in terms of the lessons supposedly learned from the past, with statesmanship seen as entailing this capacity. This process had a resonance in terms of public memory. The latter focused on war and politics. Thus, failure at war with France in 1744–8 was given historical depth and political point by reference to the successes under John, 1st Duke of Marlborough in 1704–9.[13] Offering a more distant perspective also seen earlier with the *Craftsman*, the loss of Minorca to French attack in 1756 led an opposition pamphleteer to reflect 'the breed of our Britons is changed from what it was when we conquered France under our Edwards and Henrys',[14] a reference to English successes under Edward III (r. 1327–77) and Henry V (r. 1413–22) in the Hundred Years' War, which had ended in 1453. Thus, the frame of reference readily went back over 400 years, which is somewhat different to the general situation today. On the other hand, Scottish nationalists make frequent reference to victory over Edward II of England at Bannockburn (1314), while the limitations on English royal government decreed in Magna Carta (1215) have been readily interpreted for a modern audience in Britain.[15]

In turn, dramatic victory over, and conquests from, France and Spain, in 1758–62, during the Seven Years' War (1756–63) led to the need for a new conceptualization of British power, one in which history played a lesser role, or, at least, could not serve to provide as pressing parallels. In Richard Brinsley Sheridan's play *The Critic* (1779), the idea that the defeat of the Spanish Armada in 1588 could serve as a model for the response to the Franco-Spanish invasion attempt of 1779 is affected by the ridicule that is such a prominent theme and method in the play. Indeed, as early examples from British history became less valuable as a basis for understanding the current situation of greatness under challenge, so, instead, there was reference back to the example of Ancient Rome, which offered an escalating comparison.

Elsewhere, the past also taught or, rather, could be used to teach, particular lessons. In eighteenth-century Austria, the repulse of the Turks from Vienna in 1683 served to demonstrate providential support for the Habsburgs. Subsequent victories over the Turks in 1683–99 and 1716–18 were celebrated in ceremonies or new churches, notably the *Karlskirche* in Vienna. In turn, these ceremonies and churches acted as a form of history, one that was more dramatic and effective than history in print, not least because it reached out to the entire population, instead of only the literate section. The Turkish defeat in 1683 still plays a role in Austrian politics today (see pp. 170–1).

In Prussia, there was reference back to the Great Elector's victory over the Swedes at Fehrbellin in 1675, in practice a relatively minor victory. This victory by his grandfather provided Frederick William I (r. 1713–40) with an example of meritorious rulership that encouraged his militarism, whereas his father, Frederick I (r. 1688–1713), had been more pacific and did not provide the model that Frederick William sought. Dynastic imaging thus offered the possibility of seeking, or rather selecting, the history required. Such a practice was also seen in China, as discussed above (pp. 72–3).

In Russia, Peter I, the Great (r. 1689–1725), a self-conscious modernizer, was less inclined to look back, not least because he aspired not only to change Russia but also to achieve more in those activities, such as warfare, that he shared with his predecessors. Whereas his father, Alexis (r. 1645–76), had, although achieving much, been checked by both Swedes and Poles, Peter was determined to overcome them, and did so. The construction, in place of Moscow, of St Petersburg, built on territory conquered from Sweden in 1703 and the capital from 1712, a window looking west, was an important rejection of the history of continuity and an affirmation, instead, of a new setting for Russia's future, and thus a new history. Peter's successors, some of whom had only a precarious linkage with the Romanov dynasty, for example Catherine the Great (r. 1762–96), proved willing to deploy the Petrine legacy, not least by living in St Petersburg.

There was also, however, a 'back to the past' movement, notably under Peter the Great's grandson, Peter II (r. 1727–30), who moved the capital back to Moscow; and historical references to a pre-Petrine (Peter the Great) past were strong then. Thus, from 1725, there were two rival histories at issue, a situation that continued in Russia during the nineteenth century in the clash between Westernizers and Slavophiles. This clash was contested in Russian culture and history, including in historical scholarship.

In the period 1650–1775, conquest and the succession of new dynasties continued to provide a prime usage for history, that of affirming a relationship with the territory that had been acquired. Existing territorial claims were deployed and developed, as by Louis XIV and his *réunion* policy of the 1680s: based on the legal history of particular principalities and families, he searched out possible feudal dependencies of territories he had already acquired, and used this process to advance fresh claims, notably in Alsace and the Spanish Netherlands (Belgium).

More generally, part of the implicit (and sometimes explicit) contract with the socio-political élite made by new rulers, and, even more, new dynasties, was that they adopted and employed the existing historical language and themes in the territory in question. This was a significant aspect of eliciting consent, as in China under the Manchus. Continuing established coronation practices and promises was a key form of this process. In Britain, this policy was an aspect of the legitimacy of the Hanoverian dynasty, which came to the throne in 1714 as a result of the Act of Settlement of 1701. At the same time, in Britain, uniquely, the new dynasty faced frequent press attacks on its position. Some were historical, as in the suggestion that the Viking attacks provided a precedent for Hanoverian rule. On 5 January 1745, *Old England*, an opposition newspaper, announced: 'Nothing gives one a better idea of the detestable consequences of England being connected with a foreign interest, than a view of the history of the kings before the [Norman] conquest.'

The process of rulers adapting was not only seen at the level of kingdoms, but also at that of territories within them. Adapting to the history and, specifically, the historical freedoms of these territories was part of the process of securing, legitimating and sustaining conquest. Frequently, this procedure entailed accepting freedoms that did not otherwise pertain in the territories already ruled by the monarch, as with the Baltic conquests made by Peter the Great and those in Alsace by Louis XIV.

This employment of history to affirm and negotiate power in the eighteenth century has been underplayed due to the focus on scholarly works of history that were designed for a wide audience, such as those of Edward Gibbon. However, this employment of history to affirm and to negotiate was a significant use, not least because it also helped define authority and to bind power. Most rulers, particularly in the first half of the eighteenth century (although definitely not Peter the Great), were greatly influenced by this historical, indeed historicized, context of their authority and power, as with their unwillingness to abandon traditional ecclesiastical arrangements. Drawing on the assumptions of divine-right monarchy, this unwillingness rested on a belief in the significance of continuity and of time-honoured systems. Louis XVI's reluctance to accept the Civil Constitution of the Clergy in 1790, and George III's refusal to accept Catholic Emancipation, which led to the fall of British ministries that backed this measure in both 1801 and 1806, were each important episodes in the political history of their states.

Similarly, a conviction of the value of long-established privileges was captured in the opposition to attempts to standardize rights and obligations by groups that held specific privileges, notably aristocrats. In political terms, this opposition was seen in the reluctance throughout to accept the statist efforts of royal governments to increase power and obtain resources and, more particularly, in hostility to the related ideas of reform and transformation held by the 'Enlightened Despots' and Enlightenment intellectuals in the second half of the eighteenth century. Thus, notably in the Austrian Netherlands (Belgium) and Hungary, there was an appeal to history to defend the privileges and practices of the past against Joseph II, who ruled the Habsburg inheritance from 1780 to 1790.

Enlightenment History

The level of the state, however, proved less secure as the basis for addressing world history. Here long-established religious interpretations remained significant, but, in the eighteenth-century West, there was a considerable effort to provide a secular account, one that could cross religious boundaries. Secular does not imply that the writers of what would subsequently be described as the Enlightenment lacked Christian values and concerns.[16] However, many did not push these to the forefront of their analysis.

Instead, there was a presentation of God in a distant, deistic fashion, with providential explanations of events no longer regarded as necessary. The clash was seen in accounts of natural phenomena, notably earthquakes, in which traditional interpretations in terms of divine judgement were challenged. The clash extended to history, as the latter provided exposition and explanation in time, and also offered a context of meaning and significance. In his *Essai sur les moeurs et l'esprit des nations* (1745–53), François-Marie Arouet alias Voltaire (1694–1778), the most prominent *philosophe* in France, wrote a world history within a universal context, rather than within a Christian or nationalist framework.[17] At the same time, it is important to note the continuing scale and range of apocalyptic history, especially the strikingly different ways of ordering past and present in terms of a millenarian understanding.[18]

The historians of the eighteenth century have attracted great attention in the academic subject of historiography, as they have been seen as anticipating much of what is regarded as modern history. Particular attention has focused on British historians, notably Henry, Viscount Bolingbroke (1678–1751), David Hume (1711–76), Edward Gibbon (1737–94), Catherine Macaulay (1731–91) and William Robertson (1721–93). These individuals appear especially relevant as products of an increasingly powerful society, Britain in the eighteenth century, in which there was a major 'public space' that was not under the control of Church and state. Moreover, alongside no pre-publication censorship in Britain from 1695, there was significant freedom there in criticism of both Church and state. This freedom was linked to a considerable measure of religious toleration and to parliamentary government, both of which were established after the overthrow of the authoritarian Catholic James II of England (James VII of Scotland) by William III of Orange in the 'Glorious Revolution' of 1688–9.

There was also a dynamic print world of bookshops, subscription libraries, cheap editions and newspaper serialization. All of these offered sponsorship and profitability that were different to those represented by the governmental sponsorship that was the norm across much of the world, including most of the West. This print world encouraged experiments with new genres.[19] British public culture of the period can be seen to prefigure that of the present age.

Unsurprisingly, seeking a pedigree for the present, modern Western historiographical attention focuses on the Enlightenment writers of the eighteenth century, their methods, and their use of the past in order to establish enlightened themes. Secular progress, in past, present and future, through the extension of freedoms, notably religious toleration, was a key theme in their writing.[20] So also was the stress on the value of commerce and its linkage to freedoms and, more generally, to limited government activity in accordance with the law. The emphasis on progress through trade and limited government provided a way for British commentators of the period, and, indeed, influential foreign observers, to link Britain, past, present and future.

Moreover, other societies could be assessed accordingly. Britain could be presented in terms of a meritorious sequence of maritime states, a sequence focused on Ancient Athens, Renaissance Venice, Golden Age Holland (1580–1650), and then Britain. Although the British liked to look back to Rome, the latter could not be presented as a maritime state. No non-Western society was included in this sequence.

The use of the past was that it apparently provided a clear guide to the future. In this, the present was located as a stage in which the future could be forwarded, or, if mistakes were made, lost. Acting like moralists, historians warned about the latter, as, more generally, did those who used history. Author of *Remarks on the History of England* (1730–1) and *Letters on the Study of History* (1735), Henry, Viscount Bolingbroke, a prominent Tory politician, who never held office after the Whigs gained power in 1714, argued that what he presented as the corruption and complacency of Whig ministries were sapping national morals and betraying national interests. His was an account in which the overthrow by William of Orange (William III) of the Stuarts, in the person of James II (and VII of Scotland), in the Glorious Revolution of 1688–9, and the subsequent establishment of parliamentary government, was not a permanent achievement, but, instead, one that could be compromised, even overturned, by poor government.

Thus, history was a continual process, one prone to the rhythmic pattern of secular decline that had also brought down Ancient Rome. The range of historical and literary reference that was possible, due to knowledge of both Classical history and Classical literature, was such that the application of references and related arguments could, in turn, be contested by reference to that period. Thus, there were different perspectives drawing on Cato and on Cicero, two leading Classical writers.[21] Newspaper references to the Classical world were frequent. The *Monitor*, an influential, populist London newspaper, in its issue of 24 December 1757, referred to the Punic

Wars between Republican Rome and Carthage in the third and second centuries BCE when calling for a more vigorous strategy against France of amphibious attacks:

> A fleet is our best security: but then it is not to lie by our walls; nor be confined to the navigation of our own coasts. The way to deliver Rome from the rivalship and hostilities of the Carthaginians was to carry fire and sword upon the African coast [ie. to attack Carthage itself]. Employ the enemy at home, and he will never project hazardous invasions.

At the same time, supporters of Continental interventionism also referred back, as with the claim that '[t]he first maxim of the Roman Republic was to be faithful to its allies'.[22]

In a more complex and detailed fashion, Edward Gibbon, in his *Decline and Fall of the Roman Empire* (1776–88), provided Ancient Rome both as an interesting story and as a lesson about the cyclical nature of power. Rome's decline and fall offered a warning to a Britain facing the crisis of the American Revolution and the post-war need for revival. The use of the Classical inheritance in public culture and debate ensured that this inheritance counted as an aspect of the national narrative in Britain.

The Classics apparently offered warnings of specific problems, for example the role of bad ministers, with Lucius Aelius Sejanus (d. CE 31), the villainous Prefect of the Praetorian Guard under the Roman Emperor Tiberius, serving as a warning about Sir Robert Walpole, the First Lord of the Treasury (and leading minister) from 1721 to 1742. Sejanus misused the power given him by Tiberius, whom he finally tried to overthrow, only to meet with just punishment. As Gibbon indicated, there was also a more general possibility of decline through corruption.

To underline the complexity of the use of the past, not least because of the variety of references that could be made, the Classics also provided a sense of positive forward movement, with Britain being presented as succeeding Rome in a process of historical development. The Classical world thus took on additional value, not only as a source of reference back, but, rather, in looking forward and being part of a broader process of stadial development, development in stages. Philosophical history, as discussed by the great Scottish philosopher David Hume, in his 'On the Study of History' (1741), proposed a comprehensive explanation of long-term trends in social development, rather than an account simply of events focused, in particular, on recovering the Classical world through antiquarian scholarship. In covering much of human activity in his masterpiece, *The Wealth of Nations* (1776), Adam Smith showed that history's processes had to be understood in order to benefit from the opportunities provided by social organization.

William Robertson's intellectually and commercially successful *History of the Reign of Charles V* (1764) and his *History of America* (1776) (both of which were widely read), in their focus on Spain's rule of its American empire, offered a warning to Britain that the wealth obtained from colonial conquest would not necessarily enhance the conquering society. This argument was especially pertinent given contemporary debates in Britain about the problems posed by wealth from India, notably in terms of political corruption. The view of imperial rule as potentially corrupting provided a way to look at the history of the British in India, and this was particularly influential in the case of the discussion surrounding the trial in 1786–95 of Warren Hastings, from 1773 to 1785 the first Governor-General of British India.

Again, Rome as an imperial power could provide an unsettling precedent. Whether, however, it was a course that had to be followed by modern Britain was less clear. Taking forward British and Dutch ideas, Enlightenment thinkers argued that modern Western states, by combining naval empire, commerce and representation, could avoid the fate of the Roman Empire.[23]

As this section has indicated, British historians of the period remain of great interest, in large part because they can be presented as still being relevant. At the same time, it is necessary to underline their atypicality. In most states, there was no comparable 'escape' from the constraints and conventions of traditional national history into writing about a progressive and relatively tolerant world history in which the individual state could be readily located, as Britain was. At the same time, it would be mistaken to see these British historians as totally escaping from these constraints and conventions.

Looked at differently, the very idea of such an escape is teleological and buys into the assumptions of the enlightened critics of *ancien régime* societies, for example Voltaire, the prominent French *philosophe*. He wrote a series of historical works criticizing the consequences of the authoritarian tendencies of these societies, notably France. A number of genres were used by Voltaire, including epic, as in *La Ligue* (*The League*, 1723), later renamed *La Henriade* (*The Epic of Henry IV*). Louis XIV's concern with *gloire* was condemned in Voltaire's *Le Siècle de Louis XIV* (1751).

While such work had critical implications for the France of Louis XV (r. 1715–74), the great-grandson and successor of Louis XIV, it also provided a way to praise contemporary France as more enlightened than previous reigns and, more critically, to use history to press for such enlightenment. Similarly, the Spanish equivalents of the French *philosophes*, the *illustrados*, presented a critical account of Spain present and past in order to justify their call for reform.[24] History, therefore, was to be useful.

At the same time, there was a tension between the use of history in such a broad-brush fashion and the more specific character of scholarly work.[25] In France, the *érudits*, who focused on textual criticism, did not write histories that provided the logical principles and ethical suppositions that were required to support the immutable laws propounded by the *philosophes*.[26]

History and Identity

History was certainly deployed in France in the debate over how best to govern the kingdom, a debate which was not to receive a more popular sanction until the summoning of the Estates General in 1789 in the wake of a growing sense of political crisis. The role of the past as the source and evidence of the right approach, a role that captured both aspects of history, as the events of the past and the accounts subsequently offered of it, was seen in this debate. In his *Histoire critique de l'établissement de la Monarchie française* (1734), the Abbé Jean-Baptiste Dubos (1670–1742) argued that the royal authority of the ruling Bourbon dynasty, which had come to power with Henry IV (r. 1589–1610), represented a rightful return to the situation under the Franks in the eighth and ninth centuries. He presented this as a return after a long period of usurpation in which the aristocracy had been too powerful, indeed acted as usurpers of rightful royal authority. For Dubos, the authority of Clovis, the Frankish conqueror, derived from that of the Roman emperors, an appropriate, albeit inaccurate, account of transmission and legitimacy.

This positive argument toward royal authority clashed with that, advanced by the Count of Boulainvilliers (1658–1722), of the nobility as playing a key positive role because they were descended from freedom-loving Franks who had conquered those weakened by imperial rule, in other words overthrowing the foreign control of Rome over what, with this conquest, became France. Moreover, Boulainvilliers, author of the posthumously published *Histoire de l'ancien gouvernement de France* (1727), claimed that Clovis had been elected by the other Franks, thus implying that consent was a key element in subsequent legitimacy.

In turn, Charles-Louis, Baron of Montesquieu (1689–1755), in his *L'Esprit des Lois* (1748), answered Dubos by stressing the need to keep despotism at a distance.[27] Montesquieu's interest in history was seen in his views on the consequences of the Viking conquest of Normandy in the early tenth century, a conquest that served Montesquieu by means of illustrating relations between the North and the South and the relationship of these links with freedom. Thus, he used history to demonstrate his general point about the impact of geography.

The historical tensions and themes that were prominent in France, and that played a role in the attitude of the nobility toward the Crown during the early stages of the French Revolution, could also be found elsewhere. An emphasis on noble rights as derived from original conquest was also the case in Hungary and Poland. Similarly, the past was pillaged in order to support differing views on the power of the Papacy vis-à-vis rulers, bishops and the laity.[28]

Scholarship was deployed not so much across the blank sheet of a silent past, but as part of a crowded present in which there were contests with rival views. Thus, in Germany, the Catholic scholar Michael Ignaz Schmidt (1736–94) offered, in his *Geschichte der Deutschen* (*History of the Germans*, Ulm, 1785–1808), a critical reading of Martin Luther, the leading founder of Protestantism, a reading that fed into established patterns of religious animosity. In Sicily, the cleric Rosario Gregorio used scholarly methods to challenge false views of the medieval past of the island. In Sweden, Sven Lagerbring introduced a criticism of source material into Swedish history, while Olof von Dalin wrote a scholarly *Svea Rikes Historic* (*History of Sweden*, Stockholm, 1747–62) which was commissioned by the Estates (Parliament) and refuted the Gothicist myths of Sweden's early history. In England, there were also appeals to an ancient constitution located in Saxon times.[29]

The radical possibilities of history were most apparent in historical understandings that distinguished the nation from the state or government, alongside the more traditional distinction between the realm and the allegedly false, as in usurping, monarch. These radical possibilities had medieval anticipations that could be driven home to seem relevant in the present.

Historical work thus had a directly political resonance. This was particularly the case in constructing national accounts of the past and thereby the present. For example, Garlieb Merkel (1769–1850), in his book *Die Letten* (*The Latvians*, 1796) and other works, attacked the Baltic German landowners who dominated Latvia for their callous treatment of the Latvian peasantry. Claiming, with reason, that the medieval German crusaders, the ancestors of the landowners, had seized the land from the Latvians, he provided a historical explanation for a modern situation he decried and, in turn, used this explanation to deplore the situation further.[30]

The construction of national accounts linked history to the range of other subjects, notably philology and ethnography, that demonstrated a distinctive identity and clothed this identity with a longstanding culture. The Bulgarian national revival began in 1762 when Paisij Xilendarski's Slavo-Bulgarian history was completed. In Serbia, the Orthodox Church kept alive cultural identity and the memory of past greatness. Henrik Porthan (1739–1804), the founder of modern studies in Finnish history and folklore, studied Finnish traditional language and literature. National accounts contributed to a developing scholarly interest in the distinctive attributes of Eastern European peoples that were under the imperial sway of the Habsburgs (Austria), Ottomans (Turkey) and Romanovs (Russia). This interest looked forward to an upsurge in nationalism in the region during the nineteenth century, an upsurge grounded in historical understanding.

At the same time, there was more than one strand in historical thinking and concern. The varied cross-currents of history in the pre-revolutionary eighteenth century extended to the attempt to analyse differing ways of understanding the past. In 1724, Bernard le Bovier de Fontenelle (1657–1757), a French man of letters and secretary of the *Académie des Sciences*, published *De l'Origine des Fables*, a rational assessment of the creation and spread of myths. He was already a defender of the Moderns against the Ancients, a major controversy of the period, notably in his *Digression sur les anciens et les modernes* (1688), and had published a *Histoire des Oracles* (1687). Later in the eighteenth century, there was growing Western interest in geology and an attempt to develop and advance a scholarly and public understanding of this deep history, and to consider its implications for traditional religious accounts of the origins of the Earth.

Conclusion

Across Europe, the emphasis on dynastic legitimacy and religious orthodoxy remained significant in the eighteenth century, but there was also a concern with the civic humanism of public good that had been articulated power-fully from the Renaissance. This approach offered a way not only to praise meritorious rulers, but also to present Western culture alongside non-Western societies, sometimes to its advantage and sometimes not so. Both past and present could then be deployed in order to make points: history served alongside travel as a form of judgement.

CHAPTER SIX

History in an Age of Revolutions, 1775–1815

> From this summary of what has taken place in other countries, whose situations have borne the nearest resemblance to our own, what reason can we have to confide in those reveries, which would seduce us into the expectation of peace and cordiality between the members of the present confederacy, in a state of separation.

Writing in the *Federalist* of 14 November 1787, Alexander Hamilton, a key figure in early American politics and a supporter of a strong federal government, was in no doubt that history could be used to demonstrate the dangers to the newly independent American colonies posed by disunion. For him, history provided an obvious corrective to 'Utopian speculations', and, to that end, he considered Classical Greece and Rome, as well as European history from the Italian Wars (1494–1559) to the eighteenth century. History offered a grounding in reality that provided a warning against what Hamilton termed 'the deceitful dream of a golden age'. In particular, he challenged, in this issue of the *Federalist*, the idea that republics and commercial powers were naturally peaceful. In the event, republics were still relatively rare and the expansion, from 1792, first of Revolutionary France (a republic) and then of Napoleon's empire, was to see the demise both of long-established republics, notably Genoa, the United Provinces and the Swiss Confederation, and of the radical replacements for these states created by the French Revolutionaries.

New versus Old

By the late eighteenth century, politics in several Western states could be established and debated as a clash between new and old, a clash opposing reform or revolution and reaction. That language, indeed, was employed, and notably with the French Revolution, which began in 1789. However, as Hamilton's journalism indicates, there was also a deployment of more specific historical arguments by those who were subsequently seen as revolutionaries. In particular, with both the American and the French revolutions, as well as with that attempted in Hungary in the 1780s, there were references to historical liberties supposedly betrayed by contemporary rulers, George III, Louis XVI and Joseph II respectively. Thus, British fiscal legislation, notably the 1763 Stamp Act, was criticized in the North American and West Indian colonies as infringing established ways of approving taxation. A reference to established ways was a standard means of discussing tax demands, but there was also a radical potential in such instances. 'No Taxation without Representation' was the call of opponents.

The argument about liberty betrayed was also used by opposition Whigs in Britain. In 1788, they turned to the Glorious Revolution of 1688–9 in order to justify calls for political change. A renewal of the Glorious Revolution was called for, and it served to justify the Whig wish to replace the ministry of William Pitt the Younger, and to define him as reactionary, not least because of the circumstances in which George III, undermining the previous Fox-North ministry, had brought him to power in 1783. 'The constitution as established in 1688' remained a standard toast in Whig clubs in the 1820s.

With more cause, those who conspired against Gustavus III of Sweden in 1792 did so with reference to the Age of Liberty that he had allegedly overthrown in 1772. In turn, Gustavus saw himself as returning Sweden to an age of a more effective monarchy and a stronger Sweden, an age that he felt had ended when the death of Charles XII in 1718 led to the Age of Liberty. History could be thus used, but, as a reminder that a number of arguments were possible and, indeed, employed at the same time, Gustavus also appealed to a less historically grounded thesis about the inherent quality of particular forms of government, in his case stronger monarchy.

The use of history in the West at the close of the eighteenth century was complex. Alongside references back, there were very dramatic calls for a new world in which the weight of the past had been severed. As so often, this latter process itself could also involve, as it usually did, a self-consciously alternative history, in the shape of a call for a revival of allegedly original values and constitutional forms. That this pattern is generally seen with revolutions, for example with the Protestant Reformation of the early sixteenth century, does not make it less significant as a use of history in particular conjunctures. Revolution, therefore, has frequently been conceptualized as part of the historical process, indeed allegedly an inevitable part, as with the use of the term *the* historical process, rather than *an* historical process. But, at the same time, there was reference to more specific historical contexts, both in making the case for revolution and in offering a frame of reference from which necessary examples and forms could be taken in planning a new future.

The American Revolution

The interaction between the conservative language of looking back and the combination of radical intent and revolutionary context is notable. At the same time, the latter could involve a form of the end of history. This process was seen in the American Revolution with the new beginnings involved in changing place names, removing statues and royal coats of arms, and other breaks with monarchy and empire. It was necessary for the new American republic, established in 1776, to create a new history and, subsequently, essential for it to make sense of the process by which independence was obtained, recognized in 1783, and maintained. Doing so involved political strife. Thus, credit was differently claimed for victory in the War of Independence (1775–83).

This dispute was entwined with the struggle between the Federalists and the Democratic Republicans. In turn, events were fed through this rivalry, and recorded accordingly. Attempts at exploiting events for partisan commemoration, as of the death of George Washington in 1799, could be highly partisan at the same time as they used the language of unity. Subsequently, Federalist war-weariness in the War of 1812–15 with Britain (notably the Hartford Convention of 1814–15, which discussed options for distancing New England from the war) was used by the Democratic Republicans to discredit the Federalists, and especially, and successfully so, in the elections of 1816 and 1820. This use of the recent past overlapped with that of the journalism of the present, and there was relatively little contrast between that journalism and the instant histories of the war that were rapidly produced.

The War of 1812–15 had failed to fulfil the goals of the Democratic Republican Madison administration, but it was then conveniently recorded and celebrated as an American triumph. This process was seen with celebrations, monuments and writings. Public memorialization helped in the seizure and presentation, for nation-building, of what was really the complexity of a difficult and divisive conflict. As such the War of 1812–15 was recorded on the model of the very different War of Independence, a process greatly eased by the fact that both were fought with Britain. Each thereby sustained the impression of the other.

The French Revolution

The embrace of change was more marked in the French Revolution than in its American counterpart. This was true not only of the abolition of monarchy and establishment of a republic in 1792 (a very different step to killing the king, even if he was guillotined in 1793), but, even more markedly, of the rejection of Christianity and all it involved, a step not taken in America. The rejection meant a new shape to the year, which could no longer be organized in terms of Christian festivals and the accompanying liturgy. In addition, rejecting Christianity entailed a new understanding of the purpose of time. The Christian calendar was abandoned, and a totally new calendar introduced in 1793: 22 September 1792, the day on which the First Republic was declared, was designated the first day of Year I.[1]

The appropriation, renaming and desecration of sites of royal and religious power, notably palaces, cathedrals and monasteries, were part of this process. The treasures of discarded cathedrals and monasteries were allocated to the *Musée des Monuments Français* founded in 1795.

The revolutionaries were committed to the new and to modernity, notably in opposition to feudalism and to heredity as a justification for rank, hierarchy and subordination.[2] A sense of the new as both present and inevitable led to a requirement that its promise be implemented.

More specifically, the idea, nature and process of public history was affected by a process of disclosure and free information. There was pressure for open diplomacy and for the publication of information on state finances. The revolutionaries made state archives open to the public as sovereignty was derived from the people.[3] The *Archives Nationales* were founded in 1790 and, in 1794, a decree made it mandatory to centralize all pre-revolutionary public and private archives.

Although the revolution had a universal message, it was also grounded in a new French nationalism, one divorced from the *ancien régime*.[4] Linked to these changes, a new history, that of present events recorded in an eulogistic fashion, was rolled out. Continuous war for France from 1792 to 1802, and from 1803 to 1814, resulted in victories and treaties that were carefully packaged, in print and in illustrations. Public commemorations marked, recorded and repeated this new history. The course of the French Revolution also brought a series of allegedly exemplary new regimes in France, each of which, in turn, was superseded as a new regime came to power.

A successful revolutionary general, Napoleon, who ran France from late 1799 to 1814, was different to these earlier regimes, in part because his regime lasted for longer. In addition, the move from a universal message contained within the promise and initial stages of the French Revolution was taken further under Napoleon, in part because of the focus on his personal position, not least after he adopted imperial status in 1804 and launched an attempt at dynasticism. Yet, like the revolutionaries, Napoleon looked back to Antiquity, fashioning, in his own iconography and that of the regime, a self-image in terms of the achievements, glamour and status of the Ancient world, especially Rome. In doing so, there was a clear counterpointing to the alleged decadence of the *ancien régime*, a decadence that encompassed politics, society and the Church. Earlier, in the shape of the major and unprecedented study of Ancient Egypt that Napoleon established when he campaigned in Egypt in 1798, history also served to contextualise the West, and notably the Christian Church.

Haiti

A very different form of revolution was offered, from 1791, in Saint-Domingue, where the overthrow of French imperial rule was an aspect of a destruction of white colonial control by blacks, many of whom were former slaves. The creation of a new history in what, in 1804, became Haiti, the first independent black state in the Caribbean, has not been studied as much as that in France has been. The pre-revolutionary cultural infrastructure in Haiti was far weaker than that in France and the revolutionary disruption and devastation in a long and bitter struggle far greater.

There was a strong need for a new history, as that of a French-ruled and white-run slave society was scarcely usable. In contrast to the Western colonies in the 'New World' once these colonies gained independence (the USA, Brazil and the one-time Spanish colonies), there was in Haiti no usable post-colonial history that could be constructed, at least in part, from an account of the colonial past. In contrast to European states that became independent from foreign imperial rule, for example Greece in 1830, there was not the link between territory and people that could be asserted as part of the process of recovering a history from before the period of this rule. At the same time, there was no strong link with Africa, the source of the population, as enslavement had violently sundered such links. Instead, it was the struggle for freedom from 1791 to 1804 that provided the key history for Haiti, not least the co-operation between blacks and mulattoes that it eventually witnessed.[5]

Change and History

On the world scale, despite pressure for new-type armies, most obviously under Selim III in Turkey (r. 1787–1806), there was no equivalent in the eighteenth century to the mutability, revolutionary change, and thus new revolutionary usage of history, seen in parts of the West. The deployment of history to support and justify revolution encouraged in the West an alertness to historical arguments as well as to the experience of change. If the contrast with non-Western societies underlined the atypical character of the revolutionary usage of history on the world scale, the challenge posed to conventional practices by the usage was also apparent.

This challenge was to play out across the nineteenth century, but, in general, it was to be the adaptability of conventional Western uses of the past that emerged most clearly then. This point underlines a more general one in the usage of history, the ability of conventional, traditional and *ancien régime* systems and cultures to adapt and develop, not least in their presentation of the continuum of past, present and future.

Such a situation clashes with the more general understanding of change in history as occurring thanks to the replacement of the old by the new, with the old seen as redundant and the new as progressive. This understanding appears intuitively correct, not least because there is a rhetoric and politics about the value of change to match, both in the modern world and in the West, more particularly in the last quarter-millennium. Indeed, the use of history proves part of the dynamic, because it is employed to demonstrate both the weaknesses of the past and the extent to which it was necessarily replaced by the present.

However, this approach, which in the early nineteenth century was conceptualized by the German philosopher Georg Wilhelm Friedrich Hegel (1770–1831) in terms of a dialectical method of thesis, antithesis and synthesis, underplays the extent to which this intuitive assumption was (and is) mistaken, and, certainly, too limited. The very use of history provides a demonstration of this point. Change, indeed fundamental change, can be seen in this usage. There was no equivalent in the eighteenth century to the introduction of compulsory mass education in some Western states in the late nineteenth century, let alone no equivalent to the visual culture of history that was produced by the cinema and television in the twentieth century. At the same time, the process of getting from 1750 to 1900, and then to today, was not one in which such transformations were obtained by the total overthrow of previous systems and idioms.

Nevertheless, previous systems and idioms, including those vindicated in established processes of historical presentation, certainly had to adapt to new requirements and contexts. The transition from a history linked to a rulership based on dynastic right to a royal government also resting on democratic sanction is a key example. This adaptation, which was not seen everywhere, involved a different emphasis in much of the writing and representation of public history, but there was also room for a high degree of continuity. In particular, monarchs had generally been presented in conventional accounts as leaders of a people. In the nineteenth century, in monarchical states, the emphasis changed, but the core understanding of the political system continued.

New republics posed a different issue, notably the USA from 1776, France from 1792, 1848 and 1870, and the Latin American republics of the nineteenth century. However, again, it was possible to look back, and history was employed to suggest a legitimacy based on long usage. American and French republicans employed the sanction of Classical republicanism, doing so in the processes of constitutional innovation as well as in the idioms of politics. Institutions such as the Senate represented a conscious use of history at least in the name chosen – a clear reference to the politics and government of Ancient Rome, at least republican Rome.

This process contrasted with that seen in some cases in the twentieth century, for example Italy under its Fascist dictator Benito Mussolini (1922–43), where the reference back was to episodes and institutions of national, rather than international, history. Thus, based in Rome, Mussolini sought to recreate imperial Rome, while the American and French republicans drew on Rome (albeit republican Rome) for legitimation and for rhetorical and symbolic resonance, but without any such sense of continuity. Instead, in the republicanism of the late eighteenth century, there was a use of world history in order to provide a relevant historical iconography and vocabulary in support of a suitable historical meaning.

This process underlines the continuities referred to earlier in this and previous chapters. Legitimation through history, and thus by means of the use of history, was the key theme. Alongside contrasts in context and differences in method and vocabulary, there were important similarities in requirements and language. At the same time, the experience of revolution in the late eighteenth century indicated the process of selection. The use of the past was highly instrumental. It was also dynamic, in that one revolution could serve as a model for another. While looking back to the Classical world, there was also a more recent appropriation of the past. The American Revolution drew on the Glorious Revolution in Britain, and, in turn, served as an inspiration for revolutions in Europe in the 1780s, including that in France. At the same time, the changing nature of the French Revolution meant that the past that was used by the French Revolutionaries, including the American Revolution, altered rapidly, a fate that more directly affected earlier stages of the French Revolution. Revolutions were/are scarcely alone in reconceptualizing, indeed devouring, the past, but they did so at an unprecedented rate.

There was also a highly moral character in the use of the past to inspire, as with Jacques-Louis David's paintings of the self-sacrifice of the heroes of Republican Rome, notably the *Oath of the Horatii* (1784–5). In America, where the radicalization of the French Revolution made it increasingly unwelcome as a frame of reference, Thomas Jefferson, President from 1801 to 1809, found moral lessons in the past and in the process of historical change. Conveniently, these led him to discern support for slavery.[6]

A process of accumulation and selection in the use of the past can also be seen in the case of counter-revolution. However, the key issue for the counter-revolution was not the past, but the French Revolution, which was seen as an aspect of the present. Moreover, compared to the revolutionary tradition, there was less to be said about earlier episodes of counter-revolutionary activity. In particular, the struggle over American independence was not usable for opponents of the French Revolution.

Opposition to the revolution and, subsequently, from 1799, to Napoleon also made use of themes of identity. In 1813, Frederick William III summoned the Prussian people to fight against Napoleon for their king, fatherland, freedom and honour. Counter-revolutionary history drew on a range of themes and factors, including the value of continuity, the dangers of radicalism and the importance of religion. The latter was more significant in this period than is popularly appreciated, and it is worth noting the continued significance of ideas about Providence.[7]

Dynastic legitimacy and continuity remained part of the picture, with the Bourbons numbering Louis XVI's son, who had never in fact reigned or been crowned, in the succession as Louis XVII, with the titular years 1793–5. However, this element was not as crucial to the counter-revolutionary cause as dynastic factors had been at the time of the European succession wars between 1689 and 1748. In a different context to Louis XVII, the theme of continuity was also asserted with Napoleon's son, 'Napoleon II' (1811–32), who was styled King of Rome at his birth.

If cultural, like political, themes in the use of the past and the sense of development with time varied, there was a volatility created by the need to respond to the challenge of change. This need extended to cultural developments in the West, notably Romanticism. Lacking any coherent programme comparable to that of the Enlightenment *philosophes*, Romanticism has been variously defined. An older view, in which it was associated with the individual emotions of the artist, often at variance with social conventions, has been replaced by a greater emphasis on the political character of Romanticism. This involved a national consciousness that looked toward a strengthening of nationalist tendencies.[8] Both consciousness and tendencies could be presented as necessary responses to the challenge of change; they offered a way to understand the present and to shape the future, in each case deploying the past.

CHAPTER SEVEN

The Nineteenth Century: Nationalism and Public Education

National Histories

Public history became more intensive in the nineteenth century, in the shape of more visible and perceived as more important, as rival states sought to shape their histories in order to compete effectively. This statement accords with the Social Darwinism that became common in the West (and in Japan and China) in the later decades of the century, and thus presents the use of history in both instrumental and competitive terms. History appears in both those lights in the nineteenth century, as a key aspect of state-strengthening and nation-building in an age of political and public demands that were different to those of the *ancien régimes* of the eighteenth century.

In practice, however, as also for today and for other periods, there were, in addition, other uses and purposes for history – and the state was far from the only medium of historical activity. Moreover, the pressure for history, even if useful to states, did not necessarily stem from them. Thus, the wars of 1792–1815 within Europe were extensively memorialized[1] over the subsequent decades. Official commemoration played a role, but so also did efforts from a range of communities, families and individuals. Furthermore, while some of this commemoration suited government, as in Britain, Prussia, Russia and the USA, there was often a more complex account of the wars. This was particularly the case in France, as the commemoration of Napoleon and his victories proved highly unwelcome to the restored Bourbon kings of 1815–30. So also with the commemoration of Polish military activity, including in Napoleon's armies, a commemoration unwelcome to Austria, Prussia and, in particular, Russia, the three of which had finally partitioned Poland out of existence in 1795.

As another instance of the range of groups involved in using and contesting history in the nineteenth century, the growth of publishing was highly relevant. It developed notably, but not only eventually, in the West, as a capitalist industry that was driven by entrepreneurialism and enhanced by technological developments, especially steam-driven papermaking and printing, and by distribution by rail. This growth of publishing ensured that history was also used for the purpose of profit. This drive was particularly the case with popular fiction, as with Alexandre Dumas' *Les Trois Mousquetaires* (*The Three Musketeers*, 1845). Dumas (1802–70) also put history on the stage, notably with his play *Henri III* (1829), again about French history: Henry III (r. 1574–89) was a key and contentious figure in the French Wars of Religion and was eventually assassinated. However, even if only looking at publishing, the role of the state again emerges as highly significant, first, because of the importance of textbooks and other school material, and, secondly, due to the far greater literacy rates that followed the creation and expansion of state-organized and funded systems of mass education. Public education was a key element of the use of history in the nineteenth century, because history was deliberately employed in order to serve the interests of governments seeking to encourage popular support as an aspect of this education. The rapid social changes of the period, the large-scale population growth, high rate of migration, and experience of successive episodes of political radicalism, beginning with the rupture of the French Revolution,[2] encouraged a contrary drive for stabilization through public education. Far from being a later, academic, rationalization of developments, this argument was offered at the time. Time was experienced as disorientation, if not crisis. It appeared to be accelerating.[3]

Education in this context was a matter not only for, and by, the state, but also a more general social activity. Thus, writers of popular histories, as well as of historical fiction, saw themselves as taking part in a necessary process of socialization. In his *The History of England from the Reign of James II*, the first two volumes of which appeared in 1848, Thomas Babington Macaulay deliberately told his readers their story in order to invite them into 'new identities, as citizens or subjects'.[4]

Acute international competition furthered commitment to this process of attempted stabilization, as did the growth of governmental and more general concern about the rise of class-consciousness. As large numbers of workers came together in new industries and newly expanded cities, so their beliefs became a matter for anxiety and, in response, for attempted direction.

State educational systems encouraged teachers, academics, pupils and students to think in terms of state identity and of identification through the state. The publication of works in the vernacular, as opposed to in Latin or other wide-ranging cosmopolitan languages, was significant in representing and furthering this process. In particular, the age of mass education sharpened demands for a workable past, and also ensured that such a past had to be defined. The curriculum was a central requirement, and the textbook a key response. Both had to be approved. National history was emphasized in the teaching of, and by, schoolteachers.

The range of public education encompassed far more than history and, in the latter case, much more than school systems and textbooks. Public memorialization and display were also of great significance. In Belgium, independent from 1830, the Grand Place in Brussels became the site for an equestrian statue of Godfrey of Bouillon, a hero of the First Crusade. Duke of Lower Lorraine (r. 1089–95), Godfrey became Defender of the Holy Sepulchre after the capture of Jerusalem in 1099, and thus provided an appropriate pedigree for the new Catholic state which had rejected rule by the Protestant house of Orange as part of a greater Dutch-dominated Kingdom of the United Netherlands. The artistic past was part of the complete (re)invention of the national history of Belgium that followed the 1830 revolution.[5]

Statuary could be eclectic in its historical and political references, but there was a common theme of heroism. Indeed, statues were akin to the stationary poses of heroic figures in the grand operas of the period. Boudicca, Queen of the Iceni in East Anglia, who rebelled unsuccessfully against the Romans in 60 CE, was the subject of a dramatic bronze statue by Thomas Thornycroft, which was commissioned by Prince Albert, and sited from 1898 right next to the heart of the British state at Westminster Bridge. Boudicca was adopted by many Victorians as something of a national inspiration, and there was to be an (attempted) echo in praise for Margaret Thatcher.[6] As a valiant defender of his people, Alfred performed a similar role for the Victorians, but, unlike Boudicca, he could also be presented as the originator of the English state.[7] Defeated, Boudicca killed herself rather than be humiliated by the victorious Romans. A heroic death, including by suicide, was a major subject across the arts, notably in opera. Moreover, such a death provided a way for women to ennoble themselves alongside men, as with Bellini's opera *Norma* and Verdi's *Aida*, each set in the Ancient world; or, more radically, showing moral superiority to men, as with Puccini's opera *Madame Butterfly*, which was set in the modern world.

Alongside statues, paintings made national and imperial narratives more familiar, and, moreover, they could be readily reproduced.[8] In Switzerland, Frank Edouard Lossier (1852–1925) painted scenes from the medieval quest for independence, including episodes from the life of the legendary William Tell and from the Reformation. Rossini turned the former into an opera.

In Sweden, the Age of Greatness in 1611–1718 provided similar episodes, as in the *Death of Gustavus Adolphus* (1855) by Carl Wahlbom, in which the King appears as both heroic and luminous on the victorious battlefield of Lützen in 1632; and in *Bringing Home the Body of King Karl XII* (1884) by Gustaf Cederström, an inspirational depiction of valiant resolution in the face of adversity in 1718. Earlier periods were also depicted, as with Carl Gustaf Hellqvist's *Valdemar Atterday Holding Visby to Ransom 1361* (1882), a clear contrasting of oppressive foreign rule with virtuous Swedes; and Johan Sandberg's *Gustav Vasa Addressing Men from Dalarna* (1836), a linkage of the ruling Vasa dynasty with the Swedish people in the early sixteenth century at a formative period of dynastic establishment, national independence and embrace of Protestantism. Gustav Vasa (r. 1523–60), the founder of the Vasa dynasty, won national independence from Denmark.

In turn, paintings could be highly controversial, as with two Russian works that captured the role of iconic Tsars in the deaths of their eldest sons: Nikolai Ge's *Peter I Interrogates Tsarevich Aleksei Petrovich at Peterhof* (1871) and Ilia Repin's *Ivan the Terrible and His Son, Ivan, 16 November 1581* (1885). The portrayal of Peter related to the wider tension between Westernizers and Slavophiles. Hero to the former and villain to the latter, his reputation became a way to advance the debate over Russia's culture and future. The imprisoned Aleksei was an opponent of Peter's Westernizing policies.[9]

More generally, the construction of imposing national museums, libraries and archives, often in historic styles, whether Classical or neo-Gothic, and the accumulation and cataloguing of collections to put in these repositories gathered pace. The replanning of national capitals saw much space left for these buildings, which were treated in urban landscapes as the equivalent to legislative bodies. States confident in their status created such institutions, for example the Public Record Office on Chancery Lane in London. In France, the *Archives Nationales*, which had been founded in 1790, were located in a former princely palace, the Hôtel Soubise. In Stockholm, the National Museum, opened to the public in 1866, emphasized the visual arts, with imposing Nordic landscapes and monumental scenes from Swedish history being seen as a way to encourage a sense of national identity.

Archaeological finds played a significant role in the contents and organization of national museums, as attempts were made to define a pre-history that linked place and people. As a result, there was an appropriation of earlier peoples in the cause of asserting continuity. Archaeology focused on the theme of continuity, and not on the legacy of rule by imperial powers.[10] There was a stress on the association of people and place, an aspect of the essentialism of nationalism. Paintings of the mythic past contributed to an establishment of accounts of national origins, as did the publication and study of epic literature, some of it forged, as in Bohemia.

The growth of interest in national history did not drive out other accounts within states. There was also a major increase in the civic infrastructure of history, with local history societies developing across the West. Their activities, especially meetings and publications, strengthened the historical awareness of particular communities and celebrated them through their history. Potentially, there was a tension with the interests of the state and notably with the demands of newly united states, particularly Germany and Italy. This issue extended to states, such as France, that had been united for far longer, but where there was an important regional dimension to the heavily divided national loyalties over politics and religion.[11]

Thus, at one level, there was value to the state in the propagation of local history, but, at another level, there were potential or actual problems. The local dimension could also excite differences with other localities. These factors were all seen with the major Florentine Dante Festival of 1865, an opportunity for civic and national patriotism. In 1865, Florence became the capital of the kingdom of Italy declared in 1861 and Turin, the previous capital, the centre of the kingdom of Sardinia that was the military basis of the *Risorgimento*, the drive for Italian unification, boycotted the festival. Opposed to Italian unification, Pope Pius IX refused to approve the festival. Italy past was thus annexed to the current struggle for Italy in the future. Dante became an Italian symbol who was a justification for unification, as well as a Florentine hero.[12]

The same process of asserting identity through history was pushed hard by would-be countries seeking to assert their independent identity and autonomy, even independence, within empires, for example Finland and Poland in the Russian Empire. In empires, especially the Austrian and Russian, but also the British, Dutch and Danish, nationalism could represent, notably on the part of the Czechs, Poles, Irish, Belgians and Norwegians respectively, a clear rejection of imperial rule. The presentation of history owed much to a determination to assert an independent national culture. Unity and glory in the past became a key validation for a path to the future.[13]

This process looked back to the late eighteenth-century conflation of increased national consciousness with Romantic myth-making, but it was given new energy by the strength of popular nationalism. The organic and inevitable unity of the hoped-for new, or to be expanded, state was asserted. The need for assertion, and the possibility of a political transformation, led to pressure for a distinctive and exemplary history, one that built up the coherence of the people in question and also asserted their value and interests. This history was understood in the broadest sense to include ethnography, linguistics and archaeology,[14] and, in turn, these and other fields required an overarching historical account.

The process made it possible to define, substantiate and fix otherwise assertive but vague concepts, such as *das Deutsches Volk* (the German people) – or, rather, to offer a definition that could be contested. Thus, in France, there was a tension between tracing origins to the Gauls or to the Germanic invaders who overthrew imperial Rome. The former approach was favoured by supporters of the Third Republic, but conservative opponents emphasizing a Catholic identity for the nation and stressing papal links were more inclined to emphasize the Germanic period, notably because of the baptism of Clovis as France's first Christian monarch.[15]

Within empires, it was necessary to compete not only with imperial overlords, but also with other national rivals – for example, Lithuanians with Poles within the Russian Empire. To both ends, the education, and thus mobilization, of the masses was seen as crucial. In the Habsburg Empire, the respective role of the Magyars and Germans in European history, and specifically in the defence of Christendom, was an issue at dispute.[16] The Hungarians, who claimed descent from the Magyars, argued that they had played the key role in this defence, notably, but not only, in the fourteenth and fifteenth centuries. This claim challenged the historical prestige of the Germans, i.e. Austrians, and of the Habsburg dynasty, not least as victors over the Ottomans (Turks), and asserted a shared role and reputation.

Commemorative celebrations served to demonstrate an exemplary past. In Poland, the centenaries of the 1791 constitution, the 1794 Kosciuszko rebellion (heroically unsuccessful) against Russian rule, and the 1798 birth of the national poet Adam Mickiewicz, underlined a glorious past, as, in 1910, did the 500th anniversary of the major victory over the Teutonic Knights at Grunwald/Tannenberg. In turn, Germany was to seek to appropriate and control the memory of the latter by naming as Tannenberg its major victory of 1914 over Russian forces invading East Prussia. Tannenberg was not, in fact, the central site of the extensive 1914 battle, but it provided the necessary historical revenge, as well as suggesting that the modern Germans were the heirs of what were presented, in Germany, as the noble, self-sacrificing, crusading Teutonic Knights. After the First World War, the victory of 1914 was used by, and on behalf of, the victorious generals, Hindenburg and Ludendorff, to propagate myths about their real and potential roles as national saviours.

Nationalist historians were apt, in their quest to identify progress with their cause, to attribute what were seen as reactionary failings, such as feudalism, to foreign influences. Thus, feudalism in Poland was attributed to the Germans,[17] while the faults of the Irish rural economy were blamed on oppressive British control, including ownership of the agricultural land.

In turn, empires sought to affirm their role and to strengthen support by disseminating positive historical accounts.[18] Some of these accounts sought to be inclusive of their subjects, but others were more triumphalist. In Tallinn, the capital of Estonia, then part of Russia, the use of grand buildings as part of Russification was seen with the large (Russian) Orthodox Cathedral built in 1894–1900. Occupying a prominent site, the cathedral was a clear display of cultural power, not least with the removal of the statue of the Protestant reformer Martin Luther in order to make way for it. Many Estonians were Lutherans and Lutheranism was a statement about lasting German influence. The cathedral was dedicated to Prince Alexandr Nevsky, who had defeated Swedish and German (Teutonic Knights) forces in 1240 and 1242 respectively and who had been canonized by the Orthodox Church in 1547. Nevsky was commemorated with a mosaic on the side of the cathedral (as he was to be in Sergey Eisenstein's film, *Alexander Nevski* in 1938), while the mosaic on the opposite side of the cathedral depicted Count Vsevlod of Pskov, who had campaigned against the Estonians during the thirteenth century. Textbooks also reflected imperial interests, as in Ireland where the school textbooks of the National Board emphasized English constitutional history, and certainly not an account appropriate for Irish nationalists.

Imperial accounts of history looked back in order to explain their position and to demonstrate their status, most commonly in terms of a thesis of succession in which the empire in question was the heir to past ones judged appropriate and exemplary. In the West, including the USA, this process was encouraged by the prestige of the Classical past. This prestige, which was reflected in educational curricula and ethos, ensured that interest in the Classical past resonated widely, in a manner that today is most often replicated only on film, in television, or in historical novels. Thus, W. E. Gladstone, a leading British statesman, who was Prime Minister in 1868–74, 1880–5, 1886 and 1892–4, wrote extensively on Homer and his world, and found a large audience.[19] Lincoln's Gettysburg Address followed a long speech by a Harvard professor comparing the victory to that of the Athenians over Persian invaders at Marathon in 490 BCE. Thus, the Ancient world established an exemplary context and a worthy call to arms and to commemoration.

Less commonly, there was criticism of the Classical past, Jeremy Bentham (1748–1832) arguing that 'whatever Athenian arrogance may pretend, it will not easily gain credit with a discerning mind, that at so early a period of society the best of all possible laws should have presented themselves to view'.[20] A utilitarian philosopher, Bentham was a radical whose views were scarcely typical.

The development of historical consciousness on the part of those within empires who so far lacked independence served to affirm an identity. In part, this identity was more clearly historical because of the absence or limitation of political options, but, in addition, the possibility of political change encouraged the demand for a distinctive and exemplary history. As a result, history joined the arts (or, looked at differently, history joined the other arts) in depicting the past, both glorious and suffering, from the perspective of the nation and would-be state. Programmatic music, for example by Antonin Dvorak (1841–1904) and Jean Sibelius (1865–1957), the leading Czech and Finnish composers, exemplified this process. The music made reference to accounts of national history that were generally mythic and, characteristically, linked people and place. Thus, in this music, there was an emphasis on particular rivers or mountains. Sibelius wrote a series of symphonic poems based on episodes in the *kalevala*, the Finnish epic. His symphonic poem *Finlandia* (1899) was treated as akin to a national anthem.

The presentation of *pays*, to use the French term, may seem a geographical process removed from history, but, in practice, there was a close correspondence that reflected a sense of geography and history as linked and co-dependent,[21] the two contributing to interest and identity in a form of environmental interaction with human society, if not a degree of determinism. This consideration of *pays*, or the German *Heimat*, is underplayed in Anglo-American accounts of identity, and thus of the use of history, but it was very important across much of Europe and notably in would-be nations. History there was recorded in terms of particular ethnicities and landscapes, and as part of a process by which the nation was expressed or, to employ a more critical and active term, created. The process of proto-nations establishing a history extended to Jewish intellectuals advancing a call for Zionism.[22] No similar recognition was to be given to Arabs, notably in Palestine.[23]

In practice, both expression and creation were at issue because nationhood is in part a matter of prioritizing among multiple and potentially competing identities. The choice of the term, whether expression or creation, is signif-icant. Linked to this, the claim that nations arise from a conscious process of political and cultural activity, commonly by élites, relates largely to the issue of prioritizing at the time, in later discussion, and in subsequent analysis. Indeed, the historians of the period, many of whom benefited from state-supported educational systems to an unprecedented degree, made nations the object of philological, ethnographic and historical study, and were keen backers of a national approach to history.[24]

Despite the distrust of government by some historians, such as John, Lord Acton (1834–1902), Professor of Modern History at Cambridge from 1895 and the founder editor of the *Cambridge Modern History*, the state played a leading part in the development of academic history in the nineteenth century. That development owed much to a utilitarian drive for education and training, and to a commitment on the part of academics to the state, that were at variance with much of the liberal Western academic culture of the late twentieth century, although not so from modern govern-mental concerns. The nature of this academic commitment to the state varied, but the value of history and of specific historical models was under-stood to be ideological and functional.

A key influence was the development of the research university in the Protestant German lands from the late eighteenth century. German models were important to the practice and ideology of professionalism across the West, although to varying degrees. In part, this development of the research university was a top-down process, with education seen by governments as a means to succeed in a competitive international world.[25] This role, which offered a new commodification for the work of the academic, was focused on the training of public servants and, in a wider sense, committed citizens, whose first loyalty was to the state, rather than, for example, to interna-tional movements such as Catholicism. There were also more specific tasks for history: understanding the past appeared the way to grasp the future, while explaining the past from the perspective of the nation seemed the way to build up public support for the state.

Scientific History

Alongside these wider currents, the prestige of science, and the belief that research should, could, and would, yield a valuable insight, both contributed to the particular value associated with academic history. An important strand of the study of history developed, at once academic, professional and self-consciously scientific;[26] those in this strand expected special support and respect on this basis.[27] As academic culture, especially in Germany, moved from oral mediums to a greater emphasis on the written word, so the study of documents appeared the necessary method, and, as part of what Arnold Toynbee (1889–1975), author of the *History of the World* (1934–54), was to decry as 'the industrialisation of historical thought',[28] this study focused on the records of the state.

Indeed, the organization and publication of public records, and the opening of record offices, on both the national and the local scale, were important aspects of the nexus of public history and academic method, because it was argued that the records would be available to all. Political history and institutional history were seen as important and objective branches of the subject requiring lengthy work in the archives. This designation was part of the process by which the profession developed,[29] in opposition to an amateurism that was presented as lacking comparable purpose and status. However, the exclusion of women from most academic posts ensured that they were only allocated amateur roles. Indeed, their work tended to be seriously underrated.[30]

Leopold von Ranke (1795–1886), a highly influential figure who was Professor of History at Berlin from 1825 to 1871, emphasized not only the significance of history as a way to appreciate the nature of the world, but also the role of documents, the latter also seen, for example, with John Lingard's *History of England* (1819–30).[31] To Ranke, it was vital to understand texts and to link them to a narrative that was grounded in the evidence. This practice was seen in his *History of the Latin and Germanic Nations* (1824) and his *History of the Popes in the 16th and 17th Centuries* (1834–7).[32]

Ranke's interest in documents was related to his stress on the importance of international relations. He argued that foreign policy took priority in state policies[33] and greatly affected internal developments, an approach that could be more readily pursued through work on diplomatic archives, which were relatively plentiful. Ranke himself worked extensively on the substantial Venetian archives. The closeness to events of such sources, combined with their regularity, helped underline their value over hearsay, tradition and secondary literature. As governments (allowing for closure periods) opened up many of their records to researchers, so scholars grounded their histories in the state.

Ranke was also important as a teacher, making particular use of the seminar, and many of his pupils became German academics.[34] This influence was linked to the establishment of wider normative standards and to the development of a community of academic scholars.[35] In 1887, Ludwig Reiss, one of Ranke's students, was appointed to teach history at the new Tokyo Imperial University. His approach, which incorporated a causal analysis within a chronological framework, seemed to Japanese scholars to be more valuable than the established annalistic Chinese method of historical scholarship.[36]

In turn, in China, new means of understanding the past were probed in textual studies. In late-imperial classical studies (often called Confucianism), there was an epistemological and philological revolution in methodology, but it stopped short of a full-blown historicism in which the classics would simply become histories rather than classics. Such decanonization, however, gathered pace in the late nineteenth century.[37]

Ranke's context was that of a conservative Protestant and a German patriot. In common with most other intellectuals of the period, he saw God's will at work in history and was a devout supporter of German unification under the leadership of Prussia – Berlin was the home university of the German state. Ranke was very hostile to the 1848–9 radical revolution, and, in April 1849, claimed that only military force kept the peace in Berlin. Ranke applauded King Frederick William IV of Prussia's eventual move toward what he regarded as a more realistic (i.e. conservative) approach to politics. Ranke was also concerned about the state of the university, which he saw as in great disorder, with the students mostly idle, mischievous politicians. With classic conservatism, Ranke argued that it was a great pity when young men entered too soon into politics, before, as he saw it, their judgement was perfected, or their minds sufficiently stored with knowledge. Ranke's wife shared his prejudices, presenting the 'champions of liberty' who fell in 1848 as mostly belonging to the discontented rabble, and arguing that the press provided a false view of affairs.[38]

Competing for the Nation

Ranke wrote in the context of sharply contrasting and competing Protestant and Catholic accounts of the Thirty Years' War (1618–48), which served respectively to justify Prussian and Austrian hegemony in Germany. Competing accounts of German nationalism were thus joined to differing views on providential destiny.[39] Within Prussia, there were also sharply contrasting liberal and conservative accounts of Frederick the Great (r. 1740–86), who was variously presented as enlightened and as a great war leader.[40]

History was used to help secure both a view of Prussian destiny and a Prussian account of the new German state, an approach necessary given the degree to which chauvinistic nationalism was matched by a 'self-reflexive critical public attitude'.[41] Johann Gustav Droysen, another major figure in Prussian historical circles, who taught in the University of Berlin from 1859 to 1884, produced a *History of Prussian Politics* which served, in his view, as German by destiny, and vice versa. In 1851, he had produced a biography of Count Johann Yorck von Wartenburg, a Prussian Field Marshal and a hero of the 1813–14 war of liberation against Napoleon, a work that did not harm Droysen's efforts to gain an academic post.

The Prussian account affected differing treatments from elsewhere in the new state. Thus, co-operation with Britain in the Waterloo campaign in 1815, notably by Hanover, was subordinated to a viewpoint focused on Germany, with the key memory becoming that of victorious participation under Prussian leadership in the 1870–1 Franco-Prussian War,[42] a topic celebrated in Droysen's *Allgemeiner historischer Handatlas* (1886). Ironically, the German contribution to victory at Waterloo is currently being emphasized for contemporary political reasons, namely by British protagonists of the European Union who are eager to challenge what they present as a misguided xenophobic national exceptionalism.[43]

On a longer timescale, the history of the German nation was a topic that was discussed in the late nineteenth century in order to show a long-lasting identity. The German Empire created under Prussian leadership in 1871 was therefore given potent medieval forbears whose achievement had been undermined by a particularism that was now being reversed and that could be seen as redundant.

Across the West, intellectuals focused on the idea of the inherent characteristics of nations and, therefore, of national communities. This was a potentially misleading approach given what in practice was the porous nature of peoples and the more changeable, not to say transient, links with particular territories and cultural features.[44] However, the interest of many intellectuals and much of the public in natural history (biology) encouraged a racialized approach to its human counterpart.

Race was a key theme in public understandings of past, present and future, race taking priority over other forms, notably constitutions. This emphasis on race looked to Romantic ideas of nations and empires, to interest in geographical distribution,[45] to the emphasis on Darwinian competition in contemporary ideas of natural history, and to notions of providentialism. Charles Kingsley (1819–75), who became Regius Professor of History at Cambridge in 1860, sought to link natural and national history in his focus on the Teutonic race. The marginalization of such an approach in the subsequent treatment of Victorian historiography leads to a failure to appreciate its strength in public attitudes, with fictional accounts contributing to these attitudes.[46]

The public understanding and presentation of history tended to focus on wars, a process encouraged by conscription and the idea of the nation in arms.[47] This situation and the practice of competing histories contributed to a zero-sum gain approach to the past: one nationalism could only do well at the expense of another. There was scant attempt to search for themes of co-operation and mutual benefit. However, the fashionable nature in the West of some causes, such as Greek independence in the 1820s and the Italian *Risorgimento* in the 1840s–60s, ensured that specific nationalisms could win international support when rivalry between states was not an issue. As a result, these nationalisms drew on, and created, a Western historical consciousness, rather than a more limited one. At the same time, in Italy, liberal nationalism was explicitly directed against another inter-nationalism, the Papacy, because of its role, as the temporal power in the papal states (of central Italy), in opposing Italian unification. Each side in Italy deployed martyr cults as they created a history relevant to their cause.[48]

States that succeeded in gaining independence pushed the process of nation-forming most strongly. This was true of Balkan territories that broke free from the Ottoman (Turkish) empire, notably Greece, Romania, Serbia and Bulgaria. National history was developed as a subject and as an affirmation of nationhood, a process that continued into the twentieth century when its practices were greatly affected by the demands of totali-tarianism. Both in its independence struggle, and subsequently, for example when pressing territorial claims before, during and after the First World War, Greece sought to annex the strong Western Hellenism of the period to the cause of the reputation of the new state. For Greek nationalism and nation-building, Hellenism implied a cause that made divisive views inappropriate, and thereby offered a potent national myth.

Other newly independent states, for example Belgium and Italy, witnessed the same development.[49] Once independence had been won, hero and martyr cults that were suitable to the purposes of the new state were retained, while others were discarded. At a smaller scale, Luxembourg went through the same process.[50]

Outside Europe, the process was seen with the newly independent states of Latin America that replaced the Portuguese and Spanish empires from the 1810s–20s. Nation-building in this context was difficult, and different to that in Europe, because of the ethnic basis of the new states in the descendants of the Iberian conquerors, and with those inhabitants who were of Native or African (slave) descent kept from power and, indeed, recognition. The long-term creolization of European societies in Latin America, as new racial and ethnic identities were created, was a process that was not well recognized in practise. This latter situation meant that the new states could not easily look back to assert a continuity with a pre-conquest history prior to the sixteenth century. In contrast, in the Balkans the content of what could be presented as national history before Ottoman conquest in the fourteenth and fifteenth centuries was extensively deployed by the newly independent states, as well as contested within and between them.

Instead, the emphasis in Latin America was on the struggle for independence, and, notably for Venezuela and Colombia, the legacy of

Simon Bolívar, the central figure in the struggle. However, this history proved divisive, offering a reason for liberal, secular republican governments that was unwelcome to conservative, clerical rivals.

At the same time, there was a stress in Latin America on nation-building. In 1884, when compulsory, free primary education was introduced in Argentina, Argentine history was incorporated into the curriculum, while the celebration of national anniversaries through school ceremonies was also introduced. Education was seen as a way to integrate the diverse peoples of Argentina and to help create an Argentine nation that could draw on a patriotic historiography.[51] In some states, for example Mexico, an emphasis on resistance to Spanish conquest in the sixteenth century became a way to anticipate more recent liberation and nationalism. That Mexico lacked a Bolívar-like figure, and an equivalent struggle to those in Spanish South America, especially Colombia, Venezuela and Chile, encouraged a different chronological focus for the new national history.

Nation-building was also seen with non-Western states trying to resist Western imperialism and, in doing so, emulating much of the panoply of Western statehood, most obviously Japan, China, Siam (Thailand), the Ottoman Empire and Egypt. The methods of Western national consciousness and state identity were also borrowed, for example maps.

Across the world, political circumstances and context varied by state, but the common theme was that of the primacy of politics in the presentation of history. Moreover, this process was highly competitive, because historical assertion was explicitly at the expense of other states and would-be states, as well as against real, or potential, rival or opposing groups within individual states. Where religion, nationalism and the state could be linked, then there was no acute division in the presentation of the past.

In Japan, state Shinto developed as an amalgam of a longstanding religion with a new authoritarian form of government after the Meiji Restoration of 1868. Militarism and the new past played a role, with the foundation, in 1869, of Yasukuni as a pre-eminent shrine that was a symbol of nationalism and where the war dead were commemorated. As a consequence of the Second World War and the burial there of convicted war criminals, this shrine is now a divisive site (see p. 190). The Meiji slogan *fukoku kyohei* (enrich the country, strengthen the army) was taken up in 2012–13 by supporters of Shinzo Abe, the Prime Minister, who was keen on a national revitalization involving not only economic growth but also a more assertive international stance.

Across the world, contested changes within states drove forward this process of politicized nation-building. In France, the series of regime and constitutional changes, notably in 1814, 1815, 1830, 1848 and 1870, led to new public ideologies, and to new histories accordingly. As with most public history of a controversial type, these new histories focused on the recent past, for example Napoleon I's defeat at Waterloo in 1815 and the Paris Commune of 1870–1.[52] It was particularly necessary to justify the most recent changes, a process that was to be repeated after the fall of the Third Republic in 1940, of Vichy in 1944, and of the Fourth Republic in 1958. The French Third Republic, established in 1870 as a result of Napoleon III's defeat by Germany, and remaining in force until 1940, rested on a rejection of earlier monarchical systems, notably the Second Empire, that of the Emperor Napoleon III, from 1852.

At the same time, this discussion of earlier French history was broader than simply a focus on rejection of the previous regime or regimes. More generally, historical discussion was often in pursuit of contentious goals. Thus, political partisanship was one of the principal causes of historical works, and their use could, and should, be assessed accordingly. In France, constructions of national identity interacted strongly with political contention, and notably about the period from the French Revolution of 1789 on. Fear of domestic and foreign threats, as well as a belief in the sovereignty of the people, helps explain the emphasis, in the French Republic as elsewhere, on the indivisibility of the state and the universality of its powers within its boundaries.[53] The positive presentation of a republican tradition in France, as in the USA, underlines the extent to which a historically grounded nationalism was not a monopoly of the Right. In turn, Catholic legitimists actively challenged the centenary of the Revolution in 1889 as part of their incessant assault on the Third Republic.[54]

The Catholic account looked back to the Middle Ages, but engaged fully in the politics of the moment. This was an aspect of a more general process in which religion and the related interpretation of history both framed, and were used for, political ends. Thus, in Germany, there was an anti-papal account of medieval history related to the *kulturkampf*, Bismarck's anti-Catholic policy of 1871–87. In Ireland, the Anglicans emphasized the early Church's independence from Rome and presented St Patrick in a Protestant light. More generally, the relationship between Church and state was a key instance of the interaction of competing memory cultures. In Britain, pro-Catholic accounts, such as the *History of England from the First Invasion by the Romans to the Accession of William and Mary* (1819–30) by John Lingard, a Catholic priest, were challenged by works that put the Reformation central to national development and identity, such as James Froude's *History of England from the Fall of Wolsey to the Defeat of the Spanish Armada* (1856–69). This tension was matched by division over the constitutional and political heritage of the country, notably over the civil wars of the 1640s, but also looking back to the Anglo-Saxon heritage and the impact of the Norman Conquest.

In France, prejudice and history were mobilized in order to provide Catholic politicians with a platform, notably the *Union Nationale*, founded in 1892 by Theodore Garnier, a priest, which (falsely) claimed that Jews, Freemasons and Protestants were running the Third Republic and needed to be overthrown. The emancipation of the Jews by the Revolutionaries in 1791 was presented as a deliberately anti-Catholic step, and one that condemned both Jews and Revolutionaries.[55] An apparently exemplary nationalist-historical pedigree was found in Joan of Arc's struggle against the English in the 1420s–30s, a struggle given a pronounced religious dimension and with Joan treated as a providential figure. Joan's struggle against the English was a theme later used by the Vichy regime of 1940–4.[56]

A paranoia similar to that seen with the *Union Nationale* was at work elsewhere. The conspiracy theories that had been pushed to the fore in Europe at the time of the French Revolutionary War in the 1790s, a period in which there was a widespread belief in secret societies, some allegedly long-lasting,[57] influenced the subsequent account of both present politics and the recent past. In turn, these theories proved the easiest way to address anxieties stemming from the unexpected extent and unwelcome character of political and social change, particularly in, and after, the French Revolution.

Earlier concerns about secret movements, notably the Freemasons and the Illuminati, were played through a new context from the 1790s and were made more open and 'democratic', in large part through the culture of print and rising literacy. Thus, anti-Masonry took a major role in the political culture of mid-nineteenth-century USA.

More generally, the role of conspiracy in the account of recent history was an important consequence of a sense of ideological polarisation and, in turn, contributed to this polarization. The process encouraged the development of competing narratives, because there was more than one conspiracy theory. Thus, in Latin America, and in many other areas, including Iberia and France, competing historical narratives were offered by liberals and conservatives. Religion played a key role in this contrast, with the conservatives presenting the liberals not only as anti-clerical but as part, accordingly, of a longstanding conspiracy, the evidence of which could apparently be discerned across history. Accusations of Masonic plots allegedly proved part of this account. In turn, liberals claimed that conservatives represented a back-to-the-past movement. History therefore was not simply a set of issues and episodes to debate, but also a contested process.

Public education became particularly controversial in this context, with history a key subject. The past had to be won in order to secure the future, or so it seemed. The struggle over religion therefore greatly involved the issue of control over education, as in France in the 1900s.

The USA exemplified many of the tendencies referred to above. History united, but also threatened to divide, and was presented accordingly, as with conflicts with foreign powers: the Mexican War (1846–8) and the War of 1898 with Spain. In each case, recording war celebrated victory and shamed those who had failed to support it. A democratic politics helped make this process necessary, as an instant history of appropriate unity was rapidly established.

Conflict within the USA, the Civil War of 1861–5, had elements of the same factor. How the war was to be memorialized was a key element, for the idea of a war against slavery clashed with that of an attempt to suppress separatism. There were competing narratives in both the former Union and the ex-Confederacy, but, at the same time, from the 1890s, an emphasis on national reconciliation. Anniversaries of battles were used to bring veterans from both sides together. Moreover, the Civil War was followed by a nationalist era in which patriotic symbols, rituals and ceremonies, notably the flag, were matched by a focus on the teaching of American history which was increasingly prescribed in public schools. The textbooks produced accordingly were nationalistic.[58]

More generally, American educational reformers cited history as indispensable for creating citizenship, and not as a means to critical thinking. Various public service groups displayed a keen interest in promoting history as a citizen's credential. This was seen with the Daughters of the American Revolution, the Masonic textbook movement, and the Progressive educational reformers of the close of the nineteenth century. Thus, the state as the provider of national history can be anatomized to show the interests and bodies involved in this process and keen to see it succeed.

Art was employed to similar goals. The depiction of the glories of the American landscape, as with the Hudson School of painters, served a patriotic purpose. The painters of this self-consciously national school, engaged with the natural landscape, first the Hudson Valley and later the West, as sublime and morally uplifting. The writer Ralph Waldo Emerson (1803–82) presented America as a visionary poem, a country of young men, who, in 1775, had fired at Lexington 'the shot heard round the world'. He wrote this, appropriately, for the hymn sung at the completion of the Concord Monument.

The American past was also deployed by painters. For example, to take the work of the Philadelphia painter Peter Rothermel (1817–95), his *De Soto Raising the Cross on the Banks of the Mississippi* (1851) depicted an episode from 1541 when the Spaniard Hernando de Soto (c. 1496–1542) became the first European explorer to reach the Mississippi. The painting not only reflected the period's interest in American history, but also provided a pedigree that helped legitimate the expansionism of American Manifest Destiny; over the previous decade, with the settlement of the Oregon Question with Britain in 1845 and thanks to successful war with Mexico in 1846–8, America's frontier had reached the Pacific.

The painting depicted Native Americans as part of the process of expansion, respectfully contributing to the composition, whereas, in practice, de Soto, in his expedition of 1539–42, brutally pillaged the Lower Mississippi and nearby lands, for example defeating the Choctaw at modern Selma, Alabama, in 1541. Public interest in Philadelphia was shown in 1852 with the production of a play, 'The Tragedy of de Soto'.

A different echo of the past was provided by Rothermel's *State House on the Day of Germantown* (1862). Depicting an episode in Philadelphia in 1777 as battle raged nearby, this painting was an instance of the use of history painting during the Civil War to remind viewers of a past heritage of liberty, in this case the effort made in resisting the British during the War of Independence. When the painting was displayed in 1864, the crowds in Philadelphia were very numerous.

Changing World History

In the West, world history as an alternative to the national perspective declined over the century. This decline represented a major shift in the context within which developments were assessed as of significance and then discussed. In some respects, however, the world history dimension was annexed as an aspect of a rise of the imperial narrative on the part of the major Western states and the ability then to fit the remainder of the world into this narrative. The West as a whole appeared to be the history of the world as it was becoming, an approach that reflected the potent interaction of teleology, Providence, Darwinism, the extent to which the great powers were in the West, and a belief that civilizations were of differing value and strength. In specific cases, there were also historical accounts justifying Western imperialism, as in the argument that France and Italy were recreating the pre-Arab Roman presence in North Africa.[59]

Linked to a self-conscious modernization of history in terms of both content and method, there was also a move away from sacred time, as the new subject of geology made inroads into the understanding of the past, and thus into the uses of history. There was a major effort, however, in the West, especially in the early decades of the century, to interpret geology so that it did not invalidate the historical framework of theology. This effort matched the attempt to ensure that the counter-revolutionary tendencies of the period were still capable of being aligned with the idea of a belief in Progress. William Buckland, who became Professor of Mineralogy at Oxford in 1813, published his proof of the Biblical Flood, *Reliquiae Diluvianae, or Observations on the Organic Remains attesting the Action of a Universal Deluge*, following, in 1836, with his *Bridgewater Treatise*, which sought to use geology and other scientific tools to prove the power of God as shown in the Creation.

In the event, the development of the idea of uniformitarianism, especially in the *Principles of Geology* (1830–3) by Charles Lyell, Professor of Geology at King's College, London from 1831, proved a fundamental challenge to Biblical ideas such as the Flood. Uniformitarianism argued that current processes had acted over time, undermining Biblical accounts of history and when it, in turn, was challenged in the 1840s, it was by catastrophism in the shape of glaciation, and not by the Flood.[60] The long timespan involved in glaciation could not be fitted into the Biblical cataclysm of the Flood. Moreover, geology was one of the subjects that contributed greatly to the idea of evolution, notably with discussion of the age of the Earth and the extinction of animal and plant species.

The changing use of history, as knowledge of the geological past replaced sacred time and accompanying accounts of origins, transformed the understanding of man's place in Creation. Yet, it would be mistaken to see sacred history, the history of the Church, as redundant. Instead, historical works about aspects of Christianity appeared in considerable numbers across the West, and were spread outside it as an aspect of the publications of proselytism. Much was also written in support of providential accounts of history, and, indeed, there was the belief that academic history could contribute to this approach. Again, it is the varied uses of history that are notable.

CHAPTER EIGHT

The Twentieth Century: The Struggle of Ideologies

Prisons and Indian Independence

The Cellular Jail, the Indian Bastille, stands as a mute witness to the untold suffering, valiant defiance and undaunted spirit of the firebrand revolutionaries against the brutalities of the British barbarisms.

The plaque outside the Cellular Jail at Port Blair on the distant South Andaman Island in the Bay of Bengal was installed when the one-time prison was 'as a mark of respect to the freedom fighters dedicated to the nation' in 1979 by the Indian Prime Minister, Morarji Desai (1896–1995). Desai himself had been a civil servant under the British in Bombay (1918–30) before becoming a supporter of Gandhi and being imprisoned for civil disobedience. British rule had come to an end with Indian independence in 1947. He was imprisoned anew by the government of Indira Gandhi during her totalitarian Emergency of 1975–7, not, however, a point worthy of mention when the focus was on the iniquities of the British.

Reference to this plaque is not the record of the struggle of twentieth-century ideologies that would customarily be anticipated in a book on public history and historiography written by a British author, or, indeed, any other than an Indian. The emphasis, instead, would be on the extreme, authoritarian ideologies, Communism and Fascism, that helped cause, or define, struggles between, and within, states, from the Russian Revolution in 1917 to the collapse of Eastern European and Soviet Communism in 1989–91. Both of these events occurred in Europe, which reflects its centrality to the conventional historical account and to historiographical concerns. Each of these points is underlined by the American focus, in the twentieth century (as earlier), for the outside world on political and intellectual developments in Europe.

The uses of history by, and against, these authoritarian ideologies, indeed, were an important aspect of the subject of this book for the twentieth century, and will be considered later in the chapter. At the same time, these uses and ideologies tend to push to the margins other aspects of the treatment of history that were also highly significant, as well as other historiographical traditions. In particular, the rival ideologies (and uses) of empires and anti-imperial struggles were, and still are, very important, especially for the 'Third World' that was created by the collapse of extra-European empires. These ideologies and uses were also notable within Europe itself, from Ireland to the Balkans and Scandinavia, as imperialism, empire, and opposition to them, were key experiences in Europe.

As a result of these points, this chapter begins with the example of the Cellular Jail and its use by Indians to construct an account of the British Empire. This was a hostile account that made (and makes) sense of the Indian quest for independence. Port Blair was developed by the British from 1858 as a penal settlement for those who had taken part in the Indian Mutiny, or First War of Independence, against British rule. The choice of term is important, not least because the second term looks toward the struggle for independence from Britain prior to 1947. The idea of successive wars of independence plays up the Indian role in obtaining independence then, as opposed to emphasizing the British willingness to cede control and, earlier, to seek to conciliate Indian concerns by granting a considerable degree of autonomy. In practice, there was no second war of independence, even though Indian public history might prefer the idea of a Second War of Independence.

In the case of Britain, it is also possible as factors encouraging independence, first to emphasize exhaustion as a result of the Second World War, and, secondly, to stress the sympathy of the Labour government elected in 1945 – the first Labour government to enjoy a parliamentary majority – for Indian independence. It is, also, appropriate to downplay India by considering the extent to which the very logic of British imperialism was to move colonies toward independence and co-operation with Britain, a course already followed by those colonies that had gained Dominion status, notably Australia and Canada.

If the emphasis is on political, military and economic weakness as a global power, overstretch, and, more specifically, British exhaustion as a result of the Second World War, then agency also can be given to Asians, in this case to the impact of sweeping Japanese success against Britain in 1941–2 on the prestige and sense of Western superiority that were so necessary to the successful exercise of imperial control. A parallel can be offered by the impact of this success in discrediting, or at least weakening, the Dutch, French and American presence in areas conquered by the Japanese.

In the case of the British Empire, an Indian role can then be introduced by discussing those Indians, under Subhas Chandra Bose (1897–1945), who supported, and 'fought with', the Japanese – a situation paralleled in the case of Burma (Myanmar) with the People's Revolutionary Party and the Ba Maw puppet government. Again, the choice of words is significant, as 'fought with' is not the term that would be used by commentators sympathetic to Bose, although it is a term that captures a reality of close co-operation. Indeed, Bose visited the Cellular Jail while the Andamans were under wartime Japanese occupation,[1] and at a time when the Japanese were treating those islanders they suspected of supporting the British with murderous harshness.

Given that several of the anti-imperialist movements during the Second World War were pro-Axis, frequently with Fascist inclinations, it is not surprising that a racist essentialism played a role in their post-war identity. Looked at differently, such a racism was linked to their pre-war proto-nationalism and this factor, as much as opposition to the colonial powers, led them to turn to Hitler, Mussolini and imperial Japan.

Again, but as an alternative example, if the agency emphasized in Indian independence is that of Indians, the emphasis in weakening British rule of India can be placed on the Congress Party's 'Quit India' campaign of 1942, a campaign of civil disobedience against the British. In part, this campaign arose from anger at the Viceroy's commitment of India to war against the Axis without consulting nationalist leaders. In practice, this campaign failed, although it did have a highly disruptive effect. Railroads were uprooted and communications with the front line disintegrated. Most of the Indian police and civil administration remained passive and the government had to deploy 55 battalions of the Indian Army. The British realized that in case of a further dispute they could not rely wholesale on the police or administrators. Although the army was loyal, there were murmurings about a desire for independence once the war was won. Post-1947, Indian historiography underplays the genesis of Indian nationalism in the Indian army and overplays the non-violent culture of Congress.

British rule is discredited in the standard nationalist account by reference to the Bengal Famine of 1943 and the unsuccessful and unsympathetic nature of the British response to this calamity. This, however, is an account that greatly underplays the wartime difficulties of the British position, not least grave shortages of food and shipping. In short, a context of racialist attitudes is emphasized rather than the context of the practicalities of the period.

Port Blair had become the site of a cellular jail, built between 1896 and 1906, for political detainees deported from India to what seemed a distant destination. In 1921, following revelations of brutality by prison guards, it was decided to end the transportation of prisoners there and to repatriate the political prisoners. However, in turn, overcrowding in Indian jails resulted in a revival of the transportation of non-political prisoners, while political violence in India led to the dispatch of political detainees to the jail.

The latter dispatch was contentious, and notably because of hunger strikes in 1933 and 1937 against conditions in the jail. As a result of this

controversy, political prisoners were returned to mainland India. After
Japanese occupation of the Andamans in 1942–5, during the Second
World War, the British dismantled the penal settlement prior to Indian
independence in 1947.

In the case of the Cellular Jail (which is no longer complete), as now
presented to visitors, the harsh nature of the prison regime, and thus of
imperial rule, is demonstrated by both commission and omission. There is
a presentation of single cells and of night-time solitary confinement as an
abuse designed to break the spirit of prisoners, and not an explanation that
this was then advanced practice and likely to lessen the serious risks of the
spread of infection. The routine and, sometimes, deadly abuse of prisoners
in shared cells by other inmates is itself a problem in modern India. Far
from being a matter simply of colonial control, the Cellular Jail, indeed,
was constructed on lines similar to Pentonville prison in London.

Present-day information for visitors displayed as notices in the Cellular
Jail praise the hunger strikers of the 1930s as courting 'martyrdom', refer to
'brutal and sadistic torture', and describe the work the detainees did as 'soul
shattering' and 'intended to function as a form of torture'. There is a model
of a prisoner being flogged, as well as the remains of the gallows. Similarly
in Hanoi's Hoa Lo prison, there is the guillotine used by the French when
they were the colonial power, as well as mock-ups of the harsh conditions
including prisoners shackled to the ground. In contrast, the use of Hoa Lo
as a prison by North Vietnam once it became independent in 1954 is not
stressed, no more than Chinese museums take note of the large numbers
killed under Communist rule.

In Port Blair, there is a whole series of highly emotive comments in
displays around the prison: 'living hell ... today a sacred place ... the ever-
lasting flame for achieving freedom ... holy fire in memory of freedom
fighters who died here ... so that future generations could know about
the revolutionary freedom movement and appreciate the tremendous cost
at which our independence was achieved'. These iniquities were further
driven home in a 1996 film by Priyadarshan, a film entitled *Kaalapani* in
Malayalam and *Sirai Chaalai* in Tamil. As with other states expounding,
through history, the value of their independence, the Cellular Jail now
serves as an account both of a valiant struggle for freedom and of the
harshness of imperial rule, the latter apparently demonstrating the need for
this freedom.

Prisons frequently serve this purpose, and are often discussed in emotive
language and an unhistorical manner and without any contextualization,
or with a highly partisan one. Prisons, indeed, provide a key site for the
representation of the past – or, rather, one version of the past – in terms of
the present. Eastern Europe brings this feature out very well. During the
Communist era after the Second World War, an era that lasted until 1989,
prisons were used to demonstrate the evils of earlier regimes. Thus, in the
1970s, as in Brno, the capital of Moravia in what was then Czechoslovakia,

which I visited in 1978, prisons offered a nationalist theme of the iniquities of Habsburg rule which ended in 1918, with the Communist rulers of Czechoslovakia thereby presented as the defenders of national integrity against such rule. This approach flew in the face of the use of Warsaw Pact troops from other Eastern European states to suppress the liberal Communist Czech government and end the 'Prague Spring' of 1968. Those imprisoned under the subsequent autocratic Communist regime were not memorialized and were lost to view.

Once the Communist governments in Eastern Europe were overthrown in 1989, then the sites of imprisonment and torture under their rule, in turn, became objects of commemoration and visit. In Lviv in western Ukraine, the prison on Lonsky Street, where many were brutally treated, under Communist rule and under the German occupation of 1941–4, became, in 2009, the location of a National Museum and Memorial to the Victims of Occupation, although this became a subject for controversy. Germany has made a good job of explaining the harsh nature of imprisonment in East Germany under Communist rule between 1945 and 1989, as in the former *Stasi* headquarters and jail in Rostock.

It is likely that a similar process will occur in Cuba once the Castro regime ends. The memorialization there at present very much focuses on Castro's overthrow of the autocratic Batista regime in 1959, and not on the serious hardships subsequently inflicted under Castro. Instead, the theme is of teleology in action thanks to heroism. The Museo de la Revolución, housed in the presidential palace of Fulgencio Batista, the dictator (r. 1933–44, 1952–8) overthrown by Castro, provides great detail on the Cuban revolution of 1958–9. The story is then taken forward with exhibits on the 'construction of Socialism'. Alongside the museum is the boat that took Castro to Cuba in 1956 to begin the revolution, military vehicles from the 1961 Bay of Pigs invasion, and a monument to those who died in the revolutionary struggle. The museum of the Ministry of the Interior depicts exhibits relating to the numerous assassination attempts made on Castro, as well as details of other CIA and Cuban exile operations.

This account, propagated through memorialization and education, is the sole public history most Cubans now alive have encountered, but it is challenged by family narratives and by the presence of an outer world that offers a different perspective, notably the USA. Successful insularity, therefore, is a condition of a truly distinctive national history account, as also in modern North Korea.

The imperial perspective, understandably, is absent from the presentation of history at, and from, the Cellular Jail. This is scarcely surprising as public history is generally history as affirmation, not history as discussion. That some of the cases for which prisoners were imprisoned in the Cellular Jail, for example the Lahore Conspiracy case of 1915, occurred when Britain was involved in the First World War, and under very serious pressure, is not brought out. However, as with the even more controversial nationalist

Easter Rising in Dublin in Ireland in 1916, wartime concerns help explain the firm British response. Moreover, in the comparative context, which is not one that nationalist histories tend to favour, the response in Ireland was far less rigorous and bloody than that by the Russian rulers of Central Asia when rebellion occurred the same year.

In the case of India, there was particular concern about the pan-Islamicism that Turkey, Germany's ally during the First World War, sought to direct against British rule and influence. Nationalist agitation was also a threat, given the major role of India in the imperial war effort, and notably as a provider of troops. Indian troops were used by the British against the Turks in the Middle East and against German forces in Africa, China and France. As a reminder of the impact created by the choice of particular terms, consider the substitution of machine for effort and volunteers for troops.

Mention of Lahore, which is in Pakistan, the Muslim state created from the partition on British India on independence, brings out another aspect of the Cellular Jail. It was the prison for British India, but has been appropriated for modern India as if that state represents the culmination of pre-1947 nationalism. As a result, the role of what became Pakistan is not emphasized: that also was part of British India, but took a very different nationalist trajectory. In most Indian eyes, an independent Pakistan arises from a separatist aberration in this nationalist struggle and/or from malign British policies. More generally, 'generations of nationalist intellectuals have lent India's leaders a hand by writing nationalist annals of "all India"'.[2]

Moreover, other Indian perspectives are not considered at the Cellular Jail. In practice, Indians disagree about the unity and heroic status of the prisoners. The shock created for the prisoners by losing caste in being sent to prison also means more to some Indians than others, and is not emphasized in the jail. There was a particular tension between the prisoners' stance in the 1930s and that of the non-violent opposition to British rule associated with Gandhi and his policy of non-violent action.[3]

Contesting the Credit for Independence

This tension serves as a reminder that in states that became independent there was significant rivalry within the anti-imperial camp, however much this rivalry could be alleviated or at least conceptualized in terms of common opposition to the imperial power. For example, as in India, there was no one route to Irish or Israeli or Zimbabwean independence. Moreover, there were differences over the methods pursued. In the case of Israel, these differences played through into competing accounts of the national past and future once independence had been achieved. Thus, in the

1970s and 1980s, the powerful rival political parties, Labour and Likud, offered very differing views of the opposition to British rule in 1945–8, and, in particular, of the use of terrorist violence by the Irgun Zvai Leumi, a group that later was to be influential in the genesis of Likud. Who was responsible for winning Israeli independence was a key issue, as it was used to affirm a right to govern.

As a reminder of the contentious use of terms, and, especially the resonance of history in the present age, and the legitimation it offers and challenges, the term terrorist is controversial. This point is not only true in Israel where terrorist is applied to Arab opponents who use terrorist means, but not, comparably, to Jewish action against the British mandate in 1945–8. In particular, the word carries more than descriptive connotations, notably due to the 'War on Terror' launched by the USA in response to the murderous terrorist attacks by al-Qaeda on New York and Washington in 2001.

The resulting conflict with what can be variously defined, including as fundamentalist Islam or as Muslim terrorist groups and their supporters, involved a transnational struggle for support in which the account and definition of activity was significant for both sides and for others. In this context, it is scarcely surprising that the use, by the USA, and by those who wish to be its allies, of what was presented by critics, however implausibly, as terror became a difficult issue. This issue has been extended from the present (a period open to different chronological definitions) to earlier periods, as terrorism is now a term that is particularly contentious, and notably if linked to struggles for freedom and independence, each value-laden terms.

This point can be made about the methods employed in most independence struggles, not least because the methods involved are generally discussed, at least in so far as public history is concerned, in terms of the goals presented and the resulting definition of the morality of the struggle. Against this background, the opportunities for memorialization offered by prisons become of significance in advancing particular interpretations of independence struggles.

Malta: A Case Study

Violence, however, was not always a key element in the quest for independence, let alone in the discussion of the quest. In Malta, a British colony from 1800 to 1964, division between the two main political groupings, Labour and the Nationalists, affected both the path to independence from Britain in 1964 and its subsequent memorialization. As with India, the geographical unit at question, or rather the state and nation, was a major issue. Indeed, the very idea of Malta proved contentious. In the 1920s and 1930s, in opposition to British rule, prominent Nationalists played up the Italian character of Malta (and the Maltese) as an adjunct to Sicily. Indeed, prior to being given by Charles I of Spain (the Holy Roman Emperor Charles V) to the Knights of St John in 1530, Malta had been part of nearby Sicily. This *italianatà* also served as a way for the social élite to monopolize jobs and to exclude working-class Maltese, who did not speak Italian. This working class was the basis of the support for the Labour Party, and a religious dimension was added because the powerful Catholic Church was seen as close to the Nationalists, and not to Labour.

In the 1920s and 1930s, the Nationalists played down the extent to which being linked with Italy would simply mean exchanging one empire (Britain) for another, albeit a Catholic one, and also moving from rule by a liberal empire to a Fascist one. Claims, then and now, by the Nationalist that being pro-Italian in the inter-war years meant opposition to colonial rule are therefore flawed.

After the Second World War, this Nationalist theme was discredited as a result of the wartime failure of Benito Mussolini, the Fascist dictator of Italy in 1922–43. Moreover, the Italian role in the Axis air assault on, and attempted blockade of, Malta in the war ensured that the memorialization in Malta of the conflict had political consequences. The Nationalists focused on independence for Malta and downplayed their earlier support for Italy, much of which was ignored and written out of the record. Modern scholarship on the point therefore resonates with its significance for the historical legitimacy of the Maltese political parties, to use a problematic concept but one that can be employed by considering what each movement said and says about its goals and history.

Debating Nationalism

The Maltese Nationalists' treatment of their history is as one with a more general rewriting of nationalism against the Western imperial powers in order to ignore, minimize or extenuate support for Germany, Italy or Japan during the Second World War. Thus, the support for Japan given by Filipino and Indonesian nationalists and by Thailand is downplayed, as are links between (anti-British) Irish nationalism and Germany in both world wars. In contrast to this approach, opponents of particular nationalists who were heavily implicated in such support, for example critics of the Indian Subhas Chandra Bose, draw attention to it. These tensions contribute to debate about what a post-colonial history should contain.[4]

More generally, there was also opposition between the anti-imperial camp and those who allied with the imperial rulers. Overlapping both groups, there was the large tranche of the population that simply went about their business, a tranche that was generally the majority. In this context, using history was both pertinent for the anti-imperial moment, indeed an important aspect of campaigning against imperial rule, and was also significant retrospectively once independence had been obtained. Indeed, in each case, the use of history represented a form of mobilization of intellectual resources that was comparable, at least in rhetoric and intention, to the mobilization of popular commitment and energy called for by those keen to assert and defend the national cause, or, rather, an image of this cause.

Once independence had been won, there was no need for such mobilization, but the account of how independence was won was carefully secured. Thus, in Morocco, after French rule ended in 1956, the role in winning independence of the Sultan, Mohammed Ibn Yusuf (who became King Mohammed V), was very much pushed in the state-centred nationalist historiography. Other narratives that lessened this role, drew attention to other factors, and saw the then Sultans as playing a part in the earlier spread and maintenance of French power, were all downplayed. Morocco had become a French protectorate in 1912.[5] History was deployed in neighbouring Algeria in the cause of both the independence struggle against France and the argument that there was a distinct Algerian nation, a highly problematic thesis.[6]

Moreover, newly independent states claimed that they had had a pre-colonial tradition of sovereignty and unity. Academic arguments that such claims were frequently unfounded and that what unity had been achieved owed much to Western imperialism, an imperialism that entailed the use by locals of Western resources, as in Rwanda,[7] proved unwelcome, and lacked traction in public history. Thus, the degree to which India was a British creation was downplayed, not least by neglecting the ephemeral nature of earlier Mughal control in southern India in the late seventeenth century. Other Indian rulers had not controlled the far south. Similarly, Sri Lanka was a creation of British rule, as was Pakistan, Malaysia, Nigeria, Kenya and South Africa, and other colonies.

In post-colonial states, such as India, the idea of statehood and political legitimacy was presented as resting on an historical continuity that had allegedly been ruptured by British conquest and rule. A negative account of Western imperialism was necessary, not only to give an additional meaning to the process of national liberation, but also in order to provide a stronger logic for both state and country. Ironically, Western imperial territorialization and concepts of identity and political authority were used by the post-colonial states, and notably with the retention of imperial frontiers. At the same time, the difficulties created by this retention, not least in including different ethnic groups in the new state while dividing other groups, and in proving inconvenient economically, became a way to blame imperial rule for problems, especially in Africa.

The post-independence rethinking of the colonial period led to a greater emphasis on resistance to colonial rule, for example by the Maroons of

Jamaica in the eighteenth century, and in India. However, this emphasis tended to involve a misleading treatment of much earlier resistance in terms of later, nationalistic, state-building, anti-colonialism. Thus, the role of Islam in opposition to British rule in nineteenth-century India is downplayed. Moreover, the standard approach in the post-independence rethinking ignores or underplays the emergence of local colonial élites willing to co-operate with imperial rulers.

Consideration of the colonial period was also potentially problematic as it posed a major question mark against the success of post-colonial governments in improving living standards, in maintaining stability and the rule of law, notably the integrity of contracts, and in limiting corruption. In contrast, in many states, the rule of law appears to have deteriorated since imperial rule ended, while corruption has become more serious. In India, corruption has become especially prominent over the last decade, compromising the ability of government to fulfil its functions. Corruption is linked to more systemic political factors, in the shape of the use of the post-independence state to advance particular interests, notably religious, ethnic and regional. As such, public history is part of a larger process of self- and sectional interest as well as self- and sectional identification.

Independence was/is a key theme in public memorialization in former colonies, as in street names, public holidays and stamps. Museums emphasize the struggle for independence, for example the impressive Military History Museum in Hanoi. In Ho Chi Minh City (Saigon until 1975), one-time capital of South Vietnam, a replica of the North Vietnamese tank that stormed the gates of the presidential palace in 1975, a celebrated moment in the end of the independent, pro-Western south, can be found in the palace, now renamed the Reunification Palace.

Adopting a focus on the collapse of empires puts the national dimension first, rather than the transnational perspective entailed by an emphasis on ideologies such as Communism. Yet, instead of assuming a stark dichotomy, it is more pertinent to note that these transnational ideologies were largely played out in a national context. Moreover, they are recalled and used largely in those terms. Since newly independent states seek to offer an incorporating myth, the resulting theme is generally that of an ideology of national freedom in which nationalism played the key role, and, indeed, is given agency. This is also the case in Communist states, providing a particular historical pedigree to their ideological message. In Cuba, nationalist opposition to America and to American influence receives key attention in the account of Castro gaining and securing power.

It would be easy to suggest a sequential pattern, with the ideological struggle, that closed with the defeat of Nazism and imperial Japan in 1945, followed by an emphasis on decolonization in the Western empires. Between 1945 and 1975, this decolonization led to a change in control over people that was unprecedented for such a brief period in world history. That approach, however, underrates the extent to which nationalism also played a major role in the policies of the totalitarian states involved in the power politics of 1918–45, while the nationalist striving for independence and identity, moreover, set part of the agenda in 1900–1945. Many states became independent in 1900–45, including Norway, Ireland, Poland, Czechoslovakia, Hungary, Finland, Estonia, Latvia, Lithuania, Panama, Albania, Iraq and Saudi Arabia.

Once independent, successor-states employed history to help forge national identities and to respond both to the legacy of imperial control and to subsequent developments.[8] In Czechoslovakia, which, in 1918, won independence from Habsburg rule in the Austrian empire, St Wencelas and Jan Hus were deployed as Czech national heroes, while, in Hungary, there was a focus on celebrating 15 March, which was the day the eventually unsuccessful Revolution of 1848 against Habsburg rule had broken out. This revolution was presented in retrospect as an heroic failure,[9] an approach also taken to describe Polish risings against Russian control in 1794, 1830 and 1863, as well as the Irish rising of 1798 against British rule. The last became more resonant as it could be seen to anticipate the (also unsuccessful) Easter Rising of 1916, while the Polish past was annexed to the service of newly independent Poland, notably in the successful resistance to Soviet invasion in 1920.

The emphasis throughout was on earlier opposition to imperial control, rather than the acceptance of it that had been more common. This emphasis was linked to a stress on identity politics, and in particular on not being subsumed into the imperial identity, but, instead, on maintaining a sense of national difference. This argument was of great importance to Irish nationalists as Ireland had. in practice. taken a major role in the British Empire, including producing many volunteer troops, both Catholic and Protestant, during the First World War.

Moreover, the past was deployed in order to support territorial claims which were very much presented in nationalist terms. Ethnic arguments, of the 'here be Romanians' type, were deployed, but, in these, and other, cases, the argument from history ('here were and should be Romanians') was highly important. Thus, Greece backed its demands for territory from the Ottoman Empire by reference to Classical Antiquity and, increasingly, to Byzantium, the Eastern Roman Empire, with its capital in Constantinople, that had lasted until 1453. In attempting to gain control of western Anatolia after the First World War, the Greeks made frequent reference, for both foreign and domestic audiences, to the integral role of Ionia (its then name) in the Classical Greek world. This approach extended to nomenclature, with a refusal in Greece to use the term Istanbul and, instead, a continued employment of Constantinople. So also with Izmir and Smyrna, the principal city in western Anatolia. While these arguments persuaded Greek opinion and won support from Britain, they were destroyed by the complete nature of Turkish military success in 1921–2.

There were also many would-be states whose independence was suppressed in the period 1900–45, including Korea, which was annexed by Japan, and Ukraine, Armenia, Georgia and Azerbaijan, all of which were conquered by Soviet (Communist) forces in the Russian Civil War that followed the Russian Revolution of 1917. Each of these cases involved attempts to create an appropriate history, as well as moves by rivals and opponents to suppress this history. There was the added complication that it was not initially clear that the Communist movements in these states were going to be expected to subordinate any nationalist aspirations to membership in a Soviet Union that, in practice, proved to be highly centralist.

As in the nineteenth century, this process of national assertion involved competition with other national movements. Thus, in Ukraine, there was bloody opposition, in what is now western Ukraine, to Polish nationalism and expansionism. National assertiveness could also be directed against minorities that were not part of a rival nationalism, for example Jews in Ukraine. Jews suffered greatly from being a cosmopolitan element in a period in which nationalism was largely defined in exclusive, rather than inclusive, terms. This definition was furthered by the emphasis on an historical approach, that of ancestral rights, rather than the inclusive conse-quences of considering who lived in an area at the current moment.

An emphasis on history served to assert rights and identities. This was true of states and would-be states. For example, a deliberate concern with history was important to those seeking to maintain Korean identity during the period of Japanese rule from 1910 to 1945. The Japanese sought to subsume Korean historical and cultural identity under a dominant Japanese past or presented Korea as historically inferior.[10] In response, Korean intellectuals tried to use history to preserve, articulate or expand Korean identity.[11]

Ireland

A very different instance of national assertiveness was offered by the trans-formation of Irish nationalism into a sectarian Catholicism that denied equality to the Protestant Irish living in the newly independent Irish Free State established under the Anglo-Irish Treaty of December 1921. The Irish Revolution remains highly controversial in academic circles,[12] let alone among the public.

The emphasis on Irish nationalism has led to a marked neglect of the large numbers of Irish Catholic volunteers who had fought for George V in the First World War. This neglect extended to a failure to put much effort into constructing or maintaining war memorials. The latter were (and are) a form of memorialization that was, at once, public and open to private reflection, and that also joined the state to the individual community offering a particular realization of nationhood.

In contrast, the far smaller number involved in the Easter Rising of 1916 against British rule were actively commemorated. Endowed with great symbolism, their defiance was presented as a crucial element in winning Irish independence.[13] That a survivor of the rising, Eamon de Valera, leader of Sinn Féin, the nationalist party, in 1917–26, was in power in Ireland for much of the period from 1932 to 1973, contributed greatly to this situation, and also to the related ambivalence about the commemoration of the Irish Civil War of 1922–3, as he had been a member of the defeated rebels in the latter, rebels who had rejected a compromise, partition, peace with Britain. De Valera was happy to refer back to the arrival of the English in Ireland in the twelfth century in his grievances against them. Moreover, Irishmen who fought for Britain in the Second World War were branded as traitors and barred from jobs in the civil service. They were only pardoned in 2013.

More generally, the positive aspects of English control from the twelfth century to 1921 were underrated once Ireland became independent, as is still the case. Museum displays on Irish history concentrate on the glories of Celtic civilization in the 'Dark Ages' of the second half of the first millennium CE, emphasizing Ireland's contribution to European (including English) culture at a time when Europe was assailed by 'barbarians'. In contrast, in the Irish museums there is then relatively little on the period of English rule, until the story resumes with the struggle for independence and the subsequent period of history.

The standard Irish image is of lost centuries, their gloom punctuated by cruel episodes, notably the fate of the besieged towns of Wexford and Waterford at the hands of Oliver Cromwell and his invading English Protestant troops in 1649, and the Irish Famine of 1846–8, the deadly consequences of which are blamed on the British government. These episodes are presented in a very bleak fashion, with scant mention, for example, of the brutalities inflicted by the native population on recent Protestant settlers in the Irish Rising of 1641, brutalities that played a part in the treatment subsequently meted out in 1649.

Moreover, the major role played by the Irish in the development of the English, and then the British, empire, is downplayed. The Irish played a key part in supplying food for the navy in the eighteenth century and troops for the army in the nineteenth. The underplaying of the imperial connection also ensures that the riches of Anglo-Irish culture, famously represented by the writers Jonathan Swift and Oscar Wilde, are undervalued or treated essentially as Irish. Parallels can be drawn with the somewhat misleading accounts of Scotland's and Wales's history offered not only by nationalists but also by 'public intellectuals', such as Kenneth Morgan for Wales.[14]

New Nationalisms

Creating an appropriate history was also the case in the early twentieth century for states that were already independent, but where independence was redefined, in response to major political changes, in terms of a new nationalism. This was particularly the case in Turkey, from the Young Turks' revolution in 1908 and, even more, the Kemalist takeover in 1922; with China from the replacement of the Manchu dynasty by a republic in 1911–12; and with Persia (Iran) after Qajar rule was overthrown in 1921: the Pahlevi dynasty, overthrown by the Islamic Revolution in 1978–9, actually replaced the Qajars in 1925. A similar process had already occurred with the Meiji Restoration in Japan in 1868–9.

New republics or reformist rulers provided a history that justified the new developments and argued that the problems of the present stemmed from the difficulties of the past systems of rule. Thus, in China and Turkey, there was an attack on the previous imperial systems. This was especially the case in China where the Manchu dynasty could be presented as non-Chinese. As a result, a nationalist account separated dynasty from people, and did so in the context of a developmental nature of history that contrasted with the classic Chinese account of the past. In the case of Turkey, the Central Asian origins of the Ottomans led some to see the dynasty as separate to the people, but the Turkish character of the population could also be emphasized in order to provide a common identity. It was claimed, in China, Turkey, and Persia, that the Western presence, and the Western pressure in the past that had led to it, reflected the deficiencies of these past imperial regimes.

China

Thus, in China, the Republican government of the 1920s under Jiang Jieshi, which successfully took steps against British interests, argued that these interests, notably territorial rights and commercial privileges, were a product of past Chinese weaknesses, from the time of the First Opium War (1839–42) on, and helped explain the problems then facing China.

This thesis could also be employed by China against Japan, although, in that case, the emphasis was far more on the difficult legacy from more recent years, as Japanese pressure became a serious threat only in the 1890s. Defeat at the hands of Japan in 1894–5 could be linked to the failure of the Manchu to carry out a necessary process of strengthening through modernization.

China's demographic weight and present-day economic and political significance ensure that it deserves more attention in this book than would probably have been the case in such a study published in the late twentieth century. As with the independent non-Western states already mentioned, history was reconceptualized as an aspect of the drive for national reform, and played an important role in support of this drive. In the case of China, this drive came from the Left and preceded the Communist takeover in 1949. Dynastic history lost its relevance with the end of the empire in 1911–12, while, as a consequence of this change, the Confucian order was historically relativized, and thus ceased to be useful.[15]

The advancing of a workable history was linked to the definition of the nation. In a process seen a decade later with Turkey, China, hitherto a poorly defined concept, and from 1912, for the first time, a republic, was defined as a nation-state that had inherited the position of the Manchu dynasty and that was coterminous with it territorially. This account was then read back into Chinese history, providing a history appropriate to the concern of the modern state to demonstrate continuity and to use that continuity to serve present purposes. The dynasties of the past were annexed to the new state, a process that linked state and nation as each was defined in terms of the other.[16]

The dynamic character of China in the 1910s–40s, however, has since been shrouded by the memory of civil wars and foreign invasion then. Furthermore, the Communist regime rests in part for its history and legitimacy on downplaying these years other than in terms of Communist activities, notably the Long March and resisting Japanese invasion. Nevertheless, there were many important positive developments in this period, including a new account of identity, politics and history, with the emphasis on nationality, republicanism and China, as opposed to the dynastic continuity emphasised under the Manchu dynasty.

Turkey

In Turkey, there was a transformation in the early twentieth century of what had been a cosmopolitan, polyglot, multi-ethnic and multi-religious empire (albeit with a clear, Turkish, ruling group and dominant religion, Islam) into a would-be unitary nation-state. War played a major role, or, looked at differently, provided the key context. The loss of most of the Balkans in 1912–13, as a result of failure at the hands of Bulgaria, Serbia, Montenegro and Greece in the First Balkan War, was followed, during the First World War, with the loss of modern Israel, Palestine, Syria, Lebanon, Jordan, Iraq, and of the Turkish parts of what became Saudi Arabia.

These changes greatly reduced the diversity of what had been the Ottoman Empire. However, the response to these crises, as well as to the far greater catastrophe of international intervention and control under the Treaty of Sèvres of 1920 that followed the war, reflected an aggressive national set of values, based on an exclusive ethnic nationhood, that left no room for what were defined as unwelcome non-Turkish groups, princi-pally Armenians and Greeks. The resulting large-scale brutalization and expulsion of people was linked to a destruction of their historical imprint, notably with the burning of churches and other sites that were at once monuments and living presences. Much of Smyrna (Izmir) was burned down after it was seized in September 1922, while all surviving Christian men of military age were deported to the interior, where many were killed.

History was thereby bifurcated, as exile communities kept alive their history and burnished it anew in terms of an account of experiencing brutality and expropriation. This was a history through suffering compa-rable to that of the Jewish account of Imperial Russia after the pogroms of its last decades. A very different history was offered within Turkey, one from which the Greeks and Armenians had been excluded, while a separate identity was denied the Kurds, whose separatism was suppressed by force in 1937.[17]

The struggle for national survival left a secular nationalism in the shape of the Kemalist tradition (after Kemal Ataturk, the independence leader and first President), and the role of Ataturk's legacy remains significant in modern Turkey, nearly a century later. The legacy is defended by secularists, but is criticized by the Prime Minister, Recep Tayyip Erdogan, not least in 2013 when he introduced restrictive regulations on the advertising and consumption of alcohol. Referring to Ataturk and his successor as President, Ismet Inonu, Erdogan told Parliament that they were 'a pair of drunks' and asked: 'Why are their laws sacred and one that is ordered by religion [Islam] deemed objectionable?'

Nationalism in the Early Twentieth Century

The conflicts of Europe and the Middle East after the First World War ensured that groups with rival identities clashed and then strengthened and refracted these identities in light of the murderous civil violence of the period. Mutual distrust became more potent and had a new vocabulary of experience to draw on, a process that helped radicalize collective history, as in Ireland or Poland.

More generally across the world, the process of claiming, using and contesting the past for nationalist purposes linked the nineteenth and twentieth centuries, as with cartography.[18] There were also differences across time which reflected the developing, more democratic or at least populist, nature of society. Whereas the remembrance after the Napoleonic Wars focused on states and rulers, the prime theme after the First World War was nations. War memorials listed all those killed, while the tombs of unknown soldiers testified to a national commitment and to the desire to commemorate it.

At the same time, the twentieth century also saw a resorting of hero figures to match the trajectory of both new and older states. Thus, in Bulgaria, medieval rulers who had expanded its borders, such as Symeon (d. 927), were, following failure in the First World War, downplayed as heroes and, instead, Vasil Levski, a freedom-fighter executed by the Turks in 1873, became more prominent.[19] Yet, continuing with earlier hero figures could help address the controversial nature of more recent, and current, ones. In Latin America, this process encouraged a focus on figures from the Wars of Independence, notably Simon Bolívar.

Totalitarianism and History

Using the past was given a particular force in the twentieth century by totalitarian regimes advancing new ideologies as they devoted great energy to suppressing alternative views. As a consequence, these regimes sought to be best able to put the past at the service of their totalitarian vision; they politicized the presentation of history in accordance with a clear ideology, as part of their attempt to direct national life and, indeed, history as a whole – both national history and, even, world history.

From this perspective, a utilitarian view towards education was adopted, for there was scant interest in disinterested research and teaching. There was a tendency to present a clear developmental and 'moral' account of progress in time, one that reflected the strictures of a specific ideology. While there were aspects of similar assumptions and processes in liberal societies, they were more willing to leave space for alternative views of the past.

The process of offering accounts of the past was at once complicated and simplified by the extent to which totalitarian governments also sought to focus on visions of the future. Embracing visions of the future necessarily affected the presentation of the past, but there was a common course of choosing aspects of the latter that appeared most convenient for the narrative of the individual regime and the exposition of its ideology. Nationalist themes were annexed to the ideology, or, at least, politics, of such states.

Nazi History

In Nazi Germany (1933–45), the depiction of the regime as the Third Reich (Empire) looked back to earlier periods of national power and glory, and thus presented the Nazis as the natural heir to past German greatness and its necessary, indeed inevitable, realization. In doing so, the Nazis sought to consolidate the unification of Germany under Hohenzollern Prussia in

1866–71, the basis of the Second Reich, and to cut short the possibility of a revival of regional historical narratives, for example those of Bavaria, Saxony and Hanover, each of which had recently been independent. Instead, the emphasis was on Germans, including Germans not then living under German rule, notably Austrians and those in the Sudetenland of Czechoslovakia.

Moreover, by referring to past greatness, there was a discrediting of the Weimar Republic that had accepted the 1919 Versailles Peace Settlement, and a presentation of Weimar as an aberrant interlude. Refighting the First World War by contesting its verdict, the Peace Settlement was presented as disastrous and dishonourable.

The agenda of national strength inherently answered to a different historical consciousness and set of references to that arising from racial issues. Yet, under the Nazis, past themes of national history were also linked to a very different determination to prove Aryan superiority and, at the same time, to take it as a given. As with Nazi geopolitics, there was a meshing of national and racial themes. In a process that was already established,[20] history gave force to long-term myths about Germany's role in Eastern Europe.[21]

For the Nazis, the present was located as taking forward a vision of the past that was at once national and racial. They were not unique in this, but there was a strong millenarian flavour to their project as well as an extremism in implementation. Excising Judaism, a central element in Nazi policy, was not only about controlling the present and future, but also about 'fixing the past [...] building a racial civilisation by extinguishing the symbolic authority over the past embedded in Judaism and the Bible'. Jews were presented as rival and dangerous drivers of world history.[22] Moreover, history to Hitler was a lived process that he encapsulated, so that his personal drama became an aspect of the historic (and therefore, at once, historical and timeless) mission of the German people.[23]

Culture, both German and Western, was appropriated and classified from the Nazi perspective,[24] while the Nazis used a variety of mediums to present their view of history. Alongside the written word came the visual, as well as numerous lengthy speeches and mass rallies. Film was employed in order to present appropriate parallels from German history, notably Otto von Bismarck, whom, it was implied, was a proto-Hitler, another means of linking the Third Reich to the Second, and the Nazis to the prestige of Prussia. As Bismarck, the unifier of Germany, had been Chancellor when France was defeated in 1870–1, so the auspices were good for Hitler. Moreover, at a time when the Second World War was going badly, much effort was devoted to producing Kolberg, a film that suggested that Soviet/Russian victory was not inevitable, by referring back to an heroic episode in the Seven Years' War (1756–63) under Frederick the Great (Frederick II of Prussia).

The educational system served to propagate Nazi nostrums. Alternative views were denied traction, not least by ensuring that the system was used to ensure compliance. Jews and Communists were excluded and purged from the system. And so also with the world of print and with archaeology. Nazi archaeology was under the control of the SS, with the *SS–Ahnenerbe* created by Himmler.[25]

Fascist History

Fascist Italy offers an instructive instance of the uses of history by government because it represents an intersection of a number of contexts and themes. When Benito Mussolini gained power in 1922, Italy was a relatively new state, essentially dating from 1860 and, as such, not too different in 'age' from many post-colonial states today. Like Germany, Italy was very much the product of nineteenth-century nationalism, and the use of history under Mussolini drew heavily on that tradition. Thus, as under the previous governments of Italy, there were many references back to the valorous struggles for independence and unification between 1821 and 1866. These struggles were then linked into a martial account that encompassed the First World War (1915–18 for Italy) and, even more, the conflicts of imperial conquest, under Mussolini, in Libya and, more dramatically, Abyssinia (Ethiopia). National rebirth through the sacrifice of blood proved a heady theme.

This pattern could be given a greater historical resonance, sense of purpose, and validation, by looking back to Imperial Rome. General Rodolfo Graziani, who was appointed Vice-Governor in Cyrenaica (eastern Libya) in 1930, presented his very harsh pacification of the colony, the last stage of its conquest, in terms of 'Romans' subduing 'barbarians', and in 1932 referred to the enforced peace as a *Pax Romana*.[26]

The 2000th anniversary of the birth of Augustus Caesar, the first Roman emperor (b. 63 BCE, r. 27 BCE–14 CE), was celebrated with great pomp, in Italy, in 1937–8. Mussolini began the celebrations by opening a large archaeological exhibition, and closed it by inaugurating the restored *Ara Pacis Augustae*, a large altar, built in 13 BCE, devoted to the goddess of Augustan Peace, to commemorate the peace that followed Augustus' victories in Gaul and Spain. Scholarly works were also sponsored.

These celebrations also commemorated the brutal conquest of Abyssinia (Ethiopia) in 1935–6, a conquest which had led the victorious Mussolini to proclaim the establishment of the Second Roman Empire. By exalting the first (Classical) empire, the regime praised itself, a device Mussolini was especially apt to adopt. The imperial style of rule was one he sought to annex and redefine, a style that contrasted with both the more limited scale of the Italian monarchy and the constrained powers of his predecessors as Prime Minister. The idea of a series of empires was also seen with Germany and the First, Second and Third Reichs, and in Japan with the Meiji Restoration.

The archaeological exhibition opened by Mussolini in 1937, the *Mostra Augustea della Romanità*, was organized by the Ministry of Popular Culture and was subsidized by Mussolini from his special funds. On a vast scale, the exhibition included casts of statues, models of architecture, engineering and military machines, and large maps of the empire, all with particular emphasis on Augustus and the legions (army). The exhibition served as a demonstration of the Fascist regime's alleged role in restoring Italian greatness, and became an approved site for tourists; Hitler went twice during his state visit to Rome in May 1938, the year in which the German-Italian Cultural Agreement was signed.

Anniversaries were important in the Fascist use of history. This exhibition was designed to reopen at the Universal Exhibition planned for Rome in 1942, the twentieth anniversary of Mussolini's seizure of power. The role of context is also significant. Thus, the exhibition survives today as the *Museo della Civitô Romana*, but serving a different public account of Italian history to that seen under Mussolini's Fascism. Moreover, modern Italian Fascism and pseudo-Fascism do not much play with the Roman heritage. Instead, as a reminder of the changing frame of historical reference, they struggle to come to terms with Mussolini, in turn praising and criticizing his policies. The French National Front has had a similar problem with the wartime collaborationist Vichy regime, for example using the Vichy slogan 'Work, Family, Country' in the 2002 Presidential election. There are parallel issues in Eastern Europe.

As far as Mussolini was concerned, the emphasis on a revived *Romanitas* served the need for exemplary and malleable historical reference points for a mass culture that he was seeking to impress and energize, as well as to mould. Mussolini's reconciliation of Italy with the Papacy by the Lateran Accords of 1929 could be comprehended in this Roman account, for Augustus' reign was presented with reference to the beginning of Christianity on the grounds that he ordered the census that led to Jesus' birth taking place in Bethlehem. In an historical context, Fascism therefore was seen as the culmination of the rebirth of Italy in the *Risorgimento* of the nineteenth century, bypassing the supposedly weak liberal governments and decadent Italian society of recent decades, while Fascism could also be presented as the revival both of imperial Roman strength and of the protection of its values through the diffusion of Christianity, a diffusion challenged by the breach with the Papacy under these liberal governments.

That Rome's story could be focused on Augustus, the first emperor, who was presented as an exemplary dictator who had brought glory and order out of the chaos of a degenerate republic, centred attention on Mussolini. Displacing attention from the king of Italy, Victor Emmanuel III (r. 1900–46), Mussolini could be extolled in a similar light, and was happy to use Imperial Roman iconography, symbolism and terms to glorify his own regime. An emphasis on Imperial Rome offered an exalting and exhortatory continuity that focused Italian nationalism, imperialism and religious belief on the Fascist regime.[27]

This focus provided a secure historical basis to justify the regime's interest in the new, for an embrace of the potential of an exemplary modern was also important to Fascist culture and ideology.[28] In Fascist Italy, past and future were opposed in some of the discussion of the quest for the future, both then and, indeed, more generally. However, Mussolini's positioning of his regime in terms of past new developments ensured that the weight of history appeared to guarantee the purpose of his regime.

Alongside mass rallies, new media were used by the Fascists, notably radio and film. The film *Scipio Africanus* (1937) offered an account of a famous Roman general (236–c. 183 BCE), a story that counterpointed the major defeat of the Romans by the great Carthaginian general Hannibal at Cannae (216 BCE) with Scipio's decisive success over Hannibal at Zama (202 BCE). This victory, won in Africa, led to the surrender of Carthage and the end of the Second Punic War. This account offered a parallel with the contrast Mussolini proposed between the national humiliation at the hands of Ethiopian forces at the battle of Adua (Adowa) in 1896 and his success in conquering Abyssinia (Ethiopia).

At the same time, as with other episodes in the use of history, it is necessary to discuss this use carefully. The significance of the Roman references in 1937–8 do not mean that Mussolini's historical world can necessarily be explained solely in those terms. For example, the reconciliation with the Papacy, the concordat of 1929 negotiated with Pope Pius XI, led to a selection of apparently appropriate Catholic historical references, including Saint Catherine of Siena who was presented under Mussolini as a patriotic figure, taking forward the use of her during the *Risorgimento*. Moreover, the role of the past in the regime's frame of reference should not lead to a downplaying of the extent of modernism in Fascist ideology.

Allowing for the marked difference of historical examples on offer, Mussolini's use of the past proved an influential model for autocratic conservative regimes in the 1920s and 1930s, and notably in the Mediterranean, Latin America, for example Argentina from 1930, and Eastern Europe. As, in this period of heyday for the Western colonial powers, Latin America then contained a high proportion of the world's independent states, the Mussolini model, therefore, was of considerable importance. This model, indeed style, linked past glory to an autocratic political and conservative social agenda, and thus provided a contrast with the more liberal exegesis of the past in Britain, France and the USA. National identity and unity were presented as requiring authoritarian policies and a politics of self-reliance, for example in the Brazilian *Estado Novo* (new state) established by Getúlio Vargas, President from 1930 to 1945 and again from 1950 to 1954.

In some autocratic conservative states in Europe, an ethnic consciousness that rested on a theme of national identity readily lent itself to a racism directed against Jews and ethnic minorities. These policies came to the fore during wartime co-operation with Hitler's Germany, as with the nationalist regime in Slovakia under Jozef Tiso, its President from 1939 to 1945, and in Hungary. Each regime also drew on a Catholic anti-Communism.

Francoist History

As in Italy, the authoritarian, right-wing, Nationalist Franco regime that gained power in Spain thanks to success in the Civil War (1936–9) both commemorated victory and also adopted an historical reference point that proposed a return to a past age of greatness, as well as drawing on an analysis of what had supposedly led to this greatness. In a parallel with what was presented as the expulsion of anti-Christian foreignness, in the shape of the Nationalists' left-wing, secularist Republican rivals, the regime looked back to the medieval *Reconquista* of Spain from the Moors. In particular, there was a focus on the reigns of Isabella of Castile (r. 1474–1504) and her husband, Ferdinand of Aragon (r. 1479–1516), under whom the Moors had been finally defeated, the Jews expelled, Catholic purity safeguarded, and the New World claimed for Spain.

As with most examples of the use of the past, this Francoist hankering back to past greatness had a longer provenance. It had been used as a comparison by those who focused on Spain's abject failure at the hands of the USA in the War of 1898. Nevertheless, as again with most examples of the use of the past, there were important differences in tone and usage, not least the degree of government support. The devout Catholicism, territorial expansionism, and racialism of Ferdinand and Isabella, apparently served as a suitable model for Franco.

As in Fascist Italy, the rejection of liberalism under Franco also drew on a number of currents, some of which had a stronger historical imagination and mythos than others.[29] Franco disliked all whom he held responsible for Spain's earlier weakness and current problems. In international relations, this approach meant a hatred of France and Britain, both of which had weakened Spain as an imperial power. That they were also tolerant democracies contributed to his attitude. Modern history was downplayed under Franco in favour of a past of Spain as a great imperial power.

The Francoist approach to Spain's past has nothing in common with the post-Francoist engagement with al-Andalus, the Moorish culture in the Middle Ages in what is today Andalusia. In particular, it has been argued that tolerant co-existence of Christians, Jews and Muslims in medieval Spain produced a Spanish culture that was not simply Christian. The weight placed on this co-operation and legacy is controversial, but the thesis about al-Andalus greatly contributes to the importance of medieval Spain to the post-Franco historical culture and, indeed, to the attempt to create what is presented as a modern integrationist civic politics that is also in line with Spain's past.[30]

Spain's trauma in the 1930s remains an issue that troubles its collective account of the past. Those who see themselves as the heirs of the combatants exchange blame, notably over atrocities and over whether there was justice in the cause then. In focusing on the Right's responsibility for launching the civil war in 1936, the Left largely ignore the extent to which their unsuccessful uprising against the republic in 1934 also challenged democracy and was not somehow necessary to stop Fascism, in turn, gaining power. In contrast, post-Francoist research revealed the extent to which, pursuing political goals, Franco's regime was responsible for the large-scale killing of prisoners and civilians, only, in turn, for this work to produce a reaction. Similarly, after the fall of Franco, nationalists on behalf of regions with a strong separatist tradition, notably Catalonia, produced accounts that found historical support for their case, only for the Right to emphasize the longevity of a reality of Spain.[31]

Portugal

A comparable emphasis on Catholicism was also seen with the authoritarian, right-wing *Estado Novo* (new state) regime which governed Portugal from 1926 until it was overthrown in 1974. The imperial dimension was more pronounced because, whereas Spain had few overseas possessions in 1939 when Franco came to power, Portugal was still a major imperial power, notably in Africa with colonies that stretched back to the fifteenth century. As a result, opposition to liberalism at home was offered with a heavy dose of support for a Christian vision of imperial purpose that Portugal was presented as having exemplified for centuries. In consequence, Portugal was given a key role in Christian, and therefore world, history. The history taught and celebrated focused on the Middle Ages and the Age of Discovery from the fifteenth century, and not on modern Portuguese history, which threatened to focus on divisions within the country.

That the *Estado Novo* regime set the historical agenda as part of a state ideology in which history played a major role, did not mean that it was the sole body to do so in Portugal. Instead, as in other authoritarian regimes, there were competing interests. In such regimes, the army was generally one of them. In the early 1940s, when António de Salazar, Prime Minister from 1932 to 1968, did not wish to offend the then victorious Germany, the Portuguese army thwarted his attempt to end the commemoration of the country's costly role in the First World War when, from 1916, it had backed the Allies against Germany.[32]

Similar public histories to that under Franco were to be found with autocratic conservative regimes later in the century, notably that of the ruling Greek Colonels from 1967 to 1973, and also such regimes in Latin America. Chile under General Pinochet, who seized power in 1973, holding it until 1990, provided a key instance. Alongside a recent 'history' designed to demonstrate the threat from Marxist subversion, a longer-term account, focused on nationalism, conservatism and Catholicism, was offered, both in Chile and elsewhere in Latin America, by right-wing commentators.

Communist History

In Communist states, Marxist-Leninism became a field of study, while control over education was enhanced by moving research from universities into national academies.[33] In the Soviet Union, the early Communist break with the past, as part of a self-conscious revolutionary consciousness, gave way, in the 1930s, to a cultural focus on pre-Revolutionary heroes of exalted background, such as Aleksandr Nevskii, Ivan the Terrible and Peter the Great, each presented as exemplary patriots. This was part of the process by which Joseph Stalin, dictator from 1924 to 1953, while pursuing a Leninist internationalist agenda,[34] also linked Russian imperialism and vulgar Marxism. That all three of the pre-Revolutionary heroes had played a key role in conflict with foreign foes was appropriate for the Soviet militarism and diplomatic isolation of the 1930s, notably in opposition to Germany and Poland, powers whose progenitors the three had fought.

At the same time, there was, understandably, no revival of a usage of an historical agenda in which Russian Orthodoxy and the Romanov dynasty played major roles. Thus, Stalin's embrace of nationalist historical references did not prefigure that seen with President Putin's post-Communist Russian nationalism in the 2000s and 2010s, a nationalism notably linked with Russian Orthodoxy and with an assertion of nationalist pride.

Soviet historians were pressed particularly hard to support the nostrums of government policy in the 1930s, and within an anti-intellectual context in which many were purged.[35] Such a process nearly completely closed the opportunities for a pluralist approach to the past, an approach that was particularly unwelcome in totalitarian regimes.[36] Stalin was personally interested in history and in 1938 spent much time editing the 'Short Course' of the history of the Communist Party, an account designed to demonstrate how he had overcome threats to it.

In China, Mao Zedong gained power in 1949 after victory in the Chinese Civil War over the Nationalists. The Maoist order offered its own historical myth, one in which Communist ideology played a central role, so that peasant uprisings were presented as the locomotive of history. Moreover, Mao's victory over his Communist rivals ensured that their role in the history of Chinese Communism was downplayed, ignored or denied, while his was built up, as in the case of responsibility for the miners' strike at Anyuan in 1922.[37]

The Maoist order also saw change in its portrayal of the pre-Communist past. Historical analogies and references were pursued in order to clarify, defend and make sense of policy, to government figures as well as the public audience. For example, in the Great Leap Forward period in 1958–62, Mao Zedong praised Qin Shihuangdi, the First Emperor (r. 247–210 BCE), and the Ch'in unification of the empire, suggesting, in 1958, that criticism of the authoritarian emperor (who had proscribed non-scientific books in an attempt to begin history anew) was in affect an attack on revolutionary violence and the dictatorship of the proletariat seen under Mao. In the 1970s, the reign was to be given a different role, being presented as a proto-proletarian dictatorship. Such an important reign had therefore to take a larger part in Maoist history, which meant not only a superstructure of events but also an apparent understanding of the locomotive of history in the shape of the means of production. As a result, the transition from a slave-holding society to feudalism, which Mao had earlier placed in the eleventh century BCE, was moved to the fifth or third century. This transition was important to the application of the Marxist model to Chinese history, or, rather, the shoehorning of the latter in terms of the former.[38] Nationalism was also a component. The Maoist government made use of ideas surrounding the Great Wall of China to help build revolutionary nationalism.

National histories were also annexed by other Communist states. Seeking to win over Mongol sympathy, the Communist regime in China, which ruled Inner Mongolia and competed there with Soviet influence in Outer Mongolia (the state of Mongolia), restored the Temple of Chinggis Khan (often known as Genghis Khan) in Ulanhot and, in 1954, returned the Khan's relics to Ejen-Khoroo, where a massive mausoleum was built in 1956.

A relic of a different type, the crown of St Stephen, was sought by the Communist government of Hungary. Captured by American forces in 1945, the crown was not returned, because that would be a clear form of acceptance of the legitimacy of the government, until 1978, when it was restored in a period of West–East *détente*. The crown was used by the Communist Kádár government as a symbol of national sovereignty, and not as a royal talisman.

Crowns and other regalia had more general significance. In 1815, the throne and regalia of Kandy, the last independent kingdom in Sri Lanka, were captured by the British and taken to the royal palace of Windsor Castle in Britain. George III replaced Sri Vikrama Rajasimha, the unpopular last King of Kandy, as a result of a convention with the Kandyan chiefs as well as military conquest that year. In turn, in 1934, both throne and regalia were returned as part of the British attempt to ease relations with the population in the colony, a process that had led to constitutional reforms, including universal suffrage in 1931. The State Council of Ceylon had passed a motion asking for the return of the regalia and throne, but, in 1934, the form chosen for their return was that they were presented on behalf of George V as a gift to loyal subjects. When independence for Ceylon was declared in 1948, the throne of Kandy was present and, as it were, presided over the proceedings, being located on a dais higher than that of the Duke of Gloucester.

Returning to the Communist use of the past, in 1983, East Germany celebrated the 500th anniversary of the birth of Martin Luther, the founder of the Protestant Reformation, as well as the 100th anniversary of Karl Marx's death. Luther was presented as an opponent of the corruption of a redundant *ancien régime*, and thus as a suitable nationalist for East Germany to honour alongside the founder of Communism, who was also a German. That this *ancien régime* centred in Rome and relied on the Habsburgs also made this argument geographically appropriate. Protestantism could not be presented as anti-Russian. Similarly, in Yugoslavia, Primož Truber, the 'Slovenian Luther', was treated under the Communists as an anti-Catholic hero.

The usable past extended to the social dimension, with the East Germans dwelling on the Peasants' Rebellion of 1524–5 as a key German instance of a proto-Communist revolution. This approach, which played down other interpretations of the rebellion, notably relating to the Reformation, suited the linked needs of the East German government to present themselves as nationalists and as Communists, not least by allegedly demonstrating that East Germany, rather than its capitalist rival West Germany, was the true heir of the progressive German past and of a German past presented as progressive.

Governments were not alone in encouraging an emphasis on ideological commitment in historical work, in part as an aspect of creating, defining or sustaining a civil religion. Instead, the power of ideology led many writers to press for commitment. For example, in his wide-ranging account of utopianism and popular action in the Andes, an account significantly first published in Communist Havana in 1986, the left-wing Peruvian historian Alberto Flores Galindo wrote: 'We should abandon the placid terrain of free-floating ideas and find struggles and conflicts, people and social classes, and problems of power and violence in society.'[39]

Churchill

The glorious past was also a point of reference for democratic societies, and notably when they were under pressure. In October 1940, when, in the Second World War, a vulnerable Britain, its forces driven from the European continent, faced a damaging German bombing offensive in the Blitz, Winston Churchill, the Prime Minister, wrote the foreword to an edition of *The War Speeches of William Pitt the Younger*. Pitt had been Prime Minister from 1783 to 1801 and 1804 to 1806, most of the period of the French Revolutionary War and part of the Napoleonic War, years when Britain had also been threatened with invasion. Churchill saw this struggle as an example to Britain in 1940, pressing the case for 'our determination to fight on, as Pitt and his successors fought on, till we in our turn achieve our Waterloo'.[40] Thus, drawing on history, the promise of eventual victory was held out. In the event, the victory occurred in 1945, whereas the defeat of France had taken longer, Waterloo occurring in 1815. The length of that struggle powerfully stamped it on the consciousness of experience.

Resolve did not equate with strategy, and, in the latter case, Churchill faced the different tracks offered by history, as so many who have looked to the past have done. Choices could be framed in terms of the politics arising from contrasting interpretations of Britain's supposedly inherent strategic culture, and, in particular, the politics shaped by competing 'lessons' drawn from the First World War. Churchill was sufficiently proud of his ancestor John Churchill, 1st Duke of Marlborough, a general whose fame rested on direct engagement on the Continent with the French main battle army in 1704–9, during the War of the Spanish Succession, to write a major study of him.[41]

However, Churchill favoured a more navalist account of British strategic culture, one that looked back to the 'blue water policy' of Marlborough's Tory opponents. The latter policy entailed securing naval mastery, pursuing trans-oceanic operations against French and Spanish colonies, launching amphibious attacks on vulnerable European targets, and avoiding conflict with the French main battle army. Churchill supported an indirect or peripheral strategy in both world wars, alternating in both between the Baltic/Scandinavia and the Mediterranean. Contrasts in the use of the glorious past can be seen by comparing Churchill's references to a distant past with the shorter timeframe employed in Mexico, where the revolution of 1911 dominated subsequent attention.[42]

The Second World War

Churchill's later political reputation and historical writing focused on the Second World War, on which he published a six-volume history in 1948–53.[43] The war, indeed, played a central role in the public history of all of the former combatants. Victors sought validation from accounts of this victory, although this validation had different meanings in a democracy like Britain where the war-leader could be removed in an election, as Churchill was in 1945, compared to the Soviet Union where Stalin continued in power until his death in 1953. In Britain, where it had been conducted by a coalition government, the war was diffused (and defused) as a wider social memory with an emphasis on national cohesion, whereas in the Soviet Union there was a more political focus on the role of the Communist state under Stalin in winning the 'Great Patriotic War'.

The legacy of recent history confronted issues raised by history over the longer term. For example, in the case of the Second World War, the

post-war meant not only confronting the massive slaughter and dislocation
of the war, but also a wartime destruction of cities on an unprecedented
scale. This issue created a politics of competing remembrance as plans
about what to rebuild were contested in terms of differing associations
of place and rival narratives, associations and narratives often of greater,
sometimes far greater, longevity than the war itself.[44]

The attempts by the defeated to adjust to the war reflected post-war
political contexts and exigencies. Those who were defeated and occupied
by the Axis powers had a different historical task to the Axis powers
themselves. There was no uniformity and scant consistency in either group
as the circumstances of the war interacted with those of post-war politics.[45]
Thus, in East Germany, the war was presented by the Communists, who
gained power under Soviet occupation, as an imposition by the Nazi regime
on German worker-soldiers. There was an effort thereby to create an anti-
Fascist unity, or at least friendship, with the Soviet Union, the target and
vanquisher of the Nazis. It was hoped that this unity would bring legitimacy
to the East German system which, in practice, rested on Soviet conquest and
support, including a major military presence. This attempt looked toward
the course of the Cold War and the search then in East Germany for a
theme of necessary suffering. This process was seen with the presentation
of the Berlin Wall, built in 1961, as a defensive barrier the East German
government had had to build and also in terms of the (very few) border
guards killed there. Streets, schools and youth clubs were named after
them.[46]

Conversely, in West Germany, a more positive account of both the war
with the Soviet Union in 1941–5 and the actual fighting on the Eastern
Front was offered, an account largely drained of atrocities by the German
army. Instead, discussion of the war and, specifically, of the Eastern Front,
focused on the effort made to protect the West from the Soviet threat,
and thus related it to Cold War calls about the need for West German
rearmament. It was only in the 1980s that the West German government
acknowledged the wartime crimes inflicted on the Soviet Union. Indeed, on
8 May 1985, President Richard von Weizsäcker felt able to declare 8 May
1945, the surrender date, as a day of liberation for Germany from Nazi
rule.[47]

In West Germany prior to the 1980s, the focus for the Second World
War was on Nazism and not on the wartime crimes of ordinary Germans.
Instead, the latter were presented as separate from and, indeed, victims of
the Nazi pathology. For example, among the first cases investigated by West
German courts in the late 1940s and 1950s were the killings of ordinary
German civilians in the last weeks of the war by hard-core Nazis, notably
SS squads.[48]

The extent to which there was opposition to Hitler in Germany was
exaggerated. Resistance to Hitler is memorialized at a number of sites in
Berlin, including the Plötzensee prison and in the Bendlerblock, the army

headquarters, where the main July Bomb Plot conspirators were shot in July 1944.

Cold War Reworkings

Historical experiences and identities were presented and remoulded during the Cold War, in response both to the ideological struggle and to the experience of recent history. This process was very much seen with the post-war movement for Western European unification, a movement that led to the establishment in 1958 of the European Economic Community, the basis of the modern European Union. This movement itself also reflected the impact of differing narratives which had very varied public traction. The established narrative was that European unification was a reaction against the horrors of the Second World War, and that this factor motivated a determination to ensure that there were no other wars.[49] However, that narrative led to a downplaying of the extent and impact of wartime co-operation within the new German empire, notably between Germany and Vichy France, but also with elements in the Benelux countries. Moreover, other themes of European co-operation looked back to older twentieth-century movements, notably anti-Communism, particularly Catholic anti-Communism.

From this perspective, the Second World War was simply a stage, albeit an increasingly important one, in the development of understandings and practices of European identity. This stage cleared a path for a new practice and vocabulary of Europe, notably by discrediting the parties of the Right and by ending German imperialism. However, in advancing Soviet power to the Elbe, the war ensured that anti-Communism became even more significant to European identity, while reviving the Communist versus Catholic axis in Eastern Europe, particularly in Poland and Hungary. At the same time, the extensive enforced population moves after the close of the war, for example Poles from western Ukraine, moved the boundaries of these long-established clashes, as well as continuing (far less bloodily) the processes by which the Germans had recently murderously transformed the ethnic complexity of Eastern Europe.

Alongside geopolitics, timing was significant to historicized identity. The Holocaust, which eventually became very important to the identity of the new Europe, was relatively insignificant in the European discussion of the war in the two decades after 1945, both west and east of the Iron Curtain. Moreover, there was a reluctance then to insert it in the historical narrative and analysis – a reluctance not only in Germany, but also more widely – and the war was not memorialized accordingly. Holocaust memory was confronted mainly by adapting the old frameworks of anti-Fascism and anti-totalitarianism.[50]

The situation changed from the late 1960s, particularly in France and Germany, but even so, there was equivocation and hesitation. In the 1980s, German officials perceived the United States Holocaust Memorial Museum in Washington as 'an anti-German museum' and unsuccessfully attempted to change its contents by including references to the anti-Nazi resistance and to post-war German history.[51]

The Cold War also saw the acceleration of the decolonization referred to earlier in the chapter. As a result, across the world of the former empires (with the important exception of the one-time white settlement colonies such as Australia), much of the history of the imperial period was discarded and rewritten. Similarly, the histories of the European autocratic regimes of a variety of political persuasions were successfully discarded and rewritten, notably in 1917–19, 1944–8, 1973–5 and 1989–91. There was an overlap, in these processes, in the case of the fall of European empires (Italy, Portugal and Spain) whose overseas territories went to newly independent states and not, as Germany's had done in 1919, to other empires. In the case both of much of Europe and of most of its one-time empires, therefore, public history was repeatedly changed.

1990 was the year of German unification as a liberal republic, a key move in the new post-Communist Europe. This event and year are adopted for a dividing periodization to mark off the contemporary period; the subsequent years are treated in the next two chapters. However, many of the processes discussed in this chapter persisted after 1990. Pressure for decolonization remained an issue, with contested histories, as for example for the Falklands/Malvinas and for French Polynesia. In addition, the impact of decolonization continued to be seen with newly independent states, such as Namibia, which gained independence from South Africa in 1990. The government of Namibia since looks back to the independence struggle, as SWAPO (the South-West African People's Organization), the independence movement, became its key constituent. The independence struggle, moreover, was used to validate the government, as with the 'Heroes' Acre' outside the capital, Windhoek. In contrast, those opposed to SWAPO have been marginalized. At the same time, many Namibian communities have, in contesting 'the politics of memory' advanced by the government, (re)-instituted forms of memorialization.[52] Another form of continuity was provided by opposition to rule by non-Western states, notably by China over Tibet and by Morocco over Western Sahara.

Re-identifying

South-West Africa became Namibia on independence. There and elsewhere, anti-imperial narratives extended to the rejection of the names and memorials associated with imperialism. Thus, Ceylon became Sri Lanka in

1972 when the governing left-wing United Front introduced a new Socialist constitution. On independence in 1964, Nyasaland was renamed Malawi and Northern Rhodesia became Zambia, whereas initially there was no such change in Southern Rhodesia, where a minority White regime seized power in 1965, holding it until 1979, when British rule was briefly reintroduced. However, the country became independent in 1980 under the name of Zimbabwe. Burma, in 1989, became Myanmar, the name of the country in Burmese. The French colony of Upper Volta gained independence in 1960 and was renamed Burkina Faso in 1983.

Cities were also renamed. The capital of Southern Rhodesia, Salisbury, named after a British Prime Minister, became Harare, the capital of Zimbabwe, while Bombay became Mumbai in 1995 and Madras Chennai in 1996. Across the world, the statues of old imperial orders were discarded and their buildings were appropriated to other purposes or discarded. In contrast, the British settlement colonies, Australia, Canada and New Zealand, retained imperial names, such as Sydney and Perth, Vancouver and Halifax, and Wellington and Nelson.

Styles of architecture associated with imperial rule fell into disfavour. Thus, in Dublin in the 1960s, the association of Georgian architecture with the eighteenth-century Protestant English ascendancy harmed attempts to preserve Georgian buildings in the northern part of the inner city.[53]

Similarly, the German heritage of cities such as Breslau and Stettin was destroyed in the post-war rebuilding of them as the Polish cities of Wrocław and Szczecin. This rebuilding ensured a new memory landscape, and thereby a new basis for legitimation, one that moved from the German past to the Socialist-Realist Polish present with its focus on a utopian Communism. There was also a more specific political drive in the shape of West Germany's refusal to accept Poland's western frontier until 1970, and the consequent determination to present annexed cities as Polish rather than German. The Polish Communists actively spread the idea that Silesia and Breslau had always been Polish, with Germanization simply a layer that could and should be removed. Thus, Baroque churches, of which there were many in Breslau, were rebuilt with Gothic interiors which were held to be more Polish. Rebuilt Protestant churches were given to the Catholic Church. This effort did not extend to the synagogues and ghettos. The policies followed and the work put in made Wrocław in particular seem Polish.[54] Under Ceausescu, old neighbourhoods in Bucharest, the capital of Romania, were torn down to make way for the *Casa Poporului* (House of the People), a massive administrative building, as well as an accompanying grand boulevard.

Alongside renaming, there were also demands for apology, compensation and restitution linked to real or supposed abuses by imperial rulers, demands that led to a degree of continuity. Britain, for example, was criticized for the treatment of detainees during the Mau Mau insurrection in Kenya in the 1950s. This process extended to would-be states. Thus, accounts of the Bloody Sunday operation in Derry in 1972 became very important in the Catholic nationalist narrative of Northern Ireland. More generally, history both served the cause of present politics and also helped define identities. Indeed, the period 1900–90 provided the prime source of assumptions and references for the use of history in subsequent years.

Conclusions

The process of self-identification was variously presented as a throwing off of the imperial yoke and of abhorrent ideologies. However, this definition was also an aspect of the competition for influence and control among indigenous groups and political movements. Thus, the renaming of cities in India owed something to the Hindu nationalism of the BJP, and also to local traditions such as Bengali, Malayali etc. This Hindu nationalism in India is an important instance of the struggle for the definition of nationalism across the world. At the level of the individual state, much of the debate draws on historical arguments, while, in turn, competing modern concepts of nationality have been employed to interpret the polities and politics of the past.

In practice, many states were composite states, in part as a result of considerable migration in the colonial period across what have since been constructed as national borders, but also because of the manner in which the states were created by imperial powers. There was a willingness, in some states, for those struggling for influence and control to seek support where it could be found. This process helped give a transnational dimension to struggles at the national level. Earlier, the search for foreign support, or at least the use, if not manipulation, of the foreign presence, eased imperial penetration or, looked at differently, had underlined the processes of compromise that, in part, constituted imperialism. A search for such support was also to be seen on the part of those who later resisted imperial rule, a process which helped locate decolonization in the Cold War.

The process of co-operation in imperialism (as well as later in fighting it), however, was underplayed in post-independence public history. Instead, in part, precisely because, during and after decolonization, it was not clear how 'peoples' were to be defined, there was an emphasis, instead, on the allegedly national character of states and proto-states. As ever, present needs dictated the usable past, and the state was a key source and medium for this process.

CHAPTER NINE

Post-1990: Searching for Meaning

Remembering Empire

In February 2013, Britain's Prime Minister, David Cameron, laid a wreath at the memorial to the 1919 Amritsar massacre in India, as well as bowing his head, and standing in silence to pay respect to those who died. In the memorial book of condolence, Cameron described the massacre, in which almost 400 people were killed, as 'a deeply shameful event in British history'. Cameron added, 'we must never forget what happened here'.

The latter is a cliché frequently employed when discussing the past in terms of its relationship with the present, and vice versa. This cliché places a weight on the use of history in the present. It acts as an unintended counterpart to the frequent references to the need to break free from the weight of the past, for example by Tony Blair, then Britain's Prime Minister, at the time of the 1998 Good Friday Agreement in Northern Ireland. Remembrance and commemoration, therefore, are very finely balanced in terms of the politics of using history.

Amritsar, indeed, provides a key instance of what to critics may seem like the process of empowerment through grievance and of history by apology, a fast-rising present-day trend. More generally, the history of the British Empire has been dissected accordingly for relevant themes and images of grievance and apology. However, frequently, the relevant episodes are approached without due regard for context.

In the 2000s and 2010s, for example, there was considerable critical discussion about the harshness of the British suppression in the 1950s of insurrections in two key colonies: that by the Communists in Malaya and the Mau Mau uprising in Kenya.[1] In each case, the nature of counter-insurrectionary warfare was condemned without due regard to the more general character of such conflict in the period. Moreover, aside from the lack of comparative awareness involved, for Kenya, in references to 'Britain's *gulag*', there was a widespread failure to devote sufficient attention to the deadly violence used by the rebels, violence that was generally directed against other members of the colonial population (rather than the better-protected colonizers), and frequently with an ethnic dimension.

In the case of resisting, and then overcoming, the Mau Mau uprising in 1952–7, the British benefited from a wide-ranging social reform policy, including land reform in which the government distanced itself from the white colonists, as well as from the assistance in the counter-insurrectionary warfare of loyal Africans, including former insurgents. The latter element was subsequently downplayed in Kenyan accounts of the uprising. Yet, it proved significant both as an aspect of winning hearts and minds, and in providing troops. Alongside British regular army units and the white settler Kenya Regiment, there were loyal Africans: the King's African Riflers, Kenya Police, Kikuyu Home Guards, and former insurgents. From 1955, success against the Mau Mau led to the withdrawal of troops, and in 1956 the police took over responsibility for operations.[2]

The present plays a major role in the subsequent recollection of these insurrections. In Malaya, the rebellion was based in the Chinese population, whereas the modern state is organised round its Malay majority. The theme of apology is not pressed by the government. In contrast, in Kenya, the rebellion was based among the Kikuyu, the majority population in the modern state. Moreover, the Mau Mau rebellion has played a major role in the origin story of modern Kenya.

Cameron's visit to Amritsar, the site of the Hari Mandir (Golden Temple) containing the Granth Sahib (Sikh sacred scripture), saw a coincidence of convenience for both India and Britain. The occasion testified to Indian accounts of their national struggle, or, at least, what was presented as this struggle, and conveniently so. Cameron was shown around the site of the massacre by descendants of some of those who came under fire in 1919, and they pointed out walls where bullet holes can still be seen, as well as the Martyrs' Well where many people died after seeking shelter from the volley of bullets: at least 379 were killed and 1,200 wounded in the massacre. The book of condolence was signed before a memorial plaque declaring: 'This place is saturated with the blood of those Indian patriots who were martyred in a non-violent struggle to free India from British domination.'

As such, the massacre is implicitly contrasted with the violence used, notably in the 1980s, by Sikhs seeking independence from India for the Punjab, the very region in which Amritsar is located. Thus the highly militarized nature of the Indian response in storming sacred sites occupied by Sikh militants, particularly the Golden Temple in 1984, is implicitly excused by the plaque.

In the hyper-critical Indian press, Cameron's remarks were condemned as too late by some Indian commentators and, separately, as designed to appeal to Sikh voters in Britain. However, his remarks associated Cameron both with Winston Churchill – a positive, indeed iconic, figure in British, specifically Conservative, history – and with a goal that presented the modern British government in a benign light. Whereas Queen Elizabeth II, when she laid a wreath at the Amritsar memorial in 1997, described the massacre as a 'distressing' example of the 'moments of sadness' in Anglo-Indian history, Cameron wrote:

> This was a deeply shameful event in British history, one that Winston Churchill rightly described at the time as 'monstrous'. We must never forget what happened here, and in remembering we must ensure that the United Kingdom stands up for the right of peaceful protest around the world.

The last was a remark that spoke more to the 2010s, when Britain supports such protest, for example in Iran after the fixed 2009 election, than to the 1910s. On both sides, indeed, there was a strong ahistoricism that failed to place the massacre, a terrible event in which there was a disproportionate use of force, in the context of the difficult situation in the Punjab in 1919.[3] Britain then was faced by an unprecedented crisis of imperial over-stretch, one that was compounded in north-west India both by opposition there and by the proximity of an Afghan threat on the nearby Northwest Frontier of British India (the frontier of modern Pakistan): 1919 saw the Third Anglo-Afghan War.

Keen to encourage Indian trade with Britain, a goal he had frequently endorsed and the purpose of his visit, Cameron was scarcely going to draw attention either to this factor, or to the extent to which there is a highly selective account of independence and massacres in Indian memorialization. This selectivity is particularly the case with the large-scale confessional massacres, notably of Hindus and Muslims by each other, at the time of partition between India and Pakistan in 1947, and especially in the Punjab. Partition was a key aspect of independence. These massacres are ignored in the public memorialization of independence, although they play a major part in that by numerous families and communities.

Cameron also continued the pattern, seen under Tony Blair and Gordon Brown, his two predecessors, of apologizing, or at least regretting, the impact of empire. In 2003, as an aspect of present-day political correctness, Jack Straw, the Foreign Secretary, declared that many of the world's international disputes were due to the legacy of British imperial rule. In 2011, when visiting Pakistan, Cameron was questioned about the Kashmir question, the most sensitive issue in Pakistani-Indian relations. Underplaying the extent to which the dispute is really about sectarian and geopolitical disputes between the two powers and also arises from politics within them, Cameron replied: 'I don't want to try to insert Britain in some leading role where, as with so many of the world's problems, we are responsible for the issue in the first place.'[4]

Nor do the Indians draw attention to the selective account of independence. The Congress Party, which has governed India for most of the time since independence in 1947, has consistently drawn in part on support from the country's large Muslim minority, and has sought to keep confessionalism at bay. As a result, there is an emphasis not on memorializing the victims of sectarian violence, a divisive issue, but, instead, on commemorating the far less numerous victims of British imperial rule. Inclusion therefore operates as a factor that helps lead to a distortion of the historical record for the present-day purposes of the Indian state.

As with the focus on the slave trade in the eighteenth century, rather than on slavery in the modern world, this agenda is historicist in that it deals with a situation that is long past. In contrast, outwith this agenda of focusing blame for the slave trade on the Western imperial powers of the past (rather than other large-scale traders in slaves then, notably African and Arab traders), there is the large-scale trafficking of coerced workers today. The hard work of confronting the sex trade and other aspects of trafficking[5] is overlooked in favour of the easy target of Western misbehaviour in the past.

Similarly, the more troubling reality of sectarian violence in India is kept alive, as by massacres in the state of Gujarat in 2002 in which over 1,000 people, mostly Muslims, were slaughtered, with the state government doing little to stop the process. The federal government had proved weak a decade earlier when the Hindu activists of the Bharatiya Janata Party (BJP) destroyed the Babri Masjid, a mosque apparently built on the remains of a Hindu temple, an episode followed by anti-Muslim riots across India. Thus, there is a convenient national myth for India, but one that provides little guidance for the contemporary situation other than in terms of outrage about Britain.

Indeed, in the case of the Babri Masjid, the British colonial authorities had kept the lid on this controversy, one that reflected both origin myths and religious commitment. Ayodhya, the site of the mosque, is the reputed birthplace of Lord Rama, a legendary hero-king who was the incarnation of a Hindu god. According to Hindu activists, the temple was built on Rama's birthplace, and they claim that it was later destroyed by Muslims. In turn, the mosque was certainly built by Babur, the Mughal conqueror in the early sixteenth century. Thus, in the view of the Hindu activists, undoing a malign history allegedly linked to the Babri Masjid was at stake in the pursuit of present policies.

In order to appeal to Hindu support, and reflecting a change in Congress policy toward the communalization of policies,[6] both Congress and the BJP, founded in 1980, began activism over the issue in the mid-1980s. The law courts sought to depoliticize the issue, but with limited success. Research by the Archaeological Survey of India on whether there was a temple on the site proved inconclusive and controversial, while the government's attempt to arrange an impartial commission to probe what had led to the destruction of the mosque was thwarted by serious delay followed by contention when the report, in 2009, claimed that the destruction had been a conspiracy.[7]

It has been repeatedly argued, on behalf of post-colonial states and by Western historians critical of Western imperialism, that ethnic and sectarian divisions and rivalries essentially derived from colonialism, notably from politics of 'divide and rule'. However, there is much evidence that such divisions and rivalries preceded Western colonialism. Moreover, they could be bitter and longstanding, as in India and Africa.[8] Such an assessment provides a basis for a rethinking of the impact of Western imperialism.[9]

More generally, there is a widespread failure to appreciate the extent to which Britain and other imperial powers, both Western and non-Western, were not the conquerors of native peoples ruling themselves in a democratic fashion. Indeed, leaving aside the nature of local self-rule where it occurred, many colonies were won from other empires.

There is also a misleading tendency, not least on the part of British commentators and politicians, to blame British imperial rule for many of today's pressures and problems which stem, in reality, from population increase, modernization and globalization. In 2005, the willingness of Manmohan Singh, India's Prime Minister from 2004, a Congress Party politician, to offer a good-and-bad account of British rule caused controversy.

As an empire, Britain engaged with rival powers, the contours and purposes of whose imperial rule was sometimes harsher than those of Britain. This situation pertained in particular to Britain's leading role in opposition to the genocidal tyranny of Nazi Germany; but, in addition, Wilhelmine Germany's policies in East and South-West Africa (Tanzania and Namibia) in the 1900s were far harsher than those of Britain in that period. So also for the 1920s–30s, in contrast to the brutality employed by the Italians to suppress resistance in Libya and to conquer Ethiopia, and that of the Japanese in attempting to conquer China. However, across the political spectrum, the tendency to read the past to satisfy the present has focused anger on British rule because, as the world's leading imperial power from the late eighteenth century until the 1960s, it is so important to the foundation accounts of so many states.

More generally, grievance becomes a way both to interrogate the past and to deploy it to present effect. Grievance also offered, and offers, apparently clear guidance to the future, because it provided a warning about what could happen or was happening, and thus prefigured what could recur or continue. Actions by recent British governments, as well as the current one, for example regrets or apologies, fall into a similar pattern of decontextualized gestures. Moreover, they invite the question of the policies pursued today in good faith that will invite apology in the future – maybe, for example, eating fish and/or meat, or Britain ruling Gibraltar.

Educating for National Identity

Apologies and commemoration are aspects of trying to fix meaning to the past. Searching for meaning is a problem for all societies as they decide how best to explain the past. School curricula are key issues, but so also is the memorialization offered by statuary national holidays, and other collective experiences which today include popular television series. There is an overlap here with the next chapter, but also a difference in emphasis. Curricula have proved a particular public battlefield in recent years, notably, but not only, in Britain. This situation leads to a political focus on history that is not matched in the case of any other subject. Politicians debate what should be taught in history lessons in a way that would not be the case for chemistry.

Britain

In part, the focus, in Britain and elsewhere, on history as a school subject is a response to serious concern about the cohesion of society; there is an attempt to use the teaching of history to provide identity. Thus, in Britain, from the 1960s, crises in the position of the monarchy, parliament and the established church, as well as uncertainties arising from the decline of empire, serious economic problems, the apparently inexorable demands of the European Union, the rise of Scottish and Welsh separatism, and unprecedented mass immigration, all encouraged a sense of disassociation.

This sense of crisis was not new, but had been prefigured in earlier anxieties, notably arising from the rise, first, of the mass (male) electorate in the late nineteenth century, and, then, from concerns about Communism in the inter-war period. In response, many conservative inter-war British writers, such as Sir Arthur Bryant (1899–1985), and, indeed, Churchill with his work on John, 1st Duke of Marlborough, sought to represent and sustain an inherent patriotism. In doing so, Bryant and others, in a way that prefigured the present, confronted not only deep tensions within conservatism, not least in response to socio-economic changes and to mass culture, but also the problems of defining a popular middle-brow voice and then using it in an attempt to revive the nation. Historical writing and journalism were deployed to emphasize national roots, as were travel guides and orchestral music, in a way that was designed to be relevant not simply to the privileged few, but to all countrymen. This project had a sound basis in inter-war British society, and notably the 1920s, one that focused in particular on a patriotism linked to people and place.

However, despite a revival in the 1950s, the project collapsed in the 1960s, in part because of the withdrawal of the intellectual élite from engagement with the needs and concerns of most of the population.[10]

In large part, the attempts by British governments and politicians, both Conservative and Labour, and notably from the late 2000s, to engage with history, identity and nationalism, reflects the consequences of this collapse, and the sense of vacuum it has left.

To believe that the teaching of history could, should and would overcome this sense, and a linked fear of the very ungovernability of the nation, appears surprising, and was (and is) not what academics sought. Nevertheless, it was argued, in Britain (and elsewhere) by politicians of both Left and Right, that active citizenship required a knowledge of national history. Accordingly, the teaching of history was to be used to provide social cement, cultural purpose and political stability.

There is also the need, in Britain and abroad, to offset dangerous divisive histories. In particular, grievance history can pose major problems for government, leading to serious difficulties, internationally and domestically, and, linked to that, can escape government oversight, let alone leadership or direction. For example, the strength of Chinese popular opposition to Japan has posed issues for China's government in recent years, as well as being useful to it.

Secondly, grievance history, from the outset, can result in a harrowing of perceived domestic culprits that seriously compromises national unity. Thirdly, this history may be directed against the government, both as responsible for alleged faults in the past and because it acts as a protector of a corrupt present to this past. Indeed, resentment has been 'the matrix of ideologies of protest, on the left and on the right'.[11]

The net effect is to underline the political danger of using the past as a prime frame of reference, but this danger cannot be addressed by not acting because such a course invites other, more hostile, narratives. This concern helps account for the revival, in the 2000s, of national accounts of history as a way to tackle what was perceived as a serious crisis in public identity. This crisis owed much in Western Europe to justified fears about the attitudes of some of the Islamic population, and in Britain arose in particular from the 2005 terrorist atrocities in London. The potential content of faith-based schooling also posed a challenge, as it continues to do.

More generally, history, in Britain as elsewhere, was presented as a core way to ground patriotism. In 2006 alone, calls to remember and study British history came from the 'History Matters' campaign launched by the National Trust, English Heritage and the Heritage Lottery Fund, as well as from Prince Charles. Gordon Brown, then Chancellor of the Exchequer, proposed the idea of a national day for Britain, and advocated the flying of the British flag.

This approach gathered pace in Britain as a result of political changes. First, the replacement in 2007 of Tony Blair by Gordon Brown as Prime Minister led to the rise of a politician who had a strong engagement with history, not least due to an interest in Britishness as well as having a doctorate in history. At the same time, as a reminder of the range of explanations possible for many historical episodes as well as for much of public historiography, the policy can be discussed in terms of the determination of the Labour government, heavily dependent on Scottish support, to resist the separation of England and Scotland advanced by the Scottish Nationalists, as well as to oppose calls for a greater commitment to English interests. Brown sits in Parliament for a Scottish constituency.

As a consequence, in these and other respects, the language of Britishness became a contentious assertion of long-term values very much in relation to the needs of the present day, a long-familiar process. Moreover, the pillaging of the past for specific causes continued, serving to provide historical ammunition that was often based on a less than thorough grasp of the situation.

The Brown government's use of history provided a reminder of the political strategies involved in historiography: the past was to be presented in pursuit of both general and specific goals. The idea of history as a grounding of patriotism continued under the Conservative-dominated coalition government that took office in 2010. The key player, Michael Gove, Conservative Secretary of State for Education from 2010, called for a national narrative, providing an 'opportunity to hear our island story', that could provide pupils with a framework which he saw, correctly, as lacking in the existing syllabus, a syllabus weak both on British history and on narrative. Gove observed that what was offered was a sequence of case studies 'with no understanding of how the vivid episodes of our past become a connected narrative'. On 24 November 2010, Gove spoke in a BBC Radio Four interview of the importance of 'an understanding of this country's past'. He also made it clear in speeches that he was concerned about what he regarded as anti-patriotic accounts of British history 'trashing our past'.

In short, Gove offered what can be seen as a British version of a standard trope in America's 'culture wars' – although some of his themes had also been taken up in Britain by those of a different political persuasion. In *History in the Balance: History in English Schools 2003–7* (2007), Ofsted complained that pupils had no overview of history, and no coherent view, could not answer the 'big questions': '[T]hey often have little sense of chronology and the possibility of establishing an overarching story and addressing broader themes and issues is limited.' At that stage, Gove made his views clear:

The changes Ed Balls [then the Labour Education Secretary] announced last week would mean more of the flabby, woolly, 'theme-based' teaching this report warns us about. Ofsted underlines the importance of rigour and giving pupils a proper connected sense of what went on in the past. Ed Balls's plans for five-minute lessons and writing Churchill out of the past are the complete opposite of that, and won't give the next generation the understanding it deserves of our national story.[12]

Thus, Churchill again appeared as a totemic figure. In Britain, the existence of a national exam structure and curriculum at the school level made such arguments appear natural to politicians. After all, there has to be something in the curriculum, and it is not possible for history alone to be exempted from a national curriculum.

This issue led to controversy in 2013 when Gove pressed for a new curriculum in which there was a greater focus on the course of national history and on a chronological approach. In a speech of May 2013, Gove stated: 'The draft history curriculum is a direct attempt to address the failure – over generations – to ensure children grow up knowing the story of our islands.'[13] In part, moreover, there was an attempt to move from the academic preference, both for a focus on learning relevant study skills and methods, and for an explicit engagement with competing views and the relativism this entailed. Neither met the criteria sought by ministers. At the university level, where there is no national curriculum, it is possible, thanks to the emphasis on study skills and on studying particular topics in great detail, to emerge from a history degree knowing very little about the history of Britain while also, paradoxically, lacking any real framework of global history.

That is also the case at the school level, but, in 2013, the teaching unions responded aggressively to the proposed changes. Gove's emphasis on facts was condemned at the national conference of the National Union of Teachers by one delegate, Anne Swift, when she urged her colleagues to protect pupils from a 'Gradgrind pub-quiz curriculum'. This remark indicated the nature of historical cultural references, as most of her listeners would not have known that Gradgrind was a harsh employer in Charles Dickens' novel *Hard Times* (1854), but would have understood that the reference was to remorseless hard work.

The British debate captures the extent to which the issues of national identity and coherence have encouraged many governments to look at the presentation and teaching of history. The need, in the face of multiculturalism and concerns about being labelled racist, to distinguish nationalism from xenophobia is an important contributory factor in the discussion. Debates on national history can be seen as a response to the currents and challenges of globalization. However, that does not automatically mean that the response is simply defensive, and it is all too easy to ascribe such a negative judgment to the aspirations and activities of politicians.

USA

In the USA, the content of history teaching at the school level led to controversy which focused on the values supposedly presented by particular textbooks.[14] The debate centred on the level of individual states, as public education is organized and financed as an aspect of state (not federal) government, and overlapped (but was not coterminous) with debate in other subjects, notably, as a product of contention over evolution, biology.

There was also a federal dimension. Senator Robert Byrd's initiative in the teaching of traditional American history, which Congress approved in 2001, was a response to 'revisionist' historians in the aftermath of the National Standards controversy of the 1990s. The initiative involved $50 to $120 million a year nationally to fund history projects submitted by individual school districts around the country. In addition, in 2002, President George W. Bush, who was personally interested in reading about history, launched the 'We the People' initiative to improve the teaching of history in schools. This programme involved federal funding for the National Endowment for the Humanities (NEH) to sponsor an annual essay contest for High School students and an annual 'Heroes in History' lecture.

These and other initiatives reflected not only the politics of culture wars – an issue of particular note for Republican politicians – but also a feeling of anxiety about the acculturation of young Americans. More than content was at stake. A sense of serious cultural challenge was brought out in a 2007 American study of the transmission of historical knowledge: 'If school history is to play a major role in shaping the consciousness of today's iPod-ed, You-Tubed, Instant Messengerised, MySpaced American youth, it must find new ways to engage the cultural curriculum that engulfs them. Failing to do so only guarantees school history's irrelevance into the next century.'[15]

Curricula and Textbooks

More generally, curricula are important and, like textbooks, show not only how the histories of the states in question are discussed, but also how other states are presented.[16] In the case of India, contents were linked to the relationship between its history and wider developments, notably the historical spread, and current political role, of Islam. Thus, the BJP government of 1998–2004 both put sympathetic historians in influential positions and, working through the National Council of Educational Research and Training, produced new textbooks that suited its partisan viewpoint. These praised Hinduism, claimed that Hindu India had played a major role in scientific development, and criticised the Muslim advance in South Asia.

Both curricula and textbooks also represent the changing use of history in terms of method. For Malta, *From the Coming of the Knights to EU Membership* (2008), edited by Yosanne Vella, and with the History Teachers' Association owning the copyright, provided the first new textbook for decades and one that emphasized that documents were complicated and should not be taken at face value. This approach helped in the navigation of Malta's partisan post-independence history.

Uses of the Past

Curricula and the related textbooks, however, are only one of the ways by which history is used to provide meaning. More generally, as across time, history is seen to offer both inspiration and guide. Such utilitarianism takes a number of forms. One is the can-do usage of the past, which includes the presentation of the work of past scholars, for example Athanassios Platias and Constantinos Koliopouos' *Thucydides on Strategy: Athenian and Spartan Grand Strategies in the Peloponnesian War and Their Relevance Today* (2010). Similarly, there has been considerable reference to the lessons for the modern world, notably for contemporary businessmen, generals and others, supposedly offered by Classical Chinese Confucian thinkers, particularly Sun Tzu.

This pattern is long-established and was seen, for example, in the subsequent use of Niccolo Machiavelli's manual of statecraft, *The Prince*, which was written in 1513. Thus, the texts of the past became a subject for exegesis, a process in which historical works played a role. Indeed, the theological skills involved in the exegesis of religious works such as the Bible are useful to the assessment of how public history is interpreted and developed.

Inspiration from the past extended to the bodies of past leaders, as in Venezuela. For Hugo Chávez, the populist President (r. 1999–2013) who died in 2013, Simón Bolívar (1783–1830), the revolutionary who fought successfully for Latin American independence from Spain, and then faced domestic opposition, served as a powerful talisman. In 1992, when he mounted an unsuccessful coup, Chávez stated that Bolívar was his inspiration. Seeking to position himself in Latin American history, Chávez, as President, claimed to be leading a 'Bolivarian revolution' against the 'empire' – the latter no longer the colonial power, Spain, but now the USA. In foreign policy, Chávez drew on Bolívar for the title of his anti-American Bolivárian Alliance for the Americas. Chávez ignored the extent to which Bolívar was an Anglophile conservative. Chávez allegedly left an empty chair at meetings, stating that it was occupied by Bolívar's ghost. In 2000, Chávez, who called himself the *comandante*, gave Fidel Castro, the Communist dictator of Cuba, a replica of Bolívar's diamond-studded sword. As part of the creation of a revolutionary heritage, this sword, in turn, was given to the Museo José Martí in Havana, the museum of Cuba's liberation hero, José Martí, killed in battle with Spanish forces in 1895. Chávez saw history as made by great men and located himself accordingly.

Chávez used his account of Latin America in the long term not only for immediate political advantage, but also so as to locate more recent history that could readily be applied to this end. Thus, Chávez claimed that, immediately before he gained power, Venezuela had been weakened by a 'neo-liberalism' that he blamed on the outside power, the USA. There was a clear parallel with aspects of the modern Chinese account of history (pp. 178–9), although China does not now share Chávez's hostility to capitalism, a hostility that led to chaos in the Venezuelan economy. Critics tended to focus on Chávez's autocratic actions, but historical references were also offered by some. Many references were to past Latin American dictators, such as Argentina's Juan Péron, President from 1946 to 1955 and 1973 to 1974, but there were also references further afield. A 'tropical Mussolini' was the verdict of the left-wing Mexican writer Carlos Fuentes,[17] a verdict that captured at least the tone of Chávez's rule.

Convinced that Bolívar was poisoned by political enemies, Chávez hoped to prove this as a result of an exhumation. As he identified with Bolívar, he also thought the latter deserved a mausoleum of his own. In 2011, Bolívar's remains were disinterred from the National Pantheon in Caracas in preparation for being installed in a nearby mausoleum which, despite great cost, was still unfinished in 2013. Both processes were taken forward in 2011 when Chávez responded to the diagnosis of the cancer that ultimately killed him, by claiming that he had been infected by American secret agents, a claim taken up by his successor as President, Nicolas Maduro, who was narrowly elected in April 2013. Thus, one false history became a model for another. The idea of a lasting presence for Chávez, once dead, was also advanced by Maduro in March 2013: 'We have to keep alive his image, his voice, his thinking. More than the physical body, we have the commander in eternal memory, especially this generation who heard it, touched it, saw him.'

In debating Latin American history, both within countries and at the continental level, there is a tendency to focus on the atrocities committed by rivals, and thus to establish respective pedigrees of crime and rectitude. The tools of history employed in this process vary greatly. In 2013, the remains of Pablo Neruda, a prominent left-wing poet and ally of Salvador Allende, the Marxist president of Chile overthrown in a military coup in 1973, were exhumed. Neruda's death soon after the coup as he prepared to flee the country was officially recorded as due to prostate cancer, but it has been claimed that he was murdered, and the tests by the state Medical Legal Service are designed to establish the truth of the matter.

Exhumation as a tool of politics and history was also used in Turkey in 2012–13, in the case of Turgat Özal, the Prime Minister from 1983 to 1989 and President from 1989 to 1993, who modernized the country. In this case, exhumation was part of the government's attempt, from 2007, to discredit the military, and, in doing so, to claim both the past and key figures in it. Generals are accused of having Ozäl killed in order to prevent him from negotiating with the Kurdish rebels, the latter the aspiration of the government in the early 2010s.

As another, very different, use of the past, the employment of historians and historical method in policy-making has been encouraged.[18] In 2013, Lord Butler, a former Cabinet Secretary, called for all departments of the British Civil Service to appoint historical advisers.[19] However, this process has been less successful than for the social sciences. In part, this contrast reflects the dominant culture among academic historians.[20] This culture is a product of the degree to which, notably in the West, academic history addresses history as questions, and not the history as answers that is more generally preferred for public history. This contrast is also important in so far as historiographical emphasis and sympathy are concerned. In the case of historiography, academic historians tend to offer attention, and praise, to history as methodology and questions, and not as narrative and answers or, at least, not as answers that are deemed simplistic. Politicians, however, markedly prefer answers.

Debating Recessions

In practice, using history to learn lessons by making comparisons can be highly problematic, as the British Treasury discovered in the 1950s–70s when trying to employ an historical section for policy purposes. Moreover, according to a 2010 newspaper interview with David Muir, head of strategy for Gordon Brown, the lacklustre and unsuccessful British Prime Minister from 2007 to 2010, Brown said several times 'They're not going to turn me into Philip Snowden'. Snowden was the Chancellor of the Exchequer under Ramsay MacDonald in the 1924 and 1929 Labour governments, but both men were remembered in the subsequent Labour view of the period for selling out to the Treasury, especially when the Labour government fell in 1931, to be replaced by a National Government that most Labour politicians opposed. MacDonald abandoned his party and became Prime Minister in the National Government from 1931 to 1935. The interview with Muir continued:

> 'Gordon knew the Treasury [in the 2000s] would always make the deficit seem worse than it was,' says Mr Muir. 'He faced very similar problems to MacDonald – a changing world order and financial collapse. MacDonald chose the financial orthodoxy of the Treasury, turned his back on Labour voters, cut unemployment benefit and Labour was out of power for a generation.' Mr Brown was thinking about how he would be remembered and Mr Muir believes that unlike MacDonald – this Labour Prime Minister ultimately made the 'right choices'.

Brown's concern for the views of posterity and for a place in history, a concern frequent among politicians, was not only fed by the mythmaking of Labour's own history, but also by the reading of the past. In 2008, Brown, who had a history doctorate based on research on left-wing inter-war British politicians, spent his summer holiday reading the book on the Great Depression of the 1930s by Ben Bernanke, the Chairman of the (American) Federal Reserve, as well as the critical emendation by the then Treasury Permanent Secretary on an original paper by John Maynard Keynes (1883–1946) advocating reflation. Brown concluded that Keynes was correct.[21] Controversy over the wisdom of Keynesian reflation was again to the fore during the Conservative-led Coalition government in the early 2010s.

The use of Keynes, a supporter of deficit financing, served critics of Conservatism, notably in arguing that Britain had taken a wrong turn with the neo-liberalism of Margaret Thatcher's government (1979–90). A very different use of the Depression was offered by David Cameron when he warned, on 12 November 2010 at the G20 summit in Seoul, that the global economy risked a return to the 1930s: 'The fear we should all have is a return to what happened in the 1930s: protectionism, trade barriers, currency wars, countries playing beggar-my-neighbour policies – trying to do well for themselves but not caring about the rest of the world. That is the danger.'

Opponents of reflation in the early 2010s referred back not to the monetary stability of the 1930s in Britain, but to the legacy of the recent Labour government, that of 1997–2010. The potential frame of reference was affected by political need (refuting Labour), chronological proximity, and the relevance and reference this process offered politicians, commentators and voters. In contrast, the 1930s was difficult territory for making points about the value of sound finances in the shape of cutting government expenditure or, to its critics, austerity. Labour's memory of the 1930s, in terms of the serious crisis in traditional areas of heavy industry and mining, and the accompanying high rates of unemployment, has triumphed over the more complex reality of the coincidence of this situation with significant growth in new industrial sectors in the South of England, notably in white goods and cars.

The same regional and sectional contrast was true of the Thatcher years and the recession of the early 1980s, and this contrast affected the very different accounts of her government following her death in 2013. Moreover, one of her own major references to history, when speaking in 1983 in favour of Victorian values, had itself created controversy, with claims that she underrated the positive role of the state in Victorian Britain. Her position toward government was different from that taken by Obama during the 2012 American presidential campaign. However much rhetoric played a role for both Thatcher and Obama, there was indeed a significant contrast between them. Attaching a value to politicians and policies by linking them to an appropriate historical reference point was a practice deployed anew in 2013 with frequent, but contested, parallels between Thatcher and Churchill as champions of freedom. That Churchill never created an 'ism' made his legacy easier to use.

The relationships between economic recessions and, on the other hand, political causes and consequences were given added bite by the case of Weimar Germany (1918–33), the democratic political system and culture destroyed by Hitler. The legacy of failure in the face of Hitler long contributed to a negative portrayal of Weimar, but a number of factors, including the present crisis in Europe, have made the example of Weimar appear not only pertinent but also less of a failure.[22] The impact of the gold standard in the failure of Weimar has recently been cited as a warning about the problems posed by the Euro, another fixed exchange system.[23]

Belief in the Past

Strongly entrenched beliefs about the past affect the accessibility of history for particular uses. Shaking such beliefs proves extraordinarily difficult. Instead, they tend to ebb only when new collective memories take their place. The First World War offers a clear instance of a strongly entrenched focus. In Britain, the emphasis is on the heavy casualties of trench warfare, notably in the Battle of the Somme (1916), and not on eventual victory in the offensive operations in the closing months of the war in late 1918. This emphasis leads to a stress on the futility of the struggle that was not, in fact, the prime response of most survivors.

The frame and intensity of historical reference varies by individual, and more generally by group, whether by generation, ethnicity, religion or nation. This frame also changes, so that references can appear anachronistic. Thus, in November 2012, Boris Johnson, the Conservative Mayor of London, compared the Socialist ministers of the Hollande government in France to the radical and violent *sans-culottes* of the 1789 French Revolution. Such a reference would have meant a lot in Britain a century ago, not least with much of the public aware of the account of the Revolution in Charles Dickens' novel *A Tale of Two Cities* (1859). By 2012, however, cultural awareness and its historical counterpart were very different.[24]

Warnings about the dangers of military intervention in the domestic conflicts of foreign states have similarly been updated, so that to discuss the failed French intervention in Mexico in 1861–7, or the international intervention in the Russian Civil War in 1919–21, the latter an unsuccessful intervention in which Churchill was heavily involved, would now be considered anachronistic. Instead, references are updated as history is reframed in the present. American intervention in Vietnam in the 1960s and early 1970s for long was the citation, but, in 2013, at a time of debate over the wisdom of such intervention in Syria, the focus is on the lessons learned from doing so in Iraq a decade earlier.

Searching for meaning in history takes place at a number of levels, across different chronological scales, and for a range of reasons. To argue that none of these is value-free might not be regarded as surprising, but requires emphasis because of the general tendency in public history to imply that such objectivity is the goal and is readily possible. Thus, in 2013, three former Supreme Court justices were appointed by the Cypriot President to investigate all 'civil, criminal and political offences' that led to the collapse of the country's financial sector.

Moreover, it is easily apparent that the search for meaning from the past is conditioned by the contexts for both search and meaning. The primacy of political considerations and of the national/state level is clear across the world. The histories of individual states are so different that the meaning that is contested varies enormously.

History and Papal Reputation

For example, the election, in March 2013, of Cardinal Jorge Mario Bergoglio as the first Latin American Pope, Francis I, had a very different meaning among Latin American countries, all of which have a majority Catholic population. The meaning was different in Costa Rica, a state with a generally benign and democratic recent history, and even in Brazil, which had had a military dictatorship, compared to the meaning in the Pope's native Argentina. His role as head of the Jesuit order there from 1973 to 1979 has caused controversy, because the Catholic Church in Argentina, especially its leadership, not only failed to denounce the military junta that seized power in 1976, ruling until 1983, but, indeed, backed them. Under the junta, Argentineans were pressed by the Catholic Church to display a 'love of country' at a time when at least 8,900 suspected 'subversives' were seized and killed.

As an instance of the controversial nature of the period, estimates of those who were killed range from at least 8,900, the figure from a Truth Commission, to 30,000. The disappearance of most of those seized was a particularly brutal instance of the denial of history, as was the removal of their children, who were handed over for adoption by those viewed with favour by the regime, and thus denied their own history. The Catholic Church's role under Juan Carlos Aramburu, Cardinal-Archbishop of Buenos Aires, was widely seen in terms of complicity, not least in ignoring the murder of the left-wing Bishop of La Rioja, Enrique Angelelli.

In 2000, the Catholic Church in Argentina issued a public statement of contrition for its failure to take a stand. However, there was also blame from the Church for the regime's left-wing opponents. Moreover, these opponents criticised the Church. For example, Horacio Verbitsky, a journalist and human-rights lawyer who has criticized the Church and who is close to the Argentine government, had sat on the intelligence committee of the Montoneros, the Marxist guerrilla movement.

The issue has continued to play a role in the Argentinean politics of memory, and notably, in 2013, involving the new Pope, who has been accused of being close to the regime, indeed complicit in the kidnapping and torture of two colleagues, and, subsequently, evasive. Having said nothing for decades, the Pope now claims, notably in a 2012 book-interview *The Jesuit*, to have played a role in assisting the regime's opponents, especially by helping them escape.

The Pope's election has therefore turned Argentina's public politics into an aspect of the Catholic Church's complex attempt to engage with its difficult past. In March 2013, the Vatican spokesman, Federico Lombardi, claimed that the accusations were part of a 'Left-wing, anticlerical conspiracy'. The public (and private) response to this, and other, controversies is itself instructive, as apologists and critics search for meaning, whether in terms of Christian history and the Christian mission, or the more difficult history of the Catholic Church, as well as the complexities of Latin American politics and the Cold War.

The awareness of, and response to, these contexts varied greatly. Historical appreciation played a role in the assessment of differences – as in contrasts between Chile, where the Vicaria de la Solidaridad opposed the Pinochet dictatorship, and Argentina, where the Church was closer to the military junta which, indeed, emphasized, not least in education, a Catholic identity for Argentina.

The Catholic Church also offers narratives of the past that include a sense of grievance. Visiting Spain in November 2010, Pope Benedict XVI (r. 2005–13), a critic of the social liberalism in that once strongly Catholic country, warned of a 'strong and aggressive secularism' similar to that seen in the 1930s. It was a highly contentious reference, as the violent attacks on the Church prior to the Civil War were used by the Nationalists as a pretext for their rebellion against the Republicans in 1936.

In 2013, a further level of controversy was added by references to the response of the new Pope and his predecessor, Benedict XVI, to allegations of child sex-abuse by priests. The creation of a critical argument in terms of a history of such abuse – an argument that would not have been offered, or enjoyed such resonance, a decade ago – demonstrated the extent to which contexts for judgement could change rapidly. This issue has superseded in public attention the long controversy over whether Pope Pius XII (r. 1939–58) was a coward, if not worse, in failing to confront Nazi policy, notably the Holocaust. The change in focus reflects the altering perspective offered by passing time and altering social concerns.

As a reminder that historical references compete for attention, those who were more sympathetic to Francis I emphasized his humility, including his unwillingness to wear the more ostentatious papal costumes and to move into the luxurious papal apartments in Rome. Moreover, a break with the past that angered traditionalists, and their perception of appropriate behaviour, was seen on Maundy Thursday 2013 when, in place of washing the feet of pilgrims at St Peter's, Rome, Francis celebrated the mass at a young offenders' institute and included two women, one a Muslim, among the twelve pilgrims whose feet the Pope washed in a symbolic echo of Jesus and his twelve (male) disciples.

Historical Grievances and Politics

Grievance, about the past and the present, was an approach particularly conducive to the democratization of politics seen in many countries from the 1990s, as societies adapted not only to democracy but also to a practice of accountability and responsiveness that was far more frequent than that of elections. Indeed, the Tea Party movement in America clearly fits into this development. Populism was least fixed, and restricted, by existing constitutional forms and political practices in countries suddenly developing as democracies, notably those of Eastern Europe and, from the 2010s, some in the Arab world.

Nevertheless, mobilizing popular, specifically electoral, support by reference to history was not only an issue in such states. The rise of historical reference was also linked to the emergence in more mature democracies of political parties that owed little to the traditional class-based divide of Left and Right. This was particularly the case with the emergence of additional parties that had to find a different resonance, and notably with those of the far right that sought to use historicized notions of identity in order to mobilize popular support across a wide range.

In Austria, under Jörg Haider, its leader from 1986 to 2005, the *Freiheitliche Partei Österreichs* (FPÖ, Austrian Liberal Party) moved to the far right and challenged the Social Democrats and the conservative People's Party, the parties that had dominated post-war Austrian politics. Popular concern about immigration provided the basis for a rise in support for the FPÖ, as also with similar parties in this period in Belgium, Denmark, France, Hungary, Italy, the Netherlands, Russia, Sweden and other states. This concern focused particularly on immigration from Islamic countries, and, although that was not the sole issue, that immigration allowed a use of historical reference, notably to the longstanding struggle between the Habsburgs and the Ottoman Turks. In the parliamentary elections of 1999, the FPÖ became the second-largest party. Haider also used the Beneš Decrees of 1945, under which the possessions of the Sudeten Germans in Czechoslovakia were expropriated as a collective punishment for collaboration with Germany, to stoke up German ethnic consciousness in Austria.

In the Vienna municipal election campaign in 2010, there was not only reference to 'our Vienna blood', but also a comic strip dispatched to every household providing an account of the climactic Ottoman attack of 1683. In this comic strip, a knight resembling Heinz-Christian Strache, the leader of the FPÖ, was depicted urging a boy to use a slingshot to attack a foreigner called Mustafa, a classic Turkish name. There were echoes of pre-First World War concerns in Europe, Australia and the USA about the 'yellow peril' posed by Chinese and Japanese immigration and power, and of opposition then to Jewish immigration from Eastern Europe.

The rise of the FPÖ in Austria is a classic instance of the way in which grievance history, by mobilizing an important populist strand of cultural anger, challenges conventional conservative accounts of identity and action, or, at the least, established conservative political hierarchies. The same is the case with the Tea Party movement in the USA, while the use of an image of Churchill, Conservative leader from 1940 to 1955 and, as wartime Prime Minister, an icon of national resolve, by the far-right British National Party at the time of the 2010 general election was also instructive, as well as being highly inappropriate. Despite the strictures of critics, nationalism scarcely equates with xenophobia and racism, and the language of national belonging plays out in very different ways. Thus, in Germany, there is scant overlap between the attitudes of the extreme right and those of the governing Christian Democrats.[25]

It is not only in Austria that the character of the Ottoman Empire, as of Islamic history as a whole, is a major theme in public history. Large-scale Islamic immigration has led to the spread of this issue. For example, in Denmark, immigration has been a major issue in the last three general election campaigns, and is still a central topic. The question of assimilating immigrants has led to long and fierce debates about what it means being Danish, and about how Danish identity should be taught, both to Danes and to immigrants.

Returning to Turkey, on the one hand, there are state-supported efforts in European countries to argue that the Ottoman Empire was a largely benign culture and to present Islamic history as fundamentally positive and tolerant. On the other hand, there are indications of a very different deep history, one in which often atavistic concerns bulk large. It would be all too easy to suggest that the division in treatment reflects a split between academic, enlightened history and a more troubled and troubling assertive public discourse, but that division would be questionable.

Assertion plays a major role, in both support and criticism of Islamic culture and history. State-supported efforts, notably the exhibitions of Islamic culture, can be seen as resting on public assertion, albeit not of a populist character. In the presentation of Islamic culture in the past, fine pieces of art are detached, for admiration, from discussion of states that could be far from tolerant. Moreover, the role of large-scale enslavement in Islamic expansion, and of Muslim traders in the African slave trade, tends to be ignored, or, at the very least, greatly downplayed,[26] as is the extent to which the pattern and practice of Islamic expansion posed a fundamental challenge to many aspects of Christian culture. The generally benign portrayal of *al-Andalus*, the Muslim state and culture in medieval southern Spain, neglects the extent to which it was involved in warfare.

Losing, or at least being frightened, are key sources of grievance history; and since most societies have been defeated, or can perceive themselves as having been defeated, at least some of the time, that offers plenty of opportunities for grievances. The USA again provides a prime instance. Alongside the classic groups who can present themselves as still suffering the after-effects of oppression, namely African Americans, Native Americans and Japanese Americans who have a specific, albeit somewhat overblown, complaint about internment in the Second World War,[27] comes Southern whites. Many of these whites still adopt an ambivalent, if not combative and unrepentant, attitude to the Civil War (1861–5).

In particular, there has come a pattern of commemorating the Southern effort in this conflict without drawing attention to slavery as an issue. George Allen, Republican Governor of Virginia from 1994 to 1998, declared a Confederate History Month in that state in 1995, 1996 and 1997. Allen proclaimed the Civil War as 'a four-year struggle for independence, sovereign rights and local government control'. Elected a senator from Virginia in 2000, Allen made a racist remark in August 2006, when he was running for re-election to the Senate, and this remark probably cost him the election, and therefore the chance of running for the Republican presidential nomination in 2008.[28]

In turn, Mark Warner, the Democratic Governor from 2002–6, was unenthusiastic about backing the idea of a Confederate History Month, only for Bob McDonnell, the next Republican Governor (2010 to present), to support it. Initially, McDonnell did not mention slavery, but he was finally obliged to accept that slavery 'has left a stain on the soul of this state and nation'. Similarly, Georgia's State Senate supported April as Confederate History Month, with backing for tourism being a key rationale, and slavery pushed into the background.

Agitation over this issue was scarcely new, and there are also grounds for optimism about the willingness in the United States to accept the role of slavery and the perspectives of black and white alike.[29] Similarly, in Britain, controversy over the legacy of the slave trade is less pronounced than agreement about its iniquities. In 2008, the Racial Equality Council complained when a pub in Plymouth was named after Sir John Hawkins, a naval hero of the sixteenth century who was also a prominent slaver.[30] However, such episodes play a far smaller role in Britain than in the USA, in part because there are far fewer descendants of slaves in Britain, and in part because tension there focused on recent Muslim immigrants, whose background was not slavery.

There is also a direct political resonance in the USA that is troubling. When Southern states with Republican administration turned to challenge the healthcare legislation of the Obama administration (2009–17) by arguing that it represented a federal infringement on states' rights, references to the secessionism of the Civil War were disturbing and linked to the racist aspect of some of the opposition to President Obama and his policies.

Moreover, the Tea Party movement has shown how episodes from the past can suddenly be developed with a strong dynamic in particular political contexts. Southern secessionism scarcely offers a national resonance comparable to the Boston Tea Party, but it plays into a feeling among much of the American white working class that it has been disempowered and that it lacks a rallying cry and cause comparable to the role of Civil Rights in African-American identity and interests. In practice, the American working class, white and non-white alike, has been hit hard by industrial relocation in part due to the pressures and opportunities arising from globalization.

The 150th anniversaries of Civil War episodes from 2011 to 2015 provided and will provide opportunities for contention. Indeed, the Secession Gala held at Charleston on 20 December 2010 to celebrate the 150th anniversary of South Carolina's decision to declare independence aroused controversy, not least because critics (correctly) claimed that the role of maintaining slavery in secessionism was largely ignored in the South, and notably on such occasions.

The range of factors involved in considering the past is such, however, that simple descriptions and simplistic conclusions are best avoided, for this and other issues. Alongside the competition of competing voices in the discussion of slavery and the Civil War, there are also elements of government and law. In the USA, as elsewhere, the culture of litigation often discourages formal apologies. Moreover, it is not surprising that the notion of reparations for slavery is generally not given much of a hearing.

Turning from the USA to a broader canvas, grievance history serves to link past and present, by offering continuity between them and yet also a contemporary application for the identity and interests bound up with the grievance. This application is encouraged by the extent to which victim status leads to a pressure both to control interpretation and to do better.

In the case of France, grievances are inscribed across a history in which there have been repeated turning points, each of which gave rise to a new cause of triumph or discontent and a new basis for validation or criticism. In addition, a varied past provided a crowded vocabulary of reference. Thus, hostility to Napoleonic adventurism, by both Napoleon I and Napoleon III in the nineteenth century, led French republicans on the left to find an obvious reference point of criticism from which to view Charles de Gaulle's rise to power in 1958 as Prime Minister, and his establishment of the Fifth Republic for which he was President from 1958 to 1969. That Napoleon III, a President (1848–52) who had become Emperor (1852–70), fell from power in 1870 encouraged hopes that de Gaulle, who was presented by critics as a pseudo-monarch, would do so as well. The French Left was later to see echoes of the French Revolution of 1789 in the *événements de mai*

(1968), when left-wing popular action challenged the state on the streets of Paris. Such references were taken up in films dealing with the latter, such as *Les Amants réguliers* (2010). In France, both left and right made repeated references to the past. In Paris, a 1936 demonstration in memory of those killed in the suppression of the Paris Commune by the forces of the more Conservative National Government in 1871 included posters depicting other heroes of the French past who could be appropriated by the left, including Voltaire and Diderot, both eighteenth-century Enlightenment writers, and Zola, a left-wing nineteenth-century writer. That 1936 was the year of a Popular Front movement under attack from the right encouraged this harnessing of the past. More generally, constructions of French identity have very much interacted with political contention within France, and notably between left and right.[31]

Across the world, searching for meaning in national narratives provided commentators and politicians with much to discuss in the late 2000s and early 2010s, as the response to economic crisis, notably in the West, but also in Japan, led many groups to lose a sense of confidence in the future. Moreover, aside from austerity sapping confidence on the right as well as the left, traditional progressive panaceas had been hit by the collapse, first, in the late twentieth century, of Marxism and, then, in the early twenty-first century, of confidence in social democracy funded by a directed capitalism.

A lack of confidence encouraged a sense of drift, but there were also more specific changes in the traction of public history. For example, in the USA, the election of Barack Obama in 2008, and his re-election in 2012, made the political narrative of Civil Rights appear less relevant in the USA. Whereas this narrative had a strong historical tradition, that was not the case with gay rights, which became a more prominent issue in 2012–13. Debate over homosexual marriage and related issues led to a relevant public history, but it was less prominent in this case than with Civil Rights.

As a reminder, that this process of transformation did not only occur on the left; there were also major changes in the content and tone of American conservatism, which was part of its 'ongoing mutation as it seeks fitness for survival in a dynamic American democracy'.[32] These changes entailed a re-presentation of the history of the American right. At the same time, history was used by this right as a point of reference.

The Tea Party Pours Out Grievances

The use of the 1773 Boston Tea Party in American politics in the late 2000s and early 2010s was direct and unambiguous. This directness provided a dissenting gloss to the frequent, and misleading, reference to what was disparagingly referred to as the 'United States of Amnesia'. Indeed, Americans, whose constitution (drawn up and contested in the late eighteenth century) and political continuity encourage reference to the past for validation and example,[33] are far from unaware of history. Sarah Palin, the populist Republican Vice-Presidential candidate in 2008, told a Boston audience in 2010:

> You're sounding the warning bell just like what happened in that midnight run and just like with that original Tea Party back in 1773. I want to tell him [President Obama] 'Nah, you know, we'll keep clinging to our constitution and our guns and religion and you can keep the change'.

Reference to the Tea Party of 1773 encourages a sense of activism, and the empowerment that goes with it, and thus presents an attractive idea for populism. Moreover, the longstanding American (and non-American) need to seek validation in the past is satisfied by this episode. The Tea Party movement presents itself as an apparent demonstration of the Declaration of Independence (1776) and the Constitution in action, one linking the Founding Fathers (the winners of independence and framers of the Constitution, such as George Washington) to the present.

As such, the Tea Party apparently provides an opportunity to assert the constitutional appropriateness of conservative politics. Such an assertion is wide-ranging. Palin claimed that the Founding Fathers had wanted Americans to 'create law based on the God of the Bible and on the Ten Commandments'. In fact, this claim was no more true of the Constitution than the argument that Church and state were not treated as separate, an argument made by Christine O'Donnell, the unsuccessful Republican senatorial candidate for Delaware in 2010 and a prominent focus of Tea Party action.[34] Standing for the Republican nomination as President, Michele Bachmann, a member of the House of Representatives and a keen Tea Party figure, declared in 2012 that the first shots of the war were fired in conservative New Hampshire, which was a 'gaffe heard around the world' as they were, in fact, fired in Massachusetts, today a centre of American liberalism.

Criticism of factual error by politicians and others referring to the past is easy, and is part of the longstanding clash between public memory and critical history-writing.[35] It is also readily possible to charge that subsequent reference to the episode in 1773 is a classic instance of the fallacy of so-called presentism, and thus demonstrates the folly of assuming that history has a clear message. Indeed, different groups will always find their own message in any historical episode, as is indicated for the Tea Party of 1773 in the next paragraph. More generally, protest and defiance are much easier to understand and carry out, than government and the construction of a system of administration.

Typically, the Tea Party movement today accords with the tendency in the 1770s to look to earlier episodes of alleged tyranny. Indeed, the extent to which American writers in the 1770s invoked Charles I's efforts to tax without parliamentary consent in the 1630s, a clear touchstone of tyranny in contemporary minds in Britain as well as its American colonies, was indicative of a wider breakdown in trust.[36] In the eighteenth century, this reference to history helped in drawing a distinction between what was legal, and inappropriate, and what constitutional, and right.[37] In practice, both laws and constitutions, in content and practice, are always open to political and public revision.

Modern Tea Party activists therefore employ America's past as those they are praising also did. Moreover, as with other major symbols, the use of the historical Tea Party has in fact been very varied. As it stands primarily as an instance of defiance of authority for the sake of liberty, it has frequently been offered by those defending direct activism against government. The Tea Party was employed in the USA to justify defiance of the law by a range of pressure groups, including temperance activists keen to see alcohol banned, suffragettes demanding votes for women, the Ku Klux Klan, the Civil Rights movement, segregationists, opponents of President Richard Nixon (r. 1969–73), and radicals at the time of the Bicentennial of the Declaration of Independence (1976). The episode in 1773 was also invoked by foreigners justifying popular activism, for example Chinese nationalists opposed to Western, especially British, economic dominance in the 1920s.[38]

At the same time, however much past uses of episodes may serve as an inspiration, each particular iteration is specific. Indeed, the current use of the Boston Tea Party serves to demonstrate a historical reach that is very different from those offered by the dominant strand of liberal thought in Americas. Among liberals, there is an emphasis on the African-American Civil Rights movement, and thus an account of American history that is relatively recent and where racial justice is a key theme. The stress is not so much on the Founding Fathers, who won independence and drew up the Constitution, as it is for the right, although liberal historians drew on the Declaration of Independence (1776) as President Obama did in his Second Inaugural in 2013.

The corollary of an emphasis on Civil Rights is that the villains are other Americans, principally white Southern racists. In practice, the Civil Rights movement was also a protest against unfair local government regulations, and, in a way, against taxation without equal representation; but this protest was focused on challenging the racist attempt to deny African-Americans the vote.

This legacy remains controversial. In June 2013, to the declared deep disappointment of President Obama, the Supreme Court found part of the Voting Rights Act, a key part of the Civil Rights legislation passed in 1965, to be 'unconstitutional in light of current conditions' on the grounds that measures decreed then, in response to wrongs of the period, were no longer pertinent.

This focus on Civil Rights is contested on the right, for example with the Washington rally in August 2010 organized by Glenn Beck, a rally deliberately seeking to appropriate the symbolism and sites associated with Martin Luther King Jr., the key Civil Rights leader in the 1960s. As a reminder of the role of national holidays as commemorative encoders of the past, in 1986 Martin Luther King Day was established by Congress. Hostility to an African-American in the White House from 2009 was also readily apparent on the right, but was underestimated in the media.

On the right, the emphasis on the Boston Tea Party serves to offer an account of America's history in which African-Americans do not play much of a part, while civil rights are defined not as Civil Rights, but in a fashion focused on opposition to big government and taxation, Tea standing for 'Taxed Enough Already'. Taxation itself, which in modern America, unlike in 1773, comes from a democratically elected government, is re-presented as alien, authoritarian and excessive, allowing conservatives to see themselves as legal revolutionaries.

The focus on the Obama administration captures the present-mindedness of the Tea Party movement's historiography, in particular a sense of the ready applicability of the episode to the here-and-now. This approach is not the sole one taken in the public sphere, for, as indicated elsewhere in the book, this sphere frequently focuses on the issue of historical grievances. The Tea Party movement, in contrast, uses the past not as an inherited grievance but as an analogous call for action against what is perceived as a present grievance. Britain in 1773 serves, in this interpretation, to represent authoritarian government and refers directly to the argument that Obama, who is referred to as a tax-and-spend Socialist (a misuse of the term), is Europeanizing America. Issues of space and ideology therefore are involved alongside time, the idea of Europeanization apparently involving a challenge to American integrity. The call to arms, however, is against the American federal government, and not against modern Britain or Europe, and, ironically, the marriage in 2012 of Prince William, a direct descendant of George III, whose father, Prince Charles, is a keen supporter of the reputation of that king, excited much positive popular interest in the USA.

More generally, ideologies call on history, but, in their hands, it becomes a prophecy, and a cause of grievance, a process also seen with many politicians. In the case of history as prophecy, take for example President George W. Bush, who majored in History at Yale University and, as President, regularly read history books, speaking in 2003: 'The advance of freedom is the calling of our time [...] we believe that liberty is the direction of history.' In practice, the 'lessons of history' that were pertinent when America considered invading Iraq in 2003 offered a contrary emphasis on prudence and realism, one that was ignored.[39]

It is particularly unfortunate, however, that, just as the past again became more important in American public discussions after the end of the Cold War, so professional historians, many fascinated by theory and jargon, have abandoned much of the public field to amateurs,[40] while the trade book industry produces books like commodities. These amateurs became increasingly visible in public discourse about the past. Thus, in the USA, there are journalists, retired military officers and others whose training is not in history, but who have moved into the front ranks of history writing anyhow. Publishers know that books that have the best chance of selling are written by authors already famous, are books that strongly confirm the fondly held assumptions of a large readership, or are books that play into the public appetite for counter-intuitive 'new' revelations that dramatically 'prove' a controversial 'new' theory which, it is sometimes alleged, the professional historians have been overlooking or actively covering up.

China

The USA is scarcely alone in seeing a similar repositioning of historical reference and meaning in response to current political concerns and consumer trends. This process is especially difficult in China due to the combination of an embrace of free-market capitalism and a maintenance of the dominant position of the Communist Party. This combination poses particular problems for assessing the years under Mao Zedong, dictator from 1949 to 1976, when Communist rule was notably radical and repressive. Attempts to discuss the incompetence, cruelty and failure of the Mao regime, and its implications for the authoritarian Communist system in China, encounter difficulties there. For example, Yang Jisheng's *Tombstone: The Great Chinese Famine 1958–1962* (London, 2012), a discussion of the brutality and failure of a key Maoist policy, and one that exemplifies the catastrophic deficiencies of the governmental system under Mao, was published in Hong Kong in 2008, but is banned in mainland China. There has been some discussion of the topic in Chinese newspapers and on the internet, but this discussion is limited and conditional: there is no freedom to discuss. Chinese history in the post-Mao years is also subject to control. Thus, the Tiananmen Square massacre of reformers in Beijing in 1989 is referred to as the 'June 4th episode'.

There is also the issue of how best to address the earlier period of development under the Nationalists, the opponents of the Communists.[41] These tensions are linked to arguments about the supposed uniqueness of Chinese history and whether it requires different criteria for assessment to that used in the West. Advancing this argument, what are presented as 'Asian values', a category and theme also pushed hard in Singapore, are opposed to Western counterparts, in an apparent cultural essentialism that draws on the past.[42] 'Asian society' is presented as inherently less liberal and more cohesive, an interpretation that is conducive to governments, including the different ones of China and Singapore.

This approach, however, is flawed in its assessment of the current situation, and more generally, and, in part, rests on a failure to understand the extent to which both the nineteenth and the twentieth centuries (before, under and after Mao) revealed serious deficiencies in the effectiveness of Chinese authoritarianism.

The Chinese account of the past very much focuses on Chinese history, but, in the post-Mao era, there have also been attempts in China to learn from international history. Lessons from abroad are projected onto China. The collapse of Soviet Communism is employed as a warning about the danger of reform, as is Alexis de Tocqueville's account of the 1789 French Revolution, *The Old Regime and the Revolution* (1856).

There has also been an attempt to look at parallels in other empires. In particular, *Daguo Jueqi* (*The Rise of Great Powers*), a Chinese government study finished in 2006, attempted to determine the reasons why Portugal, Spain, the Netherlands, Britain, France, Germany, Japan, Russia and the USA became great powers. This study was apparently inspired by a directive from Hu Jintao, China's President from 2002 to 2013, to determine which factors enabled great powers to grow most rapidly. Hu is reported to have said at a 2003 session of the Communist Party's Central Committee Political Bureau that:

> China, as a late-coming great nation, should learn from and draw upon the historical experience of the leading nations of the world in their modernisation processes, as this will certainly be very beneficial in realising the strategy of catching up and overtaking the leaders in modernisation and achieving the great rejuvenation of the Chinese nation.

The study drew together government, popular interest and academe, with many scholars consulted and some reportedly briefing the Politburo. A twelve-part programme was twice broadcast on the state-owned television channel in November 2006 and an eight-volume book series was produced and sold rapidly. The president of the television channel made the utilitarian purpose of the series clear. The book project argued the value of naval power, but also the need for a dynamic economy with international trade linking the economy to naval power. The value attached to trade is seen as a lesson from the past about the significance of international co-operation.[43]

The Former Communist Bloc

China is not the sole state facing the problem of addressing the Communist past. The end of the Cold War more generally discredited Marxism as an official creed and greatly lessened its influence as a basis for analysis; the impact of the two combined to ensure a major shift in the understanding of history in states that had been Communist. This understanding was linked at the international level to the expression, revival or rise of national grievances, within the Communist bloc, particularly in the former Yugoslavia and the former Soviet Union. In Ukraine, independence from 1991 brought public attention to the Soviet government's complicity in the mass famine that began in 1933, and led to pressure for its recognition as a genocide. In January 2010, Stalin and colleagues were indeed convicted posthumously of genocide in a Ukrainian court. Religion plays a role. In Kiev, the capital of Ukraine, the National Museum of the Great Patriotic War, opened in the Soviet period and with a giant dome decorated with Communist motifs, was altered, after independence, with the addition of a Christian cross made from gun parts.

In Russia, the process of coming to terms with the Communist era has been complicated by the resurgence of nationalist history under President Putin, the key political figure from 2000. This resurgence extends to defences of much of the Stalinist period, including the Nazi-Soviet Pact of 1939 which was condemned by the Soviet Parliament during the *Glasnost* era of the 1990s. The process then of confronting the great purges of the 1930s, and the more general state violence and oppression of the Communist era, was similarly abandoned in the 2000s. Whereas only 19 per cent approved of Stalin's activities in 1998 according to public opinion polls, the percentage in 2008 was 53 and, the following year, an inscription honouring Stalin, 'We were raised by Stalin on loyalty to the people [...]', was unveiled at the restored Kursk underground railway station in Moscow. The underground rail system was regarded as one of the triumphs of the Soviet system. That such an unveiling would have been unlikely a decade earlier serves to qualify the idea that, because 'the Great Patriotic War' with Germany in 1941–5 has never ended for the citizens of the Soviet Union, state propaganda continues to strike a strong resonance with, and shape, the individual experiences and memories of the period.[44]

The failure to confront the Communist era is the case not only with public statements but also with memorials. There are few memorials to the victims of Stalinism and most of them do not make the brutality and scale of the massacres apparent. The Putin government did not respond to the idea of a national museum and monument dedicated to the victims of Communist terror.[45] In 2013, indeed, there were proposals to memorialize Leonid Brezhnev, a Soviet leader involved, as First Secretary of the Communist Party from 1964 to 1982, in repression abroad (suppressing the Czech Prague Spring in 1968) and at home, but, by 2013, applauded in public opinion polls.

Repositioning Historical References

Such a situation is far from uncommon. Across the world, the self-interest, brutalities and corruption of the twentieth century are read in terms of the interest of governing parties, and usually in order to provide an account that is not only acceptable but that supports the present situation. At the same time, regime self-interest at the national level co-exists with the attempts to create an international moral and legal order grounded on human rights and on the historical experience of their breach. The Holocaust serves as a global lesson through the internationalization of its remembrance.[46]

The Holocaust also offers an instructive account of how academic historiographical developments both interact, and do not interact, with changes in public history. Thus, the emphasis in recent years in the scholarship has been less on the extermination camps and more on the slaughter of Jews as the German forces advanced into the Soviet Union in late 1941. The latter emphasis has led to a stress on the degree of co-operation by allies, such as Romania, and by sections of the local population, for example in Latvia.[47] In this, there has been a recovering of a local memory that had been neglected or suppressed.

At the same time, the collapse of the Communist system led to a re-examination of public history, and one that involved the repositioning of national accounts. As in Romania and Hungary, the latter could involve attempts to justify wartime co-operation with Germany, attempts that were linked to the creation of acceptable historical pedigrees for present-day political movements.

The flux in European historical consciousness can also be seen in the changing image of Germany. During the Cold War, a pre-history for West Germany was discerned in the Germany that had been replaced in the nineteenth century by French conquest and, later, Prussian nationalism: the earlier situation of the Holy Roman Empire and the 'Third Germany'. The former, abolished by Napoleon in 1806, was presented as a prelude to the federalism of West Germany, and the latter was seen as a positive alternative to Prussia and Austria. Post-Cold War German reunification, in contrast, has led to a more positive account of Prussia, which had previously been associated with Imperial, Nazi and Communist Germany. Instead, an account of Prussia as tolerant of religious minorities, and not simply militaristic, has been offered, an account that has enjoyed considerable support from the German government. Aspects of political liberalism in Prussia's history have been emphasized.

Processes of change in Germany, and elsewhere, are accompanied by a new geography of the past, notably in the shape of new museums, street names, statues and celebrations. In 2004, the Museum of the Warsaw Uprising opened, commemorating the rising against German occupation in 1944. In the Communist era, in contrast, the role of the Polish Home Army in resisting the Germans was downplayed in favour of the Communist Red Army.

This post-Communist trend also entails, generally more silently, a suppression of the past, as in 1991 when the statue of Felix Dzerzhinsky was removed from Lubyanskaya Square in Moscow in response to public pressure. The founder of the Cheka, the Soviet secret police, Dzerzhinsky was a keen advocate of a murderous implementation of class warfare. Communist public art has generally been gathered away. In Sofia, the capital of Bulgaria, the Museum of Socialist Art, opened in 2011, houses the art of the Communist era (1946–89), including a large statue of Lenin, the founder of the Soviet Union, and paintings of heroic workers. The museum was originally to have been called the Museum of Totalitarian Art.

The past therefore is changing (or rather changed) in the search for present meaning – but rarely in a clear and unproblematic fashion. When Afrikaners in South Africa took from 2007 to singing *De La Rey*, a tribute to Koos de la Rey, an unyielding Boer general, this song was seen by some as a rejection of the post-apartheid South Africa, and by others as a reawakening of Afrikaner pride that was compatible with such a South Africa.

More significantly has come the process of offering an historical account of religions that remove or lessen the expression of traditional hostilities. In particular, Pope John XXIII (r. 1958–63) encouraged the Second Vatican Council to remove from the Catholic liturgy and catechisms all reference to Jews as having a collective guilt for the crucifixion of Christ.

And so also at the national level. In New Zealand, there has been an attempt to give greater voice to Maori accounts of the past, as part of a national reconciliation on the basis of equality. At the same time, this process has been criticized, as in the general election of 2005 when the centre-right opposition National Party attacked what its leader termed the 'grievance industry' centred on Maori land claims. He promised an end to the numerous claims and the reversal of any legislation granting special privileges to Maoris. He lost. What is termed by its critics 'black armband' history, with reference to the treatment of the Aborigines, has also proved highly controversial in Australia.

In a very different context, it has proved possible to adopt a new account of the past, as in the case of the Italian Gianfranco Fini, from 1987 the head of the *Movimento Sociale Italiano*, the descendant of the outlawed Fascist party. Fini had described Mussolini as 'the greatest statesman of the 20th century'. However, by 2009, he could tell the congress of the MSI's descendant, the *Alleanza Nazionale*, which he established in 1994: 'We have come to terms with our past, we have said clear words of condemnation on Italian history between the two wars.'

Conclusions

Whether or not commentators approve of particular manifestations of the presentation of the past, the habit of state direction is a powerful one, while the lack of ready alternatives to history as a means for national identity appears clear, and certainly in the West. The decline in ideological or party political commitment across much of the Western world from the 1990s is an important aspect of this stress on history. Religion cannot provide a comparable civil politics in most states, not only because of the decline in many of popular religious observance, let alone conviction, but also as a result of the weakness of the concept and practice of state churches. This weakness is in part related to the growth of religious activity outside these churches. Moreover, education across most of the world is under state, not religious, control. Thus, the state remains the prime institutional focus for accounts of history.

CHAPTER TEN

Post-1990: History Wars

China and Japan

The serious crisis in relations between China and Japan in the 2010s focused on competing claims in the East China Sea, notably to uninhabited islands that were differently named by the two powers: the Senkakus, controlled by Japan, are called Diaoyu by China. Names are also an issue in other disputes. In the South China Sea, the islands generally known as the Paracels, which are claimed by Vietnam and Taiwan, are called the Xisha by China, which has controlled them since expelling Vietnam in 1974.

In part, the use of history that was at stake in the East China Sea was a classic one, with rival territorial claims advanced through very different accounts of the situation there over the past century and before. To China, the islands are an historical part of the Taiwan prefecture of Fujian province, later the province of Taiwan, seized by Japan in 1895, and rightfully Chinese. In contrast, Japan sees the islands as part of the Ryukyu chain (now the Okinawa prefecture) that were unclaimed until discovered by Japan in 1884.

Such was the traditional agenda of diplomacy, one matched by competing claims between powers in the South China Sea, and between Britain and Argentina over the Falklands/Malvinas. The history employed in all these cases was heavily legalistic and textual in tone and content. The Japanese government's purchase of three of the islands from a private Japanese owner in 2012 raised tensions.

There was also, as was/is frequent in these cases, a broader use of history in play as major efforts were made to mobilize public support. This interpretation appears especially pertinent in the Chinese case with reference to the controversy with Japan. National coherence is very much the goal of presentist history in China, and nationalism is employed to that end. The brutal suppression by the government of the pro-democracy demonstrations in Tiananmen Square in Beijing in 1989 was followed by a major effort to use nationalism to support the Communist system.

The 1989 episode was brushed over, flag-raising ceremonies became mandatory in schools, museums were presented as 'patriotic education bases', and, in 1991, Jiang Zemin praised patriotic education as a means to stop the young worshipping the West. Jiang was the General Secretary of the Chinese Communist Party from 1989 to 2002 and President from 1993 to 2002. The West appeared as the Manichean foe in this public history,[1] which was ironic, as China was then both a strategic partner of the USA and had a key economic relationship with it.

A portrayal of past humiliation for China,[2] notably in the nineteenth century, justified a resistance to liberalism as a foreign model. Xi Jinping, the General Secretary from 2012 and President from 2013, has pressed for the fulfilment of a 'Chinese Dream', in which national self-assertion is linked to the end of what is presented as historical humiliations. The first mention of his dream of 'the great revival of the Chinese nation' was made at the National Museum in Beijing, where the 'Road to Revival' exhibit counterpoints humiliation at the hands of colonial powers with revival under the Communists. In March 2013, Xi Jinping returned to the theme when accepting the Presidency, while, in April, its inclusion in school textbooks was ordered by Liu Yunshan, in effect the party's propaganda head. This theme has also been taken up by figures linked to the Chinese military.

Moreover, the commercial nationalism sponsored by the modern Chinese government is deliberately counterposed to a free trade order of liberal universalism. The latter is presented in terms of a hostile historical pedigree, including past Western pressure to open up the Chinese economy. This thesis is encouraged by the degree to which rule by non-Chinese dynasties, notably the Manchu (1644–1912), is made acceptable with the argument (now controversial) that conquerors were absorbed by Chinese civilization and thus sinicized (made Chinese). This argument suited nationalists and could not be applied to Western or Japanese pressure.[3] In the shorter term, China's government became more nationalist from the start of the 2010s. In May 2013, China's leading state newspaper, the *People's Daily*, called for the Ryukyu Islands to be handed over to China; the most important one, Okinawa, is host to a major American base.

Particular anger is focused on the eight-nation international force that suppressed the Boxer Uprising, a violent anti-foreigner movement in 1900. The Japanese provided the largest contingent in this force, which otherwise included American and European troops. Anger today is directed not only against foreign powers, but also at those Chinese seen as collaborators with them. Sensitivity over the latter led to rage when sixty Chinese Catholics killed by the Boxers were declared saints in 2000, a decision announced on China's national day, 1 October, and treated by the Chinese government as a 'gross insult'.

As a minor theme, Chinese nationalism also offered a way to help reconcile Nationalist China (Taiwan) to Chinese Communist control, thus completing the consolidation of Communist rule over the Chinese state of the inter-war years. Such an outcome was not going to come from any stress on Communism and on ideological divisions with free-market liberalism, the latter the pattern in Taiwan. Instead, a focus on Japan, past and present, underlines the extent to which Chinese survival against Japanese attack in 1931–45 opened the way for China to offer a new nationalist agenda, one that went beyond Chinese divisions then and subsequently.[4] For similar reasons, China offered Taiwan support in a 2013 dispute with the Philippines over fishing rights.

Again, however, the focus on the state alone was/is insufficient. It is also necessary to appreciate the degree to which the China-Japanese crisis of the 2010s resonated in the public, with extensive interest shown on the Chinese internet, a situation that contrasted with the limited media opportunities earlier available. The explanations that were advanced accordingly in China in the 2010s did not reflect the iron hand of Communist Party dogma alone, as would have been the case in the 1970s and 1980s. Instead, the burgeoning internet lent itself to the more traditional forms of spreading news as rumour and gossip. At the same time, the internet gave news, rumour and gossip an immediacy and political importance otherwise lacking with these forms.

Grievance provided the easiest way to mobilize identity and to expound policy. Anti-Japanese programmes became very common on Chinese television in the early 2010s, many produced by Hengdian World Studios. The popularity of the stories of war with a villainous Japan in 1931–45 ensured their production.

Moreover, the use of grievance in this fashion by one party encouraged its use by another. The copycat nature of public history was readily apparent in rival Chinese and Japanese demonstrations in late 2010.

Like the Chinese press, which, due to its dependency, generally very much reflects the Communist Party line, much of the content on the Chinese internet linked the crisis over the East China Sea to China's historical woes, and, in particular, to the full-scale war of conquest launched by Japan in 1937. The theme in China was that history demonstrated the seriousness of Japanese expansionism for China, while the current crisis allegedly provided further evidence of the continuity of this expansionism, and thus of the lessons to be learned from history. This account, moreover, provides a rationale for the marked growth of Chinese military expenditure. Indeed, in 2002–12, China had an average annual growth in its military budget of 15.6 per cent, which suggested that, by 2022, its military budget would overtake that of the USA.

As with much of the public use of history, the Chinese discussion of relations with Japan was scarcely an approach that welcomed more than one point of view, and, in particular, the account of Japanese policy was singularly ahistorical. This approach was similar to that taken by the Communist bloc when discussing West Germany, and, notably, its rearmament in the mid-1950s. The militaristic Japanese expansionism of the 1870s–1940s was taken by China as a descriptive model for the very different constitutional system, political culture and foreign policy of modern Japan. Moreover, anything from modern Japan that appeared to fit the bill was employed ruthlessly by Chinese critics. Past aggression is used by China to pressure Japan into publicly renouncing any intention of reverting to an interventionist military posture, and, during the Cold War, played a role in Chinese opposition to the American alliance system.[5]

And, indeed, on the side of Japan, there were aspects of a treatment of history that appeared, however misleadingly, to suggest a continuity with a menacing past, a nationalism that is backward-looking in the most troubling of ways. In particular, honouring the war-dead in the Yasukuni shrine in Tokyo (see p. 107) has been presented as respecting those who were war criminals and are buried there. This practice is linked to a tendency in Japan (although not in all quarters) to deny responsibility, both for the war and for the brutalities it produced. China and South Korea are especially sensitive on this point. Korea was a Japanese colony that was brutally treated. There has been particular and longstanding anger, seen most recently in the South Korean press in early 2013, over Japanese attempts to deny the use of force to provide 'comfort women' for their troops; abduction, rape and brutality all played a major role in this episode, which involved many women in enforced prostitution. These issues are linked to a wider geopolitics of remembering and forgetting in Asia.

The growing tendency by many Japanese politicians to adopt a nationalist position is fed into what has become a potent brew of international grievance in East Asia. Current Japanese policy, such as discussion about the possibility of developing nuclear weaponry, is approached by critics in this historical context, even though the more appropriate one, in that case, is that of the already existing nuclear armaments of three nearby powers, Russia, China and North Korea, each of which challenge Japanese security. Thus, when Shinzo Abe, who became Prime Minister of Japan in 2012, declared, in early 2013, that Tokyo will 'resolutely defend our nation's land, waters and skies', such comments are interpreted as aggressive.

The majority of the Japanese Cabinet currently decry apology diplomacy. In doing so, they link a number of trends. In part, it is a question of justifying ancestors and thus family. For example, Abe's grandfather, Nobusuke Kishi, played a key role in the economic development of occupied Manchuria in the 1930s, a development that rested on conquest and that was focused on the interests of Japan. Kishi was imprisoned by the Americans as a suspected Class A war criminal and was later Prime Minister (1957–60). In April 2012, in a meeting with Diet (Parliament) members, Abe suggested that Japan was not really the aggressor in the wars of 1931–45.

In part, there are the questions of present policy and of possible future developments. Abe and many of his colleagues criticize the post-war peace settlement and, in particular, the pacifist constitution that was imposed on Japan by the American occupiers in 1947. There is pressure to acknowledge Japan's right to armed forces, to restore the role of the Emperor as head of state, to stress collective duties over individual rights, and to make it easier to revise the constitution. Abe also wishes the education law changed, because he argues that it undervalues patriotism. Hakubun Shimomura, the Education Minister, wants the war-crimes trials of 1946–8, and the Murayama statement of 1995 expressing remorse for Japanese atrocities, both repealed. He has referred to the post-war period as a 'history of Japan's destruction', in an interpretation that puts the focus on the supposed slights involved in being under America's protective umbrella, rather than on massive economic expansion from the late 1940s.

The root of this situation is attributed by Japanese revisionists to victors' justice on the part of the Americans after the Second World War. Therefore, the account of the war is regarded as of major significance. In particular, there is hostility to accepting responsibility for the war with America (1941–5) and a tendency, instead, to blame the USA for seeking to thwart Japanese policy in Asia, a policy that is presented as somehow justifying the surprise attack on Pearl Harbor. Of the nineteen in the Japanese Cabinet at the start of 2013, fourteen are members of the League for Going to Worship Together at Yasukuni, thirteen back Nihon Kaigi, a nationalist think-tank in favour of what are presented as 'traditional values', and nine belong to the parliamentary association supporting a change in history teaching at school.

The significance of the history war between China and Japan is precisely that discussion of historical episodes, and of responsibility for them, plays a major role in the current politics of the struggle, and in both China and Japan, which are, since they changed position in 2010, the second and third largest economies in the world respectively. Particular gestures, such as the visit of prominent Japanese politicians to the Yasukuni shrine, including Abe's deputy, are treated as of major significance.

The coverage of historical episodes also excites widespread attention. Thus, there is great Chinese sensitivity to the way in which the Nanjing massacre of 1937 is reported in Japan, and notably in textbooks and the media. In turn, nationalists in Japan have reportedly downplayed the scale and significance of the massacre. The treatment of the issue in Japanese textbooks and public debate has proved the basis of legal cases and continues to do so. In 2013, much of the Cabinet wanted school textbooks rewritten so as to minimize Japanese aggression even more than is already the case.

China's understanding of the force of cultural confrontation is seen with efforts to stop or censor international providers of information, notably Google, Facebook, Wikipedia and Hollywood, and also with China's use of the internet as a tool of policy, notably in hacking government and company websites. Culture as a self-conscious issue and means is more to the fore in the effort to assert the state's view of Chinese identity, as with the propagation of Confucius Institutes. The extent to which culture adds value and values to power also encourages the invention of traditions elsewhere in the region, as in Singapore and Taiwan. This invention is an aspect of a serious historically grounded cultural competition in East Asia that is ever more self-consciously organized.

An instance of the sensitivities caused by different histories arose in November 2010 when the British trade delegation, led by David Cameron, the Prime Minister, visiting Beijing was asked to remove the poppies they were wearing because they were taken to refer to the Anglo-Chinese Opium Wars of 1839–42 and 1856–60. These wars, the very title of which reflected a pejorative account of British motivation that is less than complete, were seen both as a national humiliation for China and as the cause of a far greater subsequent foreign intervention that gravely weakened China. The issue has been presented on screen with Xie Jin's film *The Opium War* (1997). The British, however, refused to put aside the poppies, which are worn in memory of the war dead. In fact, as a reminder of the slippery case of drawing parallels, the British poppies, which symbolize French poppies from the First World War battlefields of Flanders, are very different to those from which opium is derived.

The Armenian Massacres

Whereas the quarrel between Germany and Russia in early 2013 was a limited one, over the failure of the latter to return art looted by Soviet forces occupying much of Germany after the Second World War, there are other history wars of the China-Japan type, for example that between Armenia and Turkey. Again, massacres play a role, in this case the large-scale massacres of Armenians in the Turkish Empire in 1915, and the Turkish tendency to minimize or deny them, and to extenuate and contextualize the episode in terms of Armenian support for Turkey's wartime opponent, Russia, as well as the suffering of the Turkish population. Thus, books that detail the massacres can expect to be denied publication in Turkey. Those who speak on the subject in Turkey can anticipate not being invited back to lecture. The promising scholarly re-evaluation organized since 2000 by the Workshop on Armenian and Turkish Studies[6] has had little resonance in Turkish public opinion, but, across the world, academic revisionism has not generally had much impact on public history based upon debatable interpretations, if not inventions. In 2005, the Turkish Justice Minister denounced in Parliament the organizers of a conference on 'Armenians in the Late Ottoman Empire' for 'stabbing Turkey in the back'.[7]

In practice, brutal 'ethnic cleansing' by nationalists keen on a Turkish identity is now viewed by historians as the root cause of the massacres.[8]

The historical significance of this issue rests not only on the treatment of the Armenians, for whom it is the traumatic episode of their modern history, but also on what it says about Turkey's development, as nationalism helped turn the polyglot Ottoman Empire into a sectarian state, a process also marked by changing Armenian and Kurdish place names into Turkish in the 1930s.[9] Denial of the Armenian massacres has been linked to the Holocaust debate (which, in fact, is not a case of comparing like with like) and, thus, to the question of Turkey's membership of the European Union, as Holocaust denial is now a crime there.

The transition of Turkey from a polyglot into a sectarian state was seen more widely in the age of nationalism, and also reaches into the more recent world, as in the conflicts in Rwanda and Yugoslavia in the 1990s. In turn, drawing parallels can be highly controversial. Thus, a Turkish nationalist would not appreciate any suggestion of any parallel with the genocide of Tutsis in Rwanda in 1994. Reference to Yugoslavia is controversial because the argument that the Muslims of Bosnia and Kosovo posed a threat was the excuse used by Serbian nationalists to employ murderous tactics in an attempt to stop them winning independence from Serbian control. The Serbs drew on a culture in which there was frequent mention of the experience, from 1389 to 1817, of Ottoman conquest and rule. Serbian epic poetry of the past was used to encourage the killing of opponents.

The Armenian massacre issue has played out widely, with hostile coverage in other states, notably France and the USA, judged unacceptable by Turkey. A tension arises between these condemnations and the expedients of alliance politics, and this tension is important to the competing usage of history. In 2008, Admiral William Fallon, the head of US Central Command, the branch of the military dealing with the Middle East, was forced to retire, not only because of differences over policy towards Iran and Iraq, but also for criticizing Congress for considering a resolution describing the massacres as genocide. For their own history, Western states lack the official sensitivity displayed by Turkey in this case.

Persecution and the Past

The memory of persecution is a major issue and key means in contemporary history, or at least an acknowledged issue and means. This situation contributes strongly to the process by which the establishment of identity in, and through, time explains the extent to which education, celebration and reconciliation focus on accounts of the past. 'Truth commissions' can thereby serve as agents of nationalism and national identity, and, at least, produce distinctive authorized national accounts. Moreover, historiography becomes an aspect of the competition of memories, a competition that records both views of the past, and hopes and fears of the future.[10]

At the same time, the argument of persecution is also employed by perse-cutors and would-be persecutors. Thus, ignoring Germany's role in causing the First World War, Hitler presented Germany as the victim of the 1919 Versailles peace settlement, and, more specifically, focused on the alleged hardships of Germans ruled by the new states of Czechoslovakia and Poland. This process was also displayed in Nazi paranoia and propaganda about Jews who, without any cause, were presented as exploiting Germans, both in the past and in the present.

Sri Lanka

Other history wars, while also involving violence, were/are more subtle. For example, in Sri Lanka, the emphasis on a Sinhalese Buddhist national cultural identity has led to a downplaying of the integral role of the Tamil population of Sri Lanka, many of whom are Hindu. Moreover, the (accurate) presentation of the Tamils as more likely to serve the British colonial rulers from 1795 to 1948 also serves to imply that they were, and therefore are, somehow less patriotic and nationalist, and, instead, are un-Sri Lankan, like the British themselves. The two themes are linked in British colonial support for education, which proved of particular benefit to Tamils seeking employment in public service, while the Sinhalese then preferred to focus on agriculture. A harsher tone is offered by seeing this as an instance of British policies of 'divide and rule'. This approach criticizes Britain, but also serves to present Tamil assertiveness, let alone separatism, as a legacy of imperial misgovernment and one that is out of place in modern Sri Lanka.

Furthermore, distant national history is brought into the equation. This history stresses the destruction of the wonders of medieval Sri Lankan civilization, notably the ruined one-time capital cities, Andradhapura and Polonnaruwa, by invading Indians. Doing so provides another way to criticize Tamils, who are identified with the Tamils of southern India.

The process of one-siding history is extended to the very recent past with the Sri Lankan government's response to repeated international criticism of the casualties involved in the final suppression of the Tamil Tigers in 2009. Tamil accusations of human rights abuses by the army are strongly contested, and the Lessons Learnt and Reconciliation Commission estab-lished by the government in 2010 to investigate the last stage of the war cleared the army of Tamil criticisms. Although there is no comparison with the treatment of the Tamils, Sri Lanka's significant and long-established Muslim minority is also slighted by the Sinhalese Buddhist emphasis.

Even if there is no comparable episode of a brutally suppressed rebellion in recent years, the West today is scarcely separate from the process of contested history at the international level. This pattern of grievance and retribution is more frequent at this level, and works in part because states are treated as nations and are anthropomorphized in terms of supposed characteristics. As a result, good is found on one hand and bad on the other, a process particularly conducive to ideologies, whether religious or secular.

Turning Points

History to be usable has to conform to this pattern, but this is not the sole desideratum. In the search for an exemplary identity, there is also an emphasis on particular turning points and on great leaders, although, in turn, these are redefined as history is re-thought and re-fought. Thus, the First World War was, in time, overshadowed for most participants by the Second World War.[11] However in Australia, the First World War remains far more important to national identity than the Second, with the heroic, but unsuccessful, Gallipoli expedition of 1915 being the key episode which demonstrated Australian mettle and advanced its nationhood.

At present, the siege of Vienna (1683) fits the bill of necessary turning point for the Austrians. In contrast, defeat by Prussia in 1866 and the *Anschluss* (political union) with Hitler's Germany in 1938 are not seen as relevant or desirable dates for consideration. Turning to the Second World War, the Blitz stands for the British (1940) as the key event in national remembrance, the battle of Stalingrad for the Russians (1942), and Pearl Harbor (1941), the battle of Midway (1942), and the invasion of Normandy (1944) for the Americans. In 2010, the 70th anniversary of the Blitz was extensively celebrated, for example with the BBC1 news on 29 December devoting much attention to the terrible German air raid on London seventy years earlier. There were differences in tone, notably over how far to treat the attack on, and survival of, St Paul's Cathedral with reference to religious ideas. That was done with 'Thought for the Day' on Radio 4, an opportunity for spiritual reflection; but not with the *News at Ten*. Differing military histories also result in contrasting turning points; Stalingrad competes with Midway, while there is a traditional British emphasis on the victory over the Germans at El Alamein (1942).

The Second World War

Repeatedly, the Second World War acts as both moral and political reference point,[12] or is employed in that fashion. On 24 November 2010, Godfrey Bloom, a United Kingdom Independence Party member of the European Parliament, was ejected from the latter after shouting 'Ein Volk, Ein Reich, Ein Führer' ('one people, one empire, one leader', the established Nazi acclamation) at Martin Schulz, the German Social Democrat President of the Parliament. Interviewed on BBC Radio Four after his shout-in, Bloom claimed that Schulz's support for a European super-state echoed that of the Third Reich, which was certainly a misuse of historical parallels, albeit a frequent one.[13] In 2003, Schulz had been the target for similar criticism by Silvio Berlusconi, Italy's Prime Minister, when he addressed the Parliament; Berlusconi claimed that Schulz would be perfect for a film part as the head of a concentration camp.

States that lack a recent past that it is comfortable to use, most obviously Germany, find themselves in difficulties – although Austrians have been surprisingly successful in presenting themselves as victims of Hitler, in part because of the success of the musical/film *The Sound of Music*. Yet, alongside the tendency of many Austrians and Germans to focus on the travails of veterans and of those expelled from further east at, and after, the close of the war, and to ignore the enthusiasm with which, both from these groups and among their compatriots, many participated in the numerous crimes of the Third Reich, there has also come a major effort to remember these crimes.[14]

The common theme in the modern search for an exemplary historical identity is that of past adversity, with an existential threat rising to a peak in a crisis that allegedly showed the mettle of national character and thus acts as a rallying point for present and future. For China, the stress is on Japanese attack in 1931–45. This approach, however, flattens the rest of the historical landscape or treats it with reference solely to the crisis. Thus, for Britain, the 1930s become a prelude to the Blitz, and Appeasement is castigated accordingly, while the national togetherness of the Blitz in 1940 is contrasted with the divided society of the 1930s. This approach is less than completely accurate for 1940, when there were, in practice, some obvious strains in British society, as well as a difference in exposure to German bombing, but is even more misleading as far as the 1930s are concerned. Academic revision on Appeasement, however, is largely ignored.

Appeasement

Yet, criticism of Appeasement in both Britain and the USA serves as a way to limit modern debate on international relations, ironically uniting conviction commentators on the Right with the purveyors of lazy platitudes on the Left. Munich 1938 was repeatedly used as a slogan by Soviet sympathizers arguing that democratic governments, notably Britain and France, had been willing to further Nazi schemes, a claim that was really only true of the Soviet Union (in 1939–41). Munich was also employed by those on the Right pressing the need for action over particular episodes, for example Senator Joseph McCarthy, Norman Podhoretz, the editor of *Commentary*, and the supporters of the Iraq War of 2003.[15] Saddam Hussein was presented as another Hitler, and the term 'Axis of Evil', employed by

President George W. Bush, deliberately echoed the conflict with the Axis in the Second World War. Ironically, Appeasement may have given many in Britain a greater sense of morality in fighting the Second World War because it was so patently a fight that the government had done everything to avoid in 1936–9, which incidentally fulfilled one of St Thomas Aquinas' criteria for 'just war'. Similarly, lazy platitudes about the Balkans, and their alleged inherent character for violence, were reiterated during the conflicts of the 1990s in the former Yugoslavia, and as both cause and consequence of a 'devaluation of history by the public, press, politicians, and social scientists'.[16]

Grievance History

While being changed, the past is also very present for those who see themselves as the victims. An expression of anger, history as the discussion of the past also becomes the means by which this anger is deployed. Frequently, differing narratives of grievance compete. As Jack Straw, the former Labour Foreign Secretary, in 2010, in a highly partisan call for Turkey's admission into the European Union (EU), noted, with regard to the bitter and longstanding controversy between Greece and Turkey over Cyprus:

> There are two stories: one of the 'unjustifiable' Turkish invasion [of 1974]; the other of such 'violent oppression' by the Greek majority of the minority that Turkish protection was (and is) vital. Both sets of stories have truths, but because Greek Cyprus was admitted to the EU before any settlement of the island's future it is their truths which dominate EU decisions on Turkey.[17]

The use of history in such contexts provides an instructive comment on the misleading claim that contemporary history is difficult, if not impossible,[18] as more distant events, in practice, are also discussed in these terms. Grievance history may be the opposite of the far more troubling denial (of guilt) history, but, in practice, grievance histories often offer a denial of the harm suffered by others, in other words of their grievances.

Grievance history can work for, or against, the state. It can provide a discourse of unity against outsiders, including, most sinisterly, fellow citizens perceived as outsiders. This discourse can be very useful to government, but can also be highly disruptive. Chinese discussion of real and alleged mistreatment by foreign imperial powers in the nineteenth and twentieth centuries served, and still serves very successfully, as a way to suggest that weak Chinese government in those periods led to vulnerability. As such, a history of grievance is, as in modern China, a call to national discipline and resolution; but does not allow for a sophisticated analysis of the situation, or for the asking of searching questions. Alongside grievance can come celebration, generally at having ended the grievance, or at least to commemorate victories over the 'oppressor'.

Learning Lessons from War?

Much politics, both domestic and international, involves the presentation of supporting historical narratives. For example, both the appeasement of Hitler at the time of the Munich crisis of 1938 and American failure in the Vietnam War were used to justify American action against Iraq, in 1991 and, even more, 2003. Historical analogies were employed to justify resolve and to argue that a failure to intervene would lead to more serious problems thereafter.[19] In 2003, Anders Fogh Rasmussen, the Danish Prime Minister, attacked the 'cohabitation' policy of the wartime Danish government with the German occupation (1940–5), in part because he wished to rally support for the pro-American interventionist foreign policy he was pursuing.

Successes were brought into the picture in order to show that earlier failure could have been avoided. Thus, victory in the Second World War served to justify opposition to Appeasement, and victory over Iraq in 1991 was employed in order to extenuate defeat in Vietnam. Colin Powell, Chairman of the American Joint Chiefs of Staff in 1991, presented victory then as owing much to learning the lessons from Vietnam, and urged veterans of the latter to understand praise for victory over Iraq as, in part, belated recognition for their effort in Vietnam.

The process of arguing from history for boldness continues. In an op-ed piece in the *Washington Post* on 19 March 2013, Richard Cohen pressed for American intervention in Syria, in order to prevent it being taken over by jihadists, ending with a reference to the danger of the crisis spreading:

> Blowback[20] is now a given. There is no sure way to avoid it, only to contain it. That can be done only by swiftly arming the moderates and pressing for as quick an end to the war as possible. Obama, as President of the United States, is in a position to save lives and avoid a regional calamity. His dithering has only made matters worse. Give the man an umbrella: He's becoming a latter-day Neville Chamberlain.[21]

Chamberlain, British Prime Minister at the time of the Munich Crisis, the politician most associated with Appeasement, and the leader replaced by Churchill in 1940, frequently carried a rolled-up umbrella and is generally depicted accordingly, although the reference may be lost on many readers of the *Washington Post*, notably young ones.

On the same page, an article by Michael Gerson, arguing that America's defence cuts and international retrenchment was feeding 'our rivals' destabilizing dreams of global realignment', inviting 'challenges that might have been avoided', again ended with an historical location: 'It is a traditional American temptation. As the memories of Munich, or the Berlin Blockade [of 1948–9 by the Soviet Union], or 9/11 [the terrorist attacks on the USA in 2001] fade, domestic and economic issues seem primary, and the world seems distant. But the threats of the world still gather, indifferent to our current mood.' Earlier in the article, Gerson wrote: 'could there be a more potent symbol of the unlearning of the lessons of 9/11 [than the defence cuts]?'

Conversely, both the Vietnam War and past British and Soviet failures in Afghanistan were used in the 2000s and 2010s to justify caution about Western intervention in Iraq, Syria, and, indeed, Afghanistan. The paper *Lessons from the Soviet Transition in Afghanistan* prepared for the British Ministry of Defence's Development, Concepts and Doctrine Centre in 2013 warned that the Soviet failure in 1979–88 prefigured that which would be faced in Afghanistan by NATO and drew attention to a large number of parallels. This paper, which was revealed in March 2013, led the Ministry to respond that it did not represent the government's thinking. Instead, contrasts between the two episodes were emphasized, although somewhat unconvincingly so. In part, this contrast represents the clash between realist and idealist interpretations of international relations. The past was used by military commentators, not only to discuss the value of particular commitments, for example intervening in Afghanistan, but also with reference to the very process of military development itself.[22]

Reconstruction: the Confederacy, Japan, Europe and Iraq

Historical parallels could (and can) be misleading, but also instructive. For example, accepting the very different contexts, there is an important parallel between the ultimately unsuccessful Reconstruction in the American South during the late nineteenth century and the failure of the occupation of Iraq from 2003 to fulfil American objectives. Once defeated in the American Civil War (1861–5), the Confederacy underwent a militarized occupation. The Union (American) army was the agency for the new order, much of it high-minded, as a major effort was made to unite the American nation, and thus help make America a world power, by remoulding the South in the image of the North. The army was responsible for looking after the freed slaves, and played a crucial role in restoring infrastructure, building bridges and running railways. Reconstruction literally occurred and achieved much, although, notably in the South, there was later a strong tendency to forget this, one that is very obvious in the dominant public history currently on offer in the South.

In the late 1860s, the occupying units of the Union army were confronted by the strength of white Southern belief in white superiority. The foundation of the Ku Klux Klan, a Confederate Veterans' movement, in 1866 was followed by several thousand lynchings of blacks, an aspect of the Southern past that most Southern whites long downplayed and continue to downplay. In contrast, lynchings take a role in the accounts of the South offered by Hollywood, which has generally adopted a liberal approach hostile to white supremacists. This violence bulks far larger in the black memory of the period, but that memory does not enjoy comparable prominence elsewhere.

In contrast, 'Civil Rights', an account of the movement for black opportunity in the 1950s and early 1960s, has received far more attention, in large part because it is a more accessible and attractive approach to the Southern issue, and appears more pertinent to modern America. At the same time, rather than seeing one narrative as replacing another, the earlier black one influenced that of Civil Rights and, to a lesser extent, the white liberal response to it. Again, as an instance of the role of the historians' choice of words, consider the removal of 'an account of' in this paragraph and also of the apostrophe marks around the first use of Civil Rights.

Because the deployment of Union troops was modest, only about 20,000 men in the South from 1867, the army, even had it been willing, was not in a position to support Reconstruction once it was challenged by widespread violence and intimidation against black Americans after the Civil Rights Act passed in 1866. By 1877, the pro-Reconstruction governments in the South had been overthrown, in part by the threat of white mob violence, in all bar three states: in each, these governments depended on the army. In the event, a political fix led to Rutherford B. Hayes becoming President after the 1876 election, but only in return for withdrawing the troops from the South. As a result, the three state governments fell.

The failure of Reconstruction led to the encoding of racism in the political order in the South, while the attempt itself helped strengthen a backward-looking bitterness on the part of Southern 'white' society. Both racism and bitterness ensured that the South did not engage with the possibilities of development that existed within a strong America now orientated on national grounds. The different white Southern historical account, instead, presents 'the South' as suffering from a lack of interest and support by a victorious Northern establishment – an account that downplays the black experience.

Depending on the political perspective, this neglect is presented as lasting until the 1930s or the late 1960s, a choice of dates that reflects the resonances of chronology and related analysis. In the 1930s, the Democrats' New Deal brought government investment, notably with the electrification linked to the dams from the Tennessee Valley Authority, a key episode in the 'New South'. In the late 1960s, Richard Nixon began the successful wooing of the Southern whites by the Republicans, a move that helped his election as President in 1968, and that transformed American politics, certainly until the late 2000s.

Meanwhile, the Americans, in the late 1940s and 1950s, played a large role in post-war reconstruction elsewhere. In doing so, they (understandably) did not draw on the experience of post-1865 Reconstruction but, instead, created, from new, a narrative of their own activity that was to be used to justify American policy in Iraq in, and after, 2003. Moreover, the Americans, both in the 1940s and 1950s and in the 2000s, presented their activity as contrasting clearly with the imperialist projects pursued, then and earlier, by the European empires, projects which the Americans saw as anachronistic.

In the American model, there was to be transformative improvement thanks to occupation, followed by a rapid return to independence. During the American occupation of Japan (1945–52), its politics and society were transformed, most obviously with a new constitution (1947) and with land reform (1946–50). This was a policy designed to change the character as well as the form of Japanese political culture, with, in particular, a lasting move from militarism. This move was intended to anchor the war crimes trials that followed the war (discussed in the opening section of this chapter), to ensure that Japan did not return to territorial expansionism, and to open Japan to American goods. At the time, Japanese conservatives, other than those on the more maverick extremes, did not contest the reality and memory of this occupation. The American decision to maintain Hirohito (r. 1926–89), the Emperor (albeit not as a sacred figure), and not to probe his responsibility for Japan's wartime policies was important to this success. This decision was underplayed by American commentators seeking an explanation of what was presented as a more general American success as an occupying power. Moreover, whereas, in 1945, the surrender of the defeated Axis governments was accepted in Germany and Japan, there was no equivalent step in Iraq in 2003.

In Western Europe, there was American occupation from 1945, with occupation zones in Germany and Austria, but also a more general process of political, economic and strategic intervention and activity linked to restructuring. Help under the Marshall Plan of economic assistance for Europe announced in 1947 by the Secretary of State, George Marshall, played a prominent part, but so also did American participation in the establishment, in 1949, of the North Atlantic Treaty Organization (NATO), as well as American support for the foundation in 1958 of the European Economic Community (EEC), the basis of the present European Union, as a result of the Treaty of Rome (1957).

The public account of American occupation was deliberately differentiated from what was (accurately) presented as the harsher experience of Soviet occupation in Eastern Europe. In the case of the infrastructure of historical research, the dominance of the Communist state was far stricter than the Western counterpart. Thus, in Romania, the Institute for World History, established in 1937, was brought under control in 1948, with most of the existing staff dismissed.

The reconstruction of Western Europe was part of a drawing-down of the post-war American occupation presence there. The USA saw the EEC as a way to stabilize Western Europe in the non-Communist world, and as a counterpart to its membership, through NATO, in the anti-Communist one. A stronger Western Europe enabled America to devote more effort to resisting Communism in East Asia, a theme not generally brought out in the public discussion in Europe. The American government was keen to encourage Franco-German reconciliation as an aspect of a necessary European self-reliance, to ensure that the EEC was pro-American, and to press for Britain to join the EEC. The last was an aspect of the long-term American strategy to move Britain from imperial power to the supporter of, indeed voice for, American interests in Europe.

This tendency of seeing others as malleable is an aspect, more generally, of much public history, as well as journalism. The national perspective (and the same point can be made about confessional and ethnic perspectives) may allow for nuances, divisions and debates in the nation in question, but there is usually a strident 'ought to have' approach to other states. Much of the discussion of Appeasement illustrates this point: Americans, able to explain why the USA did not oppose Germany in the late 1930s, nevertheless criticize Britain and France for not doing so. In contrast, academic scholarship is more willing to engage with different points of view, not least by assessing a range of sources, and by presenting international relations as a complex system.

A conviction of America's post-war success in occupation and reconstruction in Germany and Japan was linked not only to American confidence that it could control the situation in Iraq in 2003, but also to a combination of a lack of sufficient planning for post-war reconstruction, as well as particular policies, notably the disbandment of the Iraqi army and the policy of de-Baathification. In practice, these policies proved disastrous in Iraq and rallied support there for a Sunni insurrection against the American occupation. There was a failure by the Americans to understand the specific character of the individual societies, Germany, Austria, Japan and Iraq, that were occupied, and a misleading readiness to read between examples. Thus, history was employed to suggest parallels, but without the necessary grounding in historical knowledge or that of the current situation.

In particular, sectarian divides, both ethnic and religious, were far greater in Iraq than in Germany, Austria or Japan. Moreover, under Saddam Hussein, there had been a politicization of government, a destruction of Iraqi intermediate institutions, and a hollowing-out of civil society. These processes, along with other factors, ensured that the American occupation of Iraq lacked institutional and social anchors, as well as levers of co-operation. When the Iraqi government was destroyed in 2003, people focused on their sectarian and ethnic identities and animosities. These had historical roots, but had been sharpened by the divisive and brutal policies of the Saddam regime, which, in turn, fed a sense of lasting hostility.

The failure to command the expected response helped cause the disorientation that affected the occupation forces as opposition rose in Iraq from 2003, while the attempt to dictate such a response contributed greatly to the mounting chaos that engulfed Iraq with, and after, its conquest. This pattern was to be repeated in Afghanistan, notably from 2006, and the result helped convince at least one generation of American policymakers that occupation was hazardous and required an appreciation of cultural contrasts between America and the country in question. These factors affected the response to the Syria crisis in the early 2010s.

The American experience of occupation is a reminder not only of the disadvantages of using history, as opposed to thinking about it; but also of the revenge of the specific on the general. In particular, the varied occupations discussed indicate that the world is not an isotropic surface, and that its inhabitants are not readily open to the political experiments and social policies of uniformity.

2001, The War on Terror, and Historical Resonances

In America, moreover, there was an attempt to locate the terrorist attacks on New York and Washington on 11 September 2001 in an historical context. Usually this attempt entailed reference to the Japanese attack on Pearl Harbor in 1941, which brought the USA into direct participation in the Second World War, and thus appeared an appropriate reference point for the seriousness of the 'War on Terror' launched by the George W. Bush administration in response to these attacks. The comparison, however, greatly overestimated the power of al-Qaeda, and underplayed the major differences in the world situation between 1941 and 2001. Nevertheless, the comparison served to link the Americans of the early 2000s with 'the greatest generation' praised for fighting the Second World War, an important psychological and symbolic relationship. Phrased differently, the comparison sought to make this link, a link that involved a highly ahistorical parallel and one that suited the Bush administration as it suggested a comparable crisis that required wartime attitudes and emergency measures.

Other comparisons were suggested. John Lewis Gaddis, a prominent historian with links to the Bush administration, saw a precedent in the British burning of Washington in 1814, during the War of 1812, a conflict that lasted until 1815. Gaddis claimed that this British action was a surprise attack which led, subsequently, to an American emphasis on preemption as a means to ensure security, an emphasis he supported:

> The pattern set by this now barely remembered violation of homeland security is one that has persisted ever since: that for the United States, safety comes from enlarging, rather than contracting, its sphere of responsibilities.[23]

American expansion into Spanish-ruled Florida, with the First Seminole War of 1817–18, was presented by Gaddis as the first consequence of this policy of preemption.

This use of history to provide a justification in national identity, and thus to offset the more difficult need for international validation, was mistaken, however, not least because British operations around Chesapeake Bay were scarcely a surprise, indeed looked back to the American War of Independence (1775–83), notably in 1781. The British had also operated in the Chesapeake in 1813. Moreover, the First Seminole War is most appropriately considered in the context of earlier American expansionism, against both the Native Americans and Spain, rather than as a response to the British. The burning of Washington in 1814, in which the only people killed were those who fired on British forces, also indicates the danger of using the past to define supporting parallels. Whereas there was no reciprocity in devastation in 2001, there was in 1814; invading Americans had burned freely in Canada in 1813, notably destroying what is now Toronto.

The War of 1812 scarcely merits mention in a discussion of 'history wars', and certainly does not compare with the Chinese-Japanese battle over history discussed earlier. Nor does the burning of Washington compare with, for example, the Armenian massacres of 1915. Nevertheless, the War of 1812 indicates the extent to which different national accounts are possible. The conflict is scarcely remembered in Britain, although, in the then British colony of Canada, the successful repulses of more numerous invading American forces in 1812, 1813 and 1814 play an important role in the account of national formation. Moreover, this success helps provide an acceptable historical pedigree for Canadians concerned about their powerful neighbour to the south. The burning of Toronto is recorded in the Canadian account.

What Gaddis's mistaken and ahistorical use of this episode in Washington suggests is that the past may be readily pillaged for national advantage, including by a respected historian, even if a full-scale history war is not at stake. This point helps capture the significance of the national dimension of public history.

Another instance of the flawed nature of comparison was provided by some of the comments made about the 'War on Terror', including the

American use of its Cuban base of Guantanamo Bay to hold detainees. For example, the argument that there was a parallel between the Dreyfus Case of 1894–1906 in France and the American treatment of Muslims[24] rests on a comparison of very different situations.[25] The show-trial of Alfred Dreyfus, a Jewish army officer in France, for treason revealed a virulent anti-Semitism, but he was innocent. In contrast, the inmates in Guantanamo have, at least in many cases, committed terrorist acts.

Drawing Lessons from the Past

Gaddis's suggestion also indicates the degree to which academic historians, including those of repute, are very happy to embrace aspects of what is largely discussed in this book, in contrast, in terms of governmental activity. Looking to the past for lessons for the future is a frequent theme of many academics. For example, the *Prospect* list of 'our pick of the best public talks and events in April' 2013 included Richard Evans, Regius Professor of History at Cambridge, on 'The great plagues: lessons from the past, warnings for the future', and Iwan Morgan on 'The U.S. deficit habit: what are its causes and what lessons does history offer for breaking it?'.

More generally, interest in the Depression of the 1930s was much strengthened by the major recession that began in 2007.[26] There has been focus on apparent parallels between the current Eurozone Crisis and inter-war (between the two world wars) economic and political circumstances. Some of the language is misplaced, if not emotive. Referring back to the German reparations (payments) agreed as part of the 1919 Versailles peace settlement as a consequence of German responsibility for the First World War, Charles Maier, a Harvard historian, applied the example to the, very different, current crisis: 'Not only Greeks will see Germany as the collector of reparations if the new tightened enforcement mechanisms fail to yield economic recovery.'[27] In 2013, in response to the banking crisis in Cyprus and the German-imposed bailout, demonstrators displayed anti-German posters showing a photograph of Angela Merkel, the German Chancellor, with the addition of a Hitler moustache.

Many lectures and writings that seek lessons from the past are sage and draw on considerable scholarship. Many, however, also share the prescriptive pattern seen in much public history and, in particular, the tendency to admit of only one answer. The scholarly pattern of focusing on sources, and of drawing attention to the complexity of events and to the multiplicity of possible analyses, is not always seen in actual work by scholars, but such a pattern does represent an agreed goal. This point is especially valid for those who engage with the wider public, while this engagement suggests the need to make complexity more interesting and explicit.

After the Cold War in Europe

Returning to the theme of 'history wars', the end of the Cold War led to pressure for newly prominent identities, both domestic and international, in large part in response to the apparent redundancy of the domestic and transnational alignments of the Cold War. This pressure was seen in the public dimension of international relations, for example between China and Japan, as discussed earlier in the chapter.

There was also a broader reframing of the narratives that had played a role in the Cold War. This was readily apparent in the case of the defeated powers of the Second World War, for which there was an evolution of official historical narratives along with changes in collective memories. Contingencies and practical necessities played a role in both processes. For example, the need, in the face of a public opinion much of which was uneasy about the commitment of German troops abroad, to legitimate German participation in the NATO military intervention in Kosovo in 1999 led Chancellor Schroeder to present the 'ethnic cleansing' of the 1990s in the former Yugoslavia, notably by Serbia, in the same category as the atrocities of the Third Reich. Although this was not his intention, Schroeder's approach, however, implicitly relativized Nazi misdeeds, providing opportunities for German expellee organizations to demand a greater public profile in the official narrative. Contingency in the shape of the politics of the present also played a role in Austria. Although pressure for penitence over wartime conduct increased at the governmental level from the 1990s, the role of the Far Right in coalition politics in Austria acted as a contrary pressure.[28]

While apology (or not) played a role, and sometimes a major one, in political contention and public history, there was also the broader question of how the Second World War as a whole was addressed. Long-established national patterns of demonstrating that wartime conduct had been particularly successful, and, in the case of the Allies, had led to victory, continued. In some cases, the end of the Cold War led to renewed energy being devoted to this theme. Most national narratives in the West continued with few changes. Thus, the exhibit on the Second World War displayed in the *Musée de l'Armée* in the Invalides in Paris presents, at least to jaundiced American eyes, France as winning the war with a little British help, an account that understandably riles American visitors. In the Soviet Union, the Soviet account of the war was essentially reprised under President Putin, and, if with more emphasis on the Russian nation than on the Communist Party, there was still an important role for Stalin. In many ways, the extent to which the war still played a major part in public history was such that it had not yet ended.[29]

However, in Hungary, Slovakia, Croatia, Bulgaria and Romania, where there had been wartime co-operation with Germany, the analysis is now very different to that during the Communist years and there has been a degree of explanation of such co-operation, if not support for it. There are other reasons for revisionism about the war, and, again, tensions between states have played a major role, as in the case of Poland and Russia. The serious tensions that had existed when Poland was part of the Communist bloc came to the fore after the Cold War ended. Past Soviet exploitation of Poland, notably during the Second World War, was discussed at length, especially the Soviet massacre of captured Polish officers at Katyn Forest in 1940 and the failure to support the 1944 Warsaw Rising against the Germans.

There were also marked changes in the treatment of the Cold War once it had ended, again with much criticism of the Soviet Union by former members of the Communist bloc. Thus, the past interacted with the present, with animosities framed by the former affecting the latter, while the issues and anxieties of the present determined the understanding and presentation of the past.

Anti-Imperialism

The anti-imperialism discussed in Chapter Eight has also continued to be potent, and in the public and academic spheres in both former colonies and the once-imperial powers. This depiction extends from the printed page to cinema, from public commemorations to museums.[30] The competing histories of anti-imperialism can be seen in states taken over in recent decades such as Tibet, occupied by Chinese troops in 1950, and the Western Sahara, the one-time Spanish Sahara, which has been wholly ruled by Morocco since 1979. Polisario (the Popular Front for the Liberation of Saguira, Hamra and Rio de Oro) has run a guerrilla resistance against Moroccan rule in the Western Sahara, one that draws on a measure of popular support.

History is in dispute in this case. The Moroccan account looks back to a brief period, from the 1590s, when, as a result of the conquest of the Songhay Empire thanks to victory at Tonbidi in 1591, the Sultan was recognized, in terms of oaths of allegiance across a wide swathe of North-West Africa reaching to the River Niger. Indeed, the most aggressive pro-independence party, the Istiqlal Party, always claimed that achieving independence from the French Protectorate, as occurred in 1956, was only the first step and that true independence would be achieved only when these other territories, once under Morocco's Sultan, were liberated to become part of Morocco. Its leader, Allal el-Fassi, declared in 1956 that Morocco's true southern border was the Senegal River, a border that would have included Mauritania and the Spanish Sahara; while a map of Greater Morocco published in the Party's newspaper on 7 July 1956 showed

Morocco as including much of the Algerian Sahara, as well as the whole of the Spanish Sahara and Mauritania, and even part of Mali.[31] Moreover, for some years, given such pressure, Morocco resisted recognizing the independence of Mauritania. To this day, Western Sahara is Moroccan Sahara and the Southern Provinces.

In contrast, Polisario claims that what counts is recent history, maintaining that during the later years of Spanish rule a distinct national identity emerged, making the 'people of Western Sahara' separate from the other Saharan tribes, with their own identity. Fighting against Morocco and lengthy exile in refugee camps has reinforced this sense, giving greater substance to Polisario's chosen slice of history.

Scotland

Anti-imperialism extends to proto-states in the West, such as Catalonia, Scotland and Quebec, with grievance history playing a major role. In Scotland, grievance history, notably but not only by the Scottish National Party (SNP), focuses on incessant complaints about alleged victimization by England, as in Neil Oliver's *History of Scotland*, both the two BBC series (2008–9) and the book. There is also a rejection of the imperial legacy as part of an anti-British and anti-English nationalism. In the Victorian period and the early twentieth century, an emphasis on William Wallace, Robert the Bruce and the 'war of independence' was not the form of victim history it has become, in which all ills were blamed on England, but, rather, an account of why Scotland was a fit partner in Union, and not a colony.

In contrast, the increased expression from the 1960s of a distinctive historical tradition separate to that of Britain was widely linked to pressure for autonomy, if not independence. Much opprobrium focused on the Anglo-Scottish Union of 1707, which was presented as an episode of English imperialism, indeed as a reprise, in a different form, of the successive English attempts to subjugate Scotland from the 1290s to the 1540s.

The Union was widely discussed as a measure detrimental to Scotland and as obtained partly through bribery. The theme of disunity, indeed treason, as a cause of national weakness was one that was used in discussing the Union and, from then, could also be applied to present issues. The positive and nationalist reception of the American film *Braveheart* (1995), a heavily fictionalized account of the life of William Wallace, was indicative of a more general pattern of relating opposition to a foreign 'oppressor' to resisting 'betrayal' from within.

This approach represented a serious failure to appreciate the situation in the 1290s–1500s, as well as more generally the history of independent Scotland. Divisions in the latter extended to resistance to the state-building that was based on the Central Belt. In particular, Galloway, the Moray Firth, the Highlands and the Isles were all, for long, only partly incorporated in the Scottish state and nation. 'Betrayal' therefore is not a terribly helpful concept. Moreover, in the passage of the Act of Union through the Scottish Parliament in 1706, there were important issues of self-interest, notably economic and on the part of the Presbyterian Church.

These points were not well ventilated in public discussion where, indeed, academic caveats were unwelcome. With the creation of a Scottish Parliament and Executive, after the referendum following the Labour victory in the general election of 1997, the drift became very much away from a British identity, not least as separatism became an incremental process. The empire was underplayed as a theme in Scottish history. The new National Museum of Scotland in Edinburgh, opened in its current building in 2011, greatly downplays the role of the Scots in the British Empire. From the Scottish perspective, or, at least, that of Scottish nationalists, Scotland was regionalized from the 1940s, as Great Britain was no longer seen as a multinational polity, not least because of a smaller cultural engagement by, and with, Scots than in the eighteenth and nineteenth centuries. Instead, Scottish nationalists attacked what they presented as an Anglicization, or Englishization of, and by, a Lesser Britain.

At the same time, there was an anxious concern to ensure an appropriate national past of victimhood and grievance. Thus, in 2005, the discussion of nineteenth-century rural social changes created a furore. The academic argument, advanced by Michael Fry in *Wild Scots: four hundred years of Highland history*, that these were not as harsh and disastrous as was once commonly believed was bitterly criticized by those who grounded Scottish national identity on a sense of loss and suffering, of foreign exploitation and domestic betrayal.

Conclusions

History wars seen as disputes between states thus overlap with tensions within them, each feeding the other. In both cases, the use of the past coexists with demands for coming to terms with the past,[32] which is, in practice, a very unclear process not least for the historians involved.[33] 'Making peace with history' is seen in particular as a way to facilitate a post-colonial future, notably to confront the strains of multiculturalism, address human rights, and make transnationalism work.[34]

Looked at differently, the transference of responsibilities across the generations as a way to 'heal' the past[35] can serve largely for the reiteration of grievances. Moreover, the idea proposes a public history that is misleading as it offers an agreed narrative, with concomitant politicizing, including anger and apologies, rather than an attempt to appreciate the complexities of the past. These include the multiple experiences and perspectives that were involved in the past, as well as the range of causal analyses that can be grounded in a reasonable treatment of both sources and context.

CHAPTER ELEVEN

Into the Future

Europe and the Parallel of the Past?

In March 2013, Jean-Claude Juncker, the Prime Minister of Luxembourg from 1995, gave an interview with *Der Spiegel*, an influential German magazine, in which he used the First World War (1914–18) as his point of reference for a discussion of the current political crisis in the European Union. In response to the disparate national responses to that crisis, and to the austerity programmes to which it had given rise, Juncker claimed that circumstances were very similar to those of a century earlier as the First World War neared. He argued, moreover, that, despite the avoidance of large-scale conflict in Europe since 1945, the issues of war and peace there had not been laid to rest, and claimed that the conflicts in Bosnia and Kosovo in the 1990s demonstrated his point. Juncker specifically referred to the banners of Greek protestors in 2012–13 against the European Union austerity programme, banners that showed the German Chancellor, Angela Merkel, in a Nazi uniform.

Juncker also argued that sentiments had surfaced that it had been thought had been relegated to the past. This view was surprising given the vigour displayed by Greeks during the previous two decades over the Macedonian Question, not least concerning the name adopted by the newly independent former Yugoslav Republic of Macedonia – Greece claims the historical heritage of the ancient, pre-Roman state variously referred to as Macedon and Macedonia.

A keen and longstanding federalist and supporter of the Euro, Juncker encapsulated the use of history in terms of the false, but convenient, dichotomy – in this case Euro-federalism, or, as an apparent alternative, chaos leading to a catastrophic war, a thesis more generally advanced by enthusiastic supporters of the European Union. This was a Manichean, good versus evil, view, somewhat akin in its clarity to the American neo-conservative perspective during the 'War on Terror' of the 2000s. The many contrasts between the situation in 1913 and that today, not least the bellicosity of key leaders and groups, notably the German military, in 1913, the heavily armed nature of the states then, the availability of conscription so as to produce very large armies, and the limited dependence (by modern standards) on international money markets, were not mentioned, let alone discussed, by Juncker.

The relationship between Europe's past and present has been frequently mentioned in discussions about Europe's future, although not always with a sense that improvement is occurring. Thus, in 2000, Jean-Pierre Chevenement, the French Minister of the Interior, accused the German government of holding up the political system of the Holy Roman Empire as a model for Europe so as to favour German interests at the expense of national powers. This critique, and the German defence of federalism, drew on German scholarship, from the 1970s on, praising the Empire and the 'Third Germany' of the lesser states (not Prussia and Austria).[1] This emphasis aligned with the idea of the European Union as a union of the regions an idea that appeared to give force to Thomas Mann's call in 1953 for a European Germany, not a German Europe. Other states had very different preferences for themselves.

Future Use

It is easy to draw attention to the misleading use of the past in order to contest the present and to establish a dichotomy in which the future can be claimed. From the perspective of the present, the questions are how far this process of using the past will continue, and how far the frame of reference will change. The past certainly has a strong future. The identification and presentation, by self and others, of individuals, families and, in particular, the overlapping, but different, categories of nations, countries and states, is largely an expression of views about the past.

This expression of views about the past is presentist, in that it is located in, and from, the present, being expressed in terms of the assumptions, concerns and terms of today. Yet, this meaning of today only takes on value and force because it can deploy the past, and make it malleable and plastic to serve present purposes. Thus, the past is not fixed. Indeed, the future emerges in this continuum as a new version of the past. The future provides a fresh source of validation and expression for views on the past and the present, and a developing field for plunder for references and argumentation.

It is clear that the process will not alter, but it is still useful to ask how it will change in content, character and intensity. The most likely changes relate to developments in the global balance of power, to generational change, and to the impact of being in the twenty-first, rather than the twentieth, century. Rapid change in the present world, and the prospect of the same for the future, moreover, encourages not only futurology but also the appearance of historical studies that range into the future,[2] and others that consider the changing nature of the subject.[3]

A Developing Context of Reference

In the case of global power, the relative decline of Europe, a marked feature of the 2000s and 2010, will probably ensure that its history becomes less potent as a frame of reference and judgement. Comparisons, both within the West and more generally, will not necessarily focus on Europe. As far as the Europeans are concerned, the extent to which post–1945 Europe is now history means that it is ripe for inclusion in struggles to control memory, and thus to shape Europe.[4] In Britain, the same is true for the legacy of the Thatcher years.

As elsewhere, museums are part of the process: they answer to the present and look to the future even as they record the past, as with the *Musée des civilisations de l'Europe et de la Méditerranée*, a new French national museum opened in Marseille in June 2013. That it was not opened in Paris was a statement that the capital alone did not define history. The permanent exhibition in the Gallery of the Mediterranean is designed to address 'certaines grandes problématiques du monde contemporain: l'environnement, les droits de l'homme, le rapport à l'Autre'.[5] It is instructive to see what is left out, notably historical antipathies. In such a context, it is easy to understand why there is no national monument or museum in France for the Algerian war, the bitter struggle of 1955–62 against the independence movement there. This omission is the subject of complaint by the *pied-noirs*, the former French settlers in Algeria.[6]

With time, the European colonial empires will seem for their former colonies more like an episode of history, rather than its definition. However, even if they recede in accounts of nations, independence from these empires will continue to be important as the basis of state origin-accounts. As a consequence, colonial rule will probably remain a significant aspect of the history of former colonies. This process will maintain the politically convenient division between 'resisters' of imperial control and 'collaborators'. This division, however, fails to understand the contingencies, compromises and nuances of the past, not least the way in which people then understood their position.

This process is readily observed in Kenya, where the presidential election of 2013 brought Uhuru Kenyatta, son of Kenya's first president, Jomo Kenyatta, to power. His family's prestige rests on his father's role in helping obtain independence from Britain in 1963, but Kenyan history is presented without an attempt to explain why colonial rule in a country divided by tribalism also brought advantages that led some to co-operate. This point is relevant for the discussion of the Mau Mau uprising in Chapter Nine. In turn, Uhuru Kenyatta's reputation and position are affected by history in the shape, in 2013, of a planned trial at the International Criminal Court for crimes against humanity allegedly committed in the form of the bloodshed surrounding the contested presidential election in 2007.

The issue of co-operation with imperialism is raised in a new way by China's economic activity in Africa, a process frequently described as a new imperialism. The benefits stemming from this activity, in turn, bring in the question of corruption. The history of European imperialism becomes a way to discuss the nature of Chinese activity as both similar and different.

In the West, Latin America, notably Mexico, is likely to become more significant as a source of comparisons, and of references for a USA in which Hispanics play a greater role. As a consequence, North America will, to a degree, be reconfigured culturally from south to north rather than from east to west. Moreover, also within the West, Australia and Canada may play some of the role currently taken by Britain. As the twentieth century recedes and America changes in ethnic, demographic and cultural terms, so the legacy of the Second World War will become less significant and the idea of a 'Special Relationship' with Britain will seem an historical curiosity and, in part, a rhetorical flourish.

The Future History of Asia

On the global scale, East and South Asia will probably become more significant as the basis for historical analogies. Even though the relative position of the USA will probably not decline to the extent predicted at the start of the 2010s, the greater prominence of China and, to a lesser extent, India in the world economy, and as modern-day imperial powers, will, in turn, affect the use of the recent past for historical lessons. Thus, for example, the Chinese and Indian perspectives on the Vietnam War may well seem more significant in 2050 than they did in 1975, or today: China supported and armed North Vietnam during the war, while non-aligned India remained neutral.

The rise of China and India also represents a challenge to Western public history. The use of specific references within Western history to discuss these states may appear less relevant with time. In December 2010, when China boycotted the Nobel Peace Prize ceremony and refused to allow the relatives of Liu Xiaobo, the jailed dissident awarded the prize, to travel to Oslo, an obvious point of reference for critics of Beijing was provided by the previous occasion on which the medal was not presented, 1936. Then, the Nazi government would not allow Carl von Ossietzky, a pacifist

German journalist, to travel to Oslo. It is unclear how far such references will be effective in the future, or will seem relevant when 1936 is a century or longer ago.

More generally, there is already a presentation of Asian history designed to depict the West as in many respects long dependent on initiatives from the East. This approach represents a rewriting of the standard Western account of civilizational development and progress.[7] Moreover, engaging with non-Western histories at greater length challenges established conceptualizations, notably simplistic views about the non-West derived from long-established critical views by Western commentators. At the same time, more sympathetic accounts of Asian history by non-Western commentators can be not only simplistic but also very much geared to particular national interests and perspectives.

It is unclear how far the general displacement of attention, both historical and with respect to the future, from Europe will lead to a new hierarchy of national histories and/or to a transnational history with different priorities. The need to rewrite world history, already facing the challenge of providing post-Eurocentric hypotheses,[8] will be driven by this experience of change, raising anew the question of whether it is possible to write good world history.

As far as the use of history in China and India is concerned, it is unclear how far their greater global importance, and their stronger economic interaction with other countries, will lead to a commitment to world history akin to the spatial expansion and globalization in course designs that happened in the USA during the twentieth century.[9]

It will also be instructive to see how far Asian public history focuses on episodes in which Asians harmed other Asians – for example, the murderous Khmer Rouge regime in Cambodia in 1976–9, as a result of whose policies about a quarter of the population died, or the Great Leap Forward in China in 1958–62 – rather than either the iniquities of Western pressure on Asia, or episodes within the West of great brutality, notably the Holocaust. Mass killings and the response to them represent a form of contemporary 'judgement' that then serves to condemn particular regimes and related ideologies. Historical purpose is very much at stake in the reasons motivating such slaughters. The Khmer Rouge regime led by Pol Pot claimed that its achievements would be written in golden letters on the pages of history. The reality was mass killings as well as slave labour.

The content of the agenda of historical iniquity in fifty years' time will be instructive, and some of the readers of this book may well be able to note the change. The extent to which there is still a lack of acceptance in China of the disastrous and deadly consequences of Mao's 1958–62 policy of the Great Leap Forward does not offer an encouraging prospect,[10] and is accentuated by the role of censorship in China, including whatever challenges the legitimacy of the regime. In part, this failure may be a generational issue in China, although the, often strong, support for Stalin's reputation on the part of some young Russians is not a happy parallel. In part a reaction to contemporary failings or, rather, perceived failings, this support is an aspect of nationalist assertion, one in which ethnic hostility to non-Russian neighbours plays a role.

Political and Generational Dimensions

The more general issue of the relative weight to be placed on particular mass slaughters is that it is linked to the struggle over the memorialization of the period 1920–90, notably between Left and Right. Left-wing commentators are more prone to focus on Nazi (and Japanese) barbarity, ethnic violence and notably the Holocaust as well as the Japanese slaughter of Chinese civilians, while right-wing counterparts seek also to draw attention to the myriad slaughters by Communist regimes and to the bloody character of class warfare. The nature of future politics will affect how this argument develops in the public sphere.

Generational change encourages a different frame of reference. Episodes from the past become more distant. Today, some still have their resonance, for example the trenches of the First World War and the Holocaust, but in an increasingly decontextualized fashion as far as the circumstances of those episodes are concerned. Instead, the emphasis will be on such episodes as universal archetypes, however misleadingly. Thus, these cases will probably serve respectively as archetypes of futility and racism, which, in practice, misunderstands the first and underrates the second. This emphasis on archetypes is a classic way in which history is used, and one seen in particular with the narratives offered by religions. Looking to generational change in the future, migration and adoption may well increasingly change families leading to 'the construction of "global families"'.[11]

In the face of such pressures for a transnational or, indeed, amalgamated, history, there will be contrary drives to offer distinctive accounts. Nationalism, like confessionalism (religion), will provide important contexts and expressions for these contrary drives. Long-established narratives will be deployed, for example Swiss claims to continuity in distinctive political arrangements, claims that remain potent today in a country where historical myths are potent: 'populist leaders continue to point to events in the thirteenth and fourteenth centuries as the grounds for Switzerland's special nature.'[12]

Discussion of the future may appear fanciful in an historical work, but is especially valuable in this context because the public uses of history are intended to help frame the future. Indeed, the usage of the past for the purposes of the future, as interpreted in the present, is the key characteristic of using history in human experience. Other species can show attributes of aspects of a similar process, although not to the same degree. The extent to which computers will develop in a comparable direction is a matter of contention, not least over the ability to create conscious computers with an artificial neocortex.

Abraham Lincoln and Public Memorialization

Competition for the future, and rivalry over how to depict it, link the subjects of the last two chapters: governmental attempts to construct a coherent and effective public identity and memory, and the history wars between states. These elements are significant, but other uses of the past are also important in the struggle for the future. Presenting particular courses of behaviour as normative represents an important use of the past that can be seen in the commercial sector as well as the activities of government. A prime instance was presented in 2012 by the much-praised American film *Lincoln*. Produced by Steven Spielberg, this film was both critically and commercially successful. It focused on the last stage of the American Civil War in early 1865 and the passage of the 13th Amendment, abolishing slavery. In part, this was an account that was surprising for Americans, as the film showed the political horse-trading by President Abraham Lincoln that was necessary for the legislation to pass through the House of Representatives. As such, Americans were reminded that major achievements required mean political skills, an approach that served to vindicate more recent presidential conduct, or could be discussed accordingly.

Without the benefit of film treatment, there have been other episodes for which compromise can be emphasized, for example the presidency of Franklin Roosevelt (1933–45),[13] and indeed that of George Washington (1789–97). At the same time, compromise is not always a trait that is easy to present in a public history that, in the USA and elsewhere, generally prefers principle, heroism and success. In the American case, a classic instance occurred with the Cuban missile crisis of 1962. This crisis was generally presented in terms of successful American brinkmanship by the administration of President John F. Kennedy, notably blockading Cuba, a key ally of the Soviet Union. In practice, however, as academic scholarship has demonstrated, there was a compromise in which the USA accepted the Soviet proposal to remove American Jupiter missiles from Turkey, in exchange for the Soviets withdrawing medium-range missiles from Cuba.[14]

The film *Lincoln* also focused on the issue of slavery and its consequences, as a central topic in American history. This account provided an implicit means to defend Barack Obama, America's first African-American president (r. 2009–17), and also to present him as the culmination of American history, and thus as a pattern for the future. Obama himself praised the film. Moreover, by depicting Lincoln's opponents in a critical light, a harsh light was cast, by implication, on Obama's opponents. That

Lincoln was a Republican, as are Obama's opponents, served to indicate that that party had changed its role, and made it appear unworthy of its heritage.

Spielberg himself faced controversy, and for reasons that would not have excited great concern in 1865. The film has been criticized for marginalizing the role of blacks in their emancipation, a key issue in the case of agency. For example, Frederick Douglass (c. 1817–95), a former slave and prominent abolitionist, who was a confidante of Lincoln, is ignored. Yet, the film works for many Americans as a hymn to the USA; it provides a hero with whom it is possible to engage, and, through whom, development can be understood and a pattern for the future advanced.

As a reminder that varied, as well as overlapping, accounts of the past are possible, Lincoln was differently treated in another medium in 2012, with Vincent Desiderio's painting *Preservation of the Spirit*, which was commissioned by the Abraham Lincoln Foundation to commemorate the 150th anniversary of The Union League of Philadelphia, a body founded to support the Union war-effort. The painting's main focus is not Lincoln himself, but, somewhat more powerfully, a representation of Lincoln in the form of a white, rider-less horse, boots facing backwards, the manner in which Lincoln's horse appeared during his funeral procession in April 1865. With a reach to the modern different to that of Spielberg's film, the painting shows members of the American military from the Civil War to modern times marching across the landscape. Associating this with the institution in question, rather like a medieval triptych or chronicle, the military are joined by founding members of the League as well as more contemporary, representative members, including an African American and two women.

The Mediums of Impression

Focusing on film and illustration is relevant because, while the visual media already prove a major means of taking the past to the people, in the future, visual sources will probably play a greater role in mixed-media forms of exposition. An emphasis on visual material and, crucially, perception will raise questions about established explanations of proof and accuracy.

At the same time, there are significant developments in the written medium and its context. In particular, the internet, and the related democratization of opinion, to a degree bridge, or at least affect, the gap between scholarship and public views. Both means and content are central in the usage of history. The internet allows people to establish their competing positions on history and memory through their own websites and blogs, unaffected by peer review and professional standards.

Thus, the future use of history is likely to be far more democratic than that in the past. This democratic character will reflect and encourage changes in society and education. In the latter case, the nature of teaching will be transformed. The current model of universities, as distinctive institutions for the face-to-face teaching of young people, is already being replaced by a far more varied menu, including distance learning through the internet, as well as shorter and sandwich courses, and multi-age teaching. The net effect will be to challenge existing institutional provisions and hierarchies.

Changes in the method of provision of information, and in the real (and supposed) character of society, will probably lead to a frame of cultural reference for the past on the part of the public that results in a lower level of expertise in explanation and exposition than was the pattern in, say, the 1970s, still more the 1950s. The result is likely to be an expectation on behalf of the public of a clarity that, to many academic commentators, may seem like simplicity. The pressures for simplicity when discussing history on television and radio are already instructive.

Such a drive may well be furthered by a general decline of social deference, a decline that is linked to an attack on expertise and professionalism, both seen as inherently undemocratic and as constraints on accountability to the public. As popular views are frequently, if not largely, validated by conviction and emotion, experts will have a contested role and their status will be challenged. There has also been the rise of the 'secondary intellectual', such as journalists, novelists and television personalities, who supersede academic historians in public attention, and indeed often that of their students. This rise is an aspect of a general media-driven present-mindedness that is accompanied by a shrinking of public attention spans. The result is a demand for readily digested views of the past, which leads to questions about the role and future of history as an analysis of the past. The popularity of pseudo-histories is scarcely encouraging.[15]

The Fate of the West

Changes within Western culture raise the issue of the more general fate of the West, and the consequences of this fate for the use of history. In particular, there were the questions of how far Western liberal values of freedom of enquiry and expression will pertain elsewhere in the world, and what the consequences will be for the portrayal of the past,[16] as well as for normative values.

These questions are related to assessments of the character and perspective of differing political systems. It may be best to detach these assessments from the traditional geographical-cultural distinction of Western and non-Western and, instead, to consider the contrast in terms of liberal and authoritarian. To assume that the challenges facing the world, at a time of unprecedented population rise and pressure on resources, will necessarily lead to authoritarian outcomes is going too far, but there will probably be a tendency that way and, at least, notably in Asia, toward collectivist solutions that discourage dissident voices. This tendency will accentuate the manner in which the pressures for public myths end up producing hyper-nationalist narratives, frequently focused on grievances, and always leading towards simplification, both empirical and moral. Thus, the real complexities of life are obscured.[17]

A collectivism that does not tolerate dissident ideas does not mean the 'end of history', to misapply an idea of Francis Fukuyama writing about what he saw as 'the universalization of Western liberal democracy as the final form of human government', notably thanks to the acceptance of liberal economics by Asia, particularly China.[18] Historical processes will be recorded and discussed, however much the recording and discussion are slanted and biased. Moreover, authoritarian systems, still more collectivist ones, certainly in the present (as well as in the past), are less monolithic and ideologically coherent than they might seem, pretend or suggest.

Nevertheless, history, understood as an aspiration freely to provide independent accounts of the past, will be constrained by any move towards collectivism, as well as by the strengthening of authoritarian tendencies, however much the latter may be endorsed by popular support. Will Turkey, governed since 2002 by the Justice and Development (AK) party, an Islamicist party, for example, become less willing to jail journalists and others who are held to defame whatever the government holds dear? In the light of this general point, the most rewarding character of history rests on the liberal values of free inquiry and free debate, even if the use of history across time has generally not arisen from this context.

Conclusions

The future also serves as a means of speculation about present-day circumstances. To consider extraordinary technological possibilities therefore is to pose relevant questions. How far would history as a means of discussing the past be different if there was time travel to permit its examination? The suggestion here is not much, as the causes and consequences of change would still be contested for reasons focused on present-day identities and politics. The limited impact of scientific advances has been indicated by the case of psychoanalysis, which has not transformed history as it was suggested it would in the early twentieth century.[19]

Historiography in the future, indeed, will be driven more by social developments than by technological or scientific transformations. As, from Ireland to South Africa, Jamaica to Indonesia, the liberation accounts used in the immediate post-colonial period become less potent, governments in many states will need to develop new unifying national myths. This need will be accentuated by the volatility of societies with a large percentage of the population under twenty-five, societies affected by the disruptive impact of urbanization and industrialization, pressures on established networks, identities and systems of explanation, and the breakdown of patterns of deference and social control. The challenge posed by particular constructions of ethnicity and religion, and how they interact with historicized notions of identity and development, proves part of the equation. Confronting these challenges will involve explanation and exposition. As ever, the uses of history will be deployed in both creating, and responding to, problems.

CHAPTER TWELVE

Conclusions

Truth and Reconciliation

A 'peace and reconciliation centre' is to be built on the site of the Maze prison in Belfast, the capital of Northern Ireland, where, in the 1980s, ten Provisional IRA (Irish Republican Army) militants, imprisoned for terrorist offences, notably Bobby Sands in 1981, starved themselves to death. Initially, Unionist politicians, those whom the republican Provisional IRA wished to overthrow and frequently sought to kill, opposed the plan. By 2012, however, they had decided to accept it. Sharing in the legacy of reconciliation had become more important than the alternative for the bulk of the political community; although, looked at differently, this community now competed to claim the legacy. Northern Ireland was not unique in this process, and it represented a way in which history wars could be transmuted and contained. As a reminder, again, of the possibility of changing the impression created by altering the words employed, consider leaving out the phrase 'imprisoned for terrorist offences', or indeed mentioning that Sands had been sentenced in 1973 to imprisonment for possession of guns and in 1977 for the bombing of a furniture factory.

An optimist would focus on the containment of history wars through processes of reconciliation, and would see the duplication of truth and reconciliation commissions in the world from the 1990s as a way to ensure the spread of this process.[1] This process can be linked to trials, as in Guatemala in May 2013 where José Efraín Ríos Montt, the military dictator in 1982–3, was convicted of genocide and crimes against humanity, in his case against the Ixil Mayans. He was the first former head of state to be found guilty of genocide in his own country. The appropriateness of the charge of genocide, however, is unclear; 5.5 per cent of the Ixil population was killed, and the context was of a counter-insurgency struggle in which the Ixils were seen as helping the Cuban-supported guerrillas.

A pessimist would argue that serious disputes, notably between, but also within, states, are not readily susceptible to truth and reconciliation commissions unless there is already a strong determination to settle differences and to address the past accordingly. Moreover, as a different point, alongside trials in some cases, the very idea of reconciliation can often serve for a moral leavening that equates victims and persecutors. Such a process thereby ignores justice and glosses over inconvenient truths for the sake of damage limitation and stability.

Conversely, there can also be a failure to address the breadth of the problem, as in Argentina in the 2010s. There, former military officers from the military dictatorship of 1976–83 were tried for human rights abuses, but not the former radical guerrillas who had been a central part of the equation. In Côte d'Ivoire (Ivory Coast) in 2013, a Dialogue, Truth and Reconciliation Commission established in 2011 to address the bloody civil war in 2010–11 has done little bar providing a partisan criticism of the defeated presidential candidate in 2010, Laurent Gbagbo. Supporters of his victorious challenger, Alassane Ouattara, have not been indicted. In 2013, the exhumation of victims became part of the process of gathering evidence.

In part, there are very different legal principles at stake in such cases, notably the international law on human rights, as recently developed, and the attempts to reach a political solution in individual states. In Uruguay, where the 1970s saw a military dictatorship opposed by the Tupamoros guerrillas, an amnesty covering the abuses committed by both groups was supported in national referenda in 1989 and 2009, only to be repealed by Congress in 2011 after the Inter-American Court of Human Rights declared the amnesty in breach of the Inter-American Convention on Human Rights. In 2013, Uruguay's Supreme Court decided that the 2011 law from Congress, declaring the dictatorship's misdeeds crimes against humanity, and not subject to the statute of limitations, was unconstitutional because it was retroactive. Differing views of justice, authority and history were therefore at issue.

There are also serious practical issues facing attempts at truth and reconciliation, however defined. The ways in which societies come to terms with memories that are painful or divisive are bound up with different political and juridical cultures, and can also be influenced by recent events, such as regime changes.[2] The collapse of Eastern European Communism and the dissolution of Yugoslavia led to a repositioning and revival of the Macedonian question that affected bitterly competing accounts of the evacuation/removal of children from northern Greece in 1948 by the Communists shortly before their defeat in the Greek Civil War.[3] For truth and reconciliation to work, there must be a powerful interest in seeking reconciliation on the part of the political leadership, as well as consistency across the official narrative – textbooks as well as rhetoric, and a degree of coherence between government and grassroots actions. Such coherence is difficult to obtain and sustain.

For example, in the case of Israel and the German past, there are not only the questions of inter-governmental relations and compensation from Germany for the Holocaust, but also cultural issues. The decision by Israel's Chamber Orchestra in 2013 to visit Bayreuth, the centre of celebration of Wagner's music, led to discussion over at what point peace should be made with history and whether it was time for history and music to be reconciled. There is, moreover, in the case of reconciliation, the need for a degree of reciprocity, a willingness by the designated victims to accept the apology, but obtaining this is problematic.

The equivalent to the public theme of reconciliation is the academic stress on objective truth, and the two can be linked, as by the British journalist Anne Applebaum in 2010: 'If we remember the twentieth century for what it actually was, and not for what we imagine it to have been, the misuse of history for national political purposes also becomes more difficult.'[4]

History as a Battleground

However, Applebaum's view appears somewhat naïve, for, as we have seen in earlier chapters, history has been consistently used as a battleground for politics, identity and understanding. This situation has become more the case over the last 150 years, in what is a more populist age, one with a higher degree of public awareness due to mass education, mass literacy, the visual media and, eventually, the internet.

At the same time, there is an important distinction over the role of historical division arising from the situation between states and that within them. In the latter case, considered in Chapter Nine, there is a political compulsion to achieve a degree of order and cohesion; but in the former case, discussed in Chapter Ten, there is no such drive. Indeed, partly as a result, much of the discussion of contesting history and history wars relates to rivalries between states, for example that between China and Japan. Tensions linked to decolonization can be seen as a variant of this rivalry.

In these disputes, the frame of reference can be very wide. In the spring of 2013, Shinzo Abe, the determined Japanese Prime Minister, used the example of the 1982 Anglo-Argentine Falklands War to justify Japan's stance over the islands in dispute with China in the East China Sea (see p. 187). He argued that in 2013, as in 1982, it was a case of the right of international law versus aggression, and thus sought to snatch the mantle of successful resolve. Argentina is not a major commercial partner of Japan.

Offering Parallels

The use of history in this context involved the running together of cases without due concern for the complexities of context. And so also with other instances of the use of history to justify action against aggression. The appeasement of the dictators in the 1930s and the Vietnam War served, respectively, to encourage and discourage subsequent intervention. For Margaret Thatcher, British Prime Minister from 1979 to 1990, Appeasement was a serious mistake by Britain, as well as a stain on national honour, that was a spur to subsequent firmness toward the Soviet Union during the Cold War. Addressing the Czechoslovak Federal Assembly in 1990, she referred to the shame she felt as a result of the Munich agreement of 1938. This shame was not personal as, a child at the time, she had not shared in the responsibility, but reflected a consciousness of the role of her parents' generation. In 2003, George W. Bush and Tony Blair played out resistance to Hitler in the shape of the overthrow of Saddam Hussein, the dictator of Iraq.

In practice, the 'appeasement' of Iraq supposedly at issue in 2003 was far more questionable than in 1990–1, as Iraq had invaded Kuwait in 1990 and not to have responded would indeed have been appeasement. The case was different in 2003, as, far from having launched another invasion, Iraq then allegedly had weapons of mass destruction with the potential for aggression they entailed. Moreover, then and more generally, when the appeasement of the 1930s was referred to, it was only some dictatorships of the period that were considered. In particular, the Soviet Union, which attacked Poland and Finland in 1939, is not generally included in the list.

The iconic nature of Churchill was not restricted to his opposition to Appeasement and his role in the Second World War. An attempt to employ Churchill's reputation was made by David Cameron's rival Boris Johnson, the Conservative Mayor of London, when he began work in 2013 on *The Churchill Factor*, a book intended to focus on Churchill's character, life, legacy and 'meaning today'. Johnson's choice of topic was seen as significant in political terms, while the author presented Churchill as demonstrating the role of leadership:

> He is the resounding human rebuttal to all Marxist historians who think history is the story of vast and impersonal economic forces. The point of the *Churchill Factor* is one man can make all the difference.[5]

Historical parallels are also extended to the future. Thus, the Anglo-Japanese naval struggle of 1941–2 was held up in 2012 by John Maurer, Chair of the Strategy and Policy Department at the [American] Naval War College, as 'a sobering parable, a warning of potential dangers looming for the United States' from China.[6]

Criticism of the applicability of particular instances, a process that comes naturally to academic historians, however, does not capture the value of historical analogies, not just for politicians, but also for the public seeking to make sense of developments and discussion. Living in the past is an aspect of experience, and thus of discerning and defining meaning. There are also more direct lessons to be learned from the past. For example, historical awareness is important to successful military command, not least in the face of contrary pressures, including the cult of modernity and the sense of technological transformation. Furthermore, historical lessons of the value of command initiative offer a criticism to over-determined control styles.[7]

Deep Histories

The political manifestations of living in the past, or, at least, referring to it, vary, and, in doing so, indicate the range of chronologies at stake. For example, in early 2013, the state of Sabah, part of the Malaysian section of Borneo, was invaded by sea by about 200 Filipinos who claimed the state for their leader, Jamalul Kiram III, the self-proclaimed Sultan of Sulu (an island in the Philippines) who regards Sabah as his birthright. The area in dispute, about the size of Ireland, was ceded to the Sultan of Sulu by the Sultan of Brunei in 1658, but, in 1878, the Sultan leased it to the British North Borneo Company, as a result of which it became part of Malaysia in 1963. Descendants of the Sulu sultans received a nominal rent, a process that continues to this day, and Kiram states that he has documents from the 1800s proving his claim to Sabah.[8]

This small-scale episode is very different to the deep history involved, for example, in Austria's hostility to Turkey's possible accession to the European Union. This hostility reflects the extent to which war with the Ottoman Turks over centuries (but not since 1790), including two sieges of Vienna (1529, 1683), and the related religious and ethnic opposition, became important in Austrian identity. From that, this hostility has become significant in modern Austrian nationalism and politics, even though the context is very different to that of the wars between Habsburgs and Ottomans. Current or recent developments, for example Islamicist policies in Turkey in the 2000s and 2010s and authoritarian actions by the Turkish government in 2013, are fed into this equation.

Despite the difference between the examples of Sabah and Austria, there is a common feature. This common feature is not only the role of the past, but also the extent to which it is important in particular contexts. Looked at differently, these contexts are affected by, and in some cases arise from, the very politicization and representation of the past.

The Role of Present Conjunctures

Allowing for this point, the weight of the past is an issue of historical conjunctures: to understand the impact of the past, it is necessary to appreciate the history of the present and the questions posed then, and, in particular, how the issues and circumstances of today operate and interact. Although, in drawing 'lessons from history', or being 'led by examples', it is clearly necessary as the first step to know and understand what happened,[9] the writing of history is not now, and never has been, detached from present interests and controversies. It is noteworthy, for example, that women's history arose as a major subject over the last forty years, a period when equality of opportunity became a significant political and social preoccupation in the West. Indeed, even when Western academic history adopted a scientific culture and exposition in the nineteenth century, as it very much did in a society increasingly validated by science, historians did so as an aspect of a set of norms that implied clear moral values.[10]

An incautious use of historical comparisons does not contribute to quality debates. Instead, this use is an aspect of the porosity of the past and the presentness of history, the way in which the latter is deployed from current perspectives and in order to support the political issues of the day. Thus, *the* crisis, and thereby the imminent collapse, of capitalism was repeatedly cited throughout the twentieth century, while the Marxist analysis was extrapolated onto earlier ages. More generally, declinist arguments linking past, present and future prove particularly seductive: decline and failure can be blamed on opponents and also lend particular urgency to the demand for support in a given conjuncture when the alternative, allegedly, is continued decline.

This book itself is a reflection not only of the longstanding interest of this topic, but also of the extent to which it seems particularly pertinent at the moment. At a time of rapid political and economic change, if not trans-formation, there is a lack of confidence in the future, notably, but not only, in the West. There is particular unease in the West about the relative shift in political and economic power, especially to Asia. The election of a Latin American Pope in 2013 drove home Europe's relative decline. In response, transnationalism is an intellectual as well as political strategy to cope with change, indeed decline. It is also a reply to what appears to be another response, that of greater nationalism.

In both the USA and Europe, there are more particular political occasions and signifiers. An emphasis on transnationalism, rather than on the state and nation, as the building blocks of historical consciousness, appears particularly conducive to those Americans who are wary of what they present as unilateralism and xenophobic patriotism, the former seen in the invasion of Iraq in 2003 and the latter used to characterize the Tea

Party movement of the late 2000s and early 2010s. However, scepticism about transnationalism is more pronounced in the USA, not least due to widespread disappointment with, if not suspicion of, the UN.

In Europe, the emphasis on transnationalism, alongside a heritage rather than a political account of history,[11] is more particularly linked to the European Union (EU). In turn, a belief in transnationalism, as well as specific ideas associated with it, are deployed against the EU's critics and, more specifically, in order to typecast them as negative. Nationalist opposition to the EU and populism, both of the Right and of the Left, are presented as backward-looking, and as grounded in a (misplaced) nationalism that drew on history. At another level, there is also the tendency in academe to hire staff and produce scholarship across national boundaries.

Given these perspectives, and the present-minded nature of analysis, this book can be typecast as part of the debate over the value of transnationalism. While accurate to a point, such an assessment is not the full story because there is also an attempt in this work to give due weight to non-Western developments and perspectives that are not part of this debate in Europe. Moreover, the conviction here of the continued importance of both state and nation reflect the continuing significance of the first for curricula, as well as the importance of languages in expressing and sustaining distinctive historical traditions. From the transnational perspective, language can become a minor factor, 'the intrinsic relationship between local language and local histories'.[12]

However, that approach scarcely does justice to the continuing role of individual languages. In 1994, France, then under a right-wing government, passed the *Loi Toubon* making it obligatory to use French in the education system and in contracts, a measure taken against what was seen as an Anglo-Saxon globalized culture. Furthermore, the attempt to present the alternative to the transnational as the local, not least with the pejorative, or at least secondary, implications of the use of the word, says more about the attitude of globalizers, notably on behalf of English, than it does about the reality of difference.

Language is far from the sole issue. For example, in the case of cinema and television, very well-established differences between states lie 'behind the contours of a new, digital, transnational media culture in Europe'.[13] In turn, different national emphases and narratives are reflected in contrasting micro-narratives, competing as 'memories in the making' are developed. Through memories, individuals make sense of broader narratives. The state and the nation are far from the sole levels and agencies for contesting the past.[14]

There is scant sign that the processes discussed in this book are ending. At the very moment that the human environment is altering at an unprecedented rate, notably due to population growth, urbanization and social transformation, history continues to provide a key source of identity and a (related) basis for difference, confrontation and conflict. The American novelist William Faulkner (1897–1962), whose work focused on the tendrils and tensions of traditional values under pressure, observed, in *Requiem for a Nun* (1951): 'The past is never dead. It's not even past.' Indeed the past is alive largely because it has meaning and use in the present.

CHAPTER THIRTEEN

Postscript

Esta es la Historia (*This is History*, 1980) by the Cuban painter Gilberto de la Nuez (1913–92) offered the history of Cuba all in one image. All is simultaneous, including the landing of Christopher Columbus, the opening of the Spanish era; the explosion of the USS *Maine* in 1898 in Havana harbour, which helped trigger the Spanish-American War that led to Cuban independence; and Castro's revolution in 1959. Violence is a key theme in this dramatic painting. This simultaneity is that of experience, at once disconcerting but also forcing interest in what would otherwise be distant in time. This psychological response is not separate from the world of the intellect. The painting, with its episodes from across time, represents the complex nature of memory and thought, and their common presence in what is at once reflection and myth making.

Reflecting, in 1860, the year in which he became editor of the *Economist*, on pressure for constitutional change in Britain, Walter Bagehot (1822–77) was in no doubt of the value of looking to the past:

> Perhaps no subject of historical research should be so interesting just now as the practical working of our system of Parliamentary representation before 1832. The principles of representative government are again to be brought under discussion. The more that subject is discussed, the more do all thoughtful persons wish to consult the lessons of experience with respect to it.

Bagehot concluded with a reflection on the value of his study, which argued that prudence required keeping democracy at bay:

> [T]he events of the earlier part of the last century [the eighteenth] show us – demonstrate, we may say to us – the necessity of retaining a very great share of power in the hands of the wealthier and more instructed

classes. We have seen that we owe the security of our present constitutional freedom to the possession by these classes of that power: we have
learned that under a more democratic system the House of Stuart might
have been still upon the throne.[1]

The Stuarts were regarded as opposed to liberalism and Protestantism.

Such an approach, the use of the past to support the views of the present
or, at least, the presenter, is common to modern processes of argument,
as any consideration of newspapers or books considering current affairs
will reveal. At the same time, frequent reference to the past takes place in
markedly different national and international contexts, as well as economic,
cultural, religious, social, and gender contexts, with the differences arising
in part from governmental systems and activity and in part from cultural
norms. These contexts have changed greatly. The distinction between
imperial and non-imperial political systems is far less relevant than was
the case prior to the 1960s, when this contrast was important to the 'little
practices of history' such as the assessing of material worth recording and
retaining and its accumulation in archives.[2] A key contrast today is that
between societies where expression is free, and those where the past is
prescribed as an aspect of controlling the present and claiming the future.
In the latter case, aspects of the past are proscribed and public discussion
of them is not permitted.

The former type of society, that where expression is free, is more
attractive to most Western and many non-Western commentators, and
not solely to those who are liberal. Free expression does not mean that
discussion in these societies is not also affected by present politics. Indeed,
across the world, the role of present belief in the understanding of the past
underlines the plasticity of the latter, the continual process of revisionism
seen (differently) both in scholarship and in the fragile quality of an
experience and memory that reflects the interplay of the concerns of the
moment with deeper histories. As a result of such revisionism, history as
an understood and remembered activity is always in a state of becoming.[3]
Moreover, the general Whiggish or progressive approach to academic scholarship, that of greater insights through research, and thus the passing of
time, appears more problematic if the emphasis, instead, is on the reception,
not production, of scholarship. To take the point further, the public space
involved in this reception is not defined or determined by the academic
world.

The plasticity of the understanding of the past creates particular
problems from the perspective of accuracy, not least because that criterion
is not one that, in practice, plays much of a role in the public sphere, and
certainly not a dominant one: accuracy is asserted particularly loudly by
those who do not conduct scrupulous historical research. Instead, there are
other criteria to the fore. They do not necessarily compromise accuracy, but
they indicate different key factors in the understanding and use of history.

To take the USA, the most notable feature of modern public history is the emphasis on multiple narratives, and notably as a consequence of multiculturalism. The latter is readily apparent in the public schools, in universities, and in museums and related public spaces. Thus, in Philadelphia, what was for long a treatment of national independence in 1776, essentially as a celebration of the Founding Fathers, has been joined by other accounts, while the Founding Fathers are now frequently characterized by critics as white and male, with this depiction and definition intended to suggest limits to their relevance, if not being actively pejorative. The display boards on the site of what was George Washington's house in Philadelphia draw critical attention to his treatment of his slaves, and include the story of one who fled to freedom in New England, rather than return with him as a slave to Virginia.[4]

As a reminder of the diversity of narratives, a museum of Jewish American history, which focuses on the experience of immigration, has been opened nearby in Philadelphia. It provides a very different memorialization to the Holocaust museum in Washington. Indeed, the memorialization of the Holocaust, as of other mass slaughters, depends on a key aspect of the present: political support for monuments and their inscriptions. At the same time, these inscriptions also reflect what was believed appropriate. In a central position in Philadelphia, a monument to the Holocaust was erected in 1964. Presented to the city by the Association of Jewish New Americans, it carries an inscription:

Now and Forever enshrined in memory are the six million Jewish Martyrs who perished in concentration camps, ghettos and gas chambers. In their deepest agony they clung to the image of Humanity, and their acts of resistance in the forests and ghettos redeemed the honor of man. Their suffering and heroism are forever branded upon our conscience and shall be remembered from generation to generation.

This account exaggerates the extent of resistance, which, however, was an assessment that was attractive in the 1960s.

The stress on different perspectives can lead to an atomization of public history, rather than the varied voices, public debate and democratic grounding that is the goal. More particularly, this stress can result in a situation of confusion, as much as choice, and one in which anything goes as far as opinions about the past are concerned. That situation, indeed, is an aspect of modern populist societies.

Thus, to claim 'What happened then matters now', as the British magazine *History Today* does as a continued refrain on its cover, and to argue that the past throws light on modern issues,[5] at least by posing the right questions,[6] is to invite debate. Debate frequently produces the argument that history is simply a matter of opinion, a view often thrown at the expert. 'You might think China bombed Pearl Harbor in 1940. I can

tell you Japan bombed Pearl Harbor in 1941', is an answer to that reduc-
tionist approach. However, this answer does not address the widespread
reluctance to accept professional judgement or, indeed, traditional forms
of validation in a world in which, for many, opinion and emotion validate
views. The internet is another aspect of the current situation, as the success
there of conspiracy theorists and the reiteration of inaccurate information
and erroneous opinion have indicated.

Thus, the uses of history are again very much the product of a changing
society. New sets of stories are on offer, many, but far from all, reflecting
opinions that lack any validation in accuracy. The issue for educators and
professional historians is how best to engage in, and with, this world.

NOTES

Preface

1 For an important work that is effective on the global dimension, but less so on the role of states, D. Woolf, *A Global History of History* (Cambridge, 2011). See also, G. G. Iggers and Q. E. Wang, *A Global History of Modern Historiography* (Harlow, 2008). For valuable recent methodological accounts, J. Tosh, *The Pursuit of History. Aims, methods and new directions in the study of modern history* (5th edn., Harlow, 2010), L. Jordanova, *The Look of the Past. Visual and Material Evidence in Historical Practice* (Cambridge, 2012) and A. Brundage, *Going to the Sources. A Guide to Historical Research and Writing* (5th edn., Malden, MA, 2013).

2 V. Drapac, *Constructing Yugoslavia: A Transnational History* (Basingstoke, 2010); E. G. E. Zuelow (ed.), *Touring Beyond the Nation: A Transnational Approach to European Tourism History* (Farnham, 2011); 'Transnational Significance of the American Civil War', conferences at Jena 2011, Washington, 2012; the four page leaflet for *The Cambridge History of the First World War* (Cambridge, 2013) refers to the work three times as the 'transnational history' of the conflict.

3 J. Echternkamp and S. Martens, 'The Meanings of the Second World War in Contemporayr European History', in Echternkamp and Martens (eds), *Experience and Memory. The Second World War in Europe* (Oxford, 2010), p. 262. As an aspect of internationalisation, this book was based on papers from an international colloquium held in Paris in 2006 and was originally published, in 2007, in German. The English-language edition was printed in the USA and published in New York and Oxford.

4 D. Cannadine, *The Undivided Past. History Beyond Our Differences* (London, 2013), p. 263. For Cannadine's views, see also *Making History Now and Then. Discoveries, Controversies and Explorations* (Basingstoke, 2008).

5 For an approach of this type, U. Rublack (ed.), *A Concise Companion to History* (Oxford, 2011).

6 F. Fukuyama, *The End of History and the Last Man* (New York, 1992).

7 B. Anderson, *Imagined Communities: Reflections on the Origin and Spread of Nationalism* (London, 1983). For a detailed example based on parts of Poland and Ukraine, L. Wolff, *The Idea of Galicia: History and Fantasy in Habsburg Political Culture* (Stanford, CA, 2010).

8 S. Brawley, 'A Comfortable and Relaxed Past: John Howard and the Battle of History – The First Phase', *Electronic Journal of Australian and New Zealand History*, reprinted in *Australian History Teacher*, 23 (1996), pp. 13–25; T. Taylor, 'Under Siege from Right and Left: A Tale of the Australian School History Wars', in Taylor and R. Guyver (eds), *History Wars and the Classroom. Global Perspectives* (Charlotte, NC, 2012), pp. 25–50.

9 Interview with Paul Lay, editor of *History Today*, 5 March 2013.

10 D. Cannadine, J. Keating and N. Sheldon, *The Right Kind of History* (Basingstoke, 2011).

11 D. Cannadine, 'Making history. Opportunities missed in reforming the National Curriculum', *Times Literary Supplement*, no. 5737, 15 March 2013, pp. 14–15.

12 R. J. Evans, 'The history war', *Guardian*, review section, 13 July 2013, pp. 2–4.

13 www.rps.ac.uk

14 M. Kelly, 'The Kelly and the O'Kelly's', *English Historical Review*, 125 (2010), pp. 1481–92.

Prologue

1 T. S. D. M. Sheppard, *Taman Budiman. Memoirs of an Unorthodox Civil Servant* (Kuala Lumpur, 1979), p. 227; Z. M. Ali, 'Tan Sri Dato' Mubin Sheppard: Pioneer in the Conservation of Historical Buildings in Malaysia, 1950–1994', *Journal of the Malaysian Branch of the Royal Asiatic Society*, 83, 2 (2010), p. 58.

2 Information on the museum obtained in a visit in January 2013.

3 R. A. López, *Crafting Mexico: Intellectuals, Artisans, and the State after the Revolution* (Durham, NC, 2010).

Chapter One

1 F. Fukuyama, *The End of History and the Last Man* (New York, 1992). More fine-grained complexity is added to the 'end of history' paradigm in Fukuyama, *The Origins of Political Order – From Prehuman Times to the French Revolution* (London, 2012).

2 United Nations' projections in June 2013; S. Emmott, *10 Billion* (London, 2013); D. Dorling, *Population 10 Billion. The Coming Demographic Crisis and How to Survive It* (London, 2013).

3 K. Reader, *The Place de la Bastille: The Story of a Quartier* (Liverpool, 2011).

4 M. Ignatieff, *Blood and Belonging: Journeys into the New Nationalism* (New York, 1993).

5 J. Go, *Patterns of Empire. The British and American Empires, 1688 to*

the Present (Cambridge, 2011); G. Hubbard and T. Kane, *Balance: The Economics of Great Powers from Ancient Rome to Modern America* (New York, 2013); W. Murray, R. H. Sinnreich and J. Lacey (eds), *The Shaping of Grand Strategy. Policy, Diplomacy, and War* (Cambridge, 2011).

6   P. Kennedy, *The Rise and Fall of the Great Powers: Economic Change and Military Conflict From 1500 to 2000* (London, 1987).

7   S. Conrad, *The Quest for the Lost Nation: Writing History in Germany and Japan in the American Century* (Berkeley, CA, 2010).

8   N. Gilman, M. Grosack and A. Harms, 'Everyone Is Special', *The American Interest*, 8, no. 4 (March–April 2013), p. 17.

9   I have benefited from discussing this point with Douglas Hurd, the Foreign Secretary at that juncture.

10 For support for this view by economists, J. Bhagwati and A. Panagariya, *Why Growth Matters: How Economic Growth in India Reduced Poverty and the Lessons for Other Developing Countries* (New York, 2013).

11 L. Menon, 'Coming to Terms with the Past: India', *History Today*, 54, no. 8 (August 2004), pp. 28–30.

12 In Western culture, this would sometimes be referred to as the Ur-moment, with reference to the city in Mesopotamia (modern Iraq) where civilization allegedly began. Such a definition, lineage and appropriation for Western purposes appears more problematic from a South and East Asian context.

13 For an account based on support for the Standards, G. B. Nash, C. Crabtree and R. E. Dunn, *History on Trial: Culture Wars and the Teaching of the Past* (New York, 1997). For a critical view, J. P. Diggins, 'The National History Standards', in E. Fox-Genovese and E. Lasch-Quinn (eds), *Reconstructing History. The Emergence of a New Historical Society* (London, 1999), pp. 253–75.

14 R. Lerner, A. K. Nagai and S. Rothman, *Molding the Good Citizen: The Politics of High School History Texts* (Westport, CT, 1995); L. Symcox, *Whose History? The Struggle for National Standards in American Classrooms* (New York, 2002); J. Zimmerman, *Whose America? Culture Wars in the Public Schools* (Cambridge, MA, 2002).

15 W. F. Brundage, *The Southern Past: A Clash of Race and Memory* (Cambridge, MA, 2005); J. E. Cashin, 'Southern History in Global Perspective: Vagaries of War, Region, and Memory', *Journal of the Historical Society*, 11 (2011), pp. 425–39.

16 J. Hume and A. Roessner, 'Surviving Sherman's March: the Press and Georgia's Salvation Mythology', in J. L. Meriwether and L. M. D'Amore (eds), *We Are What We Remember: The American Past Through Commemoration* (Newcastle, 2012), p. 146.

17 P. Lawrence, *Nationalism: History and Theory* (Harlow, 2005); S. Berger (ed.), *Writing the Nation: A Global Perspective* (Basingstoke, 2007).

18 J. Chapman, *British Comics: A Cultural History* (London, 2011).

19 For contrasting views, Y. Alibhai-Brown, 'The battle for history is a battle for our future', *Independent*, 10 June 2013; H. Mount, 'How should we

remember?', *Daily Telegraph*, 10 June 2013; N. Biggar, 'Was Britain right to go to war in 1914?', *Standpoint*, no. 55 (Sept. 2013), pp. 40–3

20 T. Downing, *The World at War* (London, 2012).

21 Nares autobiography, Merton College, Oxford, Mss. E. 2.41, p. 1.

22 P. Seixas, 'Schweigen Die Kinder! Or, Does Postmodern History have a Place in the Schools', in P. Stearns, P. Seixas and S. Wineburg (eds), *Knowing, Teaching and Learning History* (New York, 2000), pp. 19–37.

23 T. Dooley (ed.), *Ireland's Polemical Past: Views of Irish History in Honour of R.V. Comerford* (Dublin, 2010).

24 F. Biess and R. G. Moeller (eds), *Histories of the Aftermath: The Legacies of the Second World War in Europe* (Oxford, 2010).

25 M. Fulbrook, *Dissonant Lives: Generations and Violence through the German Dictatorships* (Oxford, 2011).

26 P. Cooke, *Representing East Germany since Unification* (Oxford, 2005).

27 O. Godeanu-Kenworthy, 'Deconstructing Ostalgia: The national past between commodity and simalcrum in Wolfgang Becker's *Good Bye Lenin! (2003)*', *Journal of European Studies*, 41 (2011), p. 163; N. Hodgin, *Screening the East: Heimat, Memory and Nostalgia in German Film since 1989* (Oxford, 2011).

28 D. Clarke and U. Wölfel (eds), *Remembering the German Democratic Republic: Divided Memory in a United Germany* (Basingstoke, 2011); N. Hodgin and C. Pearce (eds), *The GDR Remembered: Representations of the East German State since 1989* (Woodbridge, 2011); R. Rechtien and D. Tate (eds), *Twenty Years On: Competing Memories of the GDR in Postunification German Culture* (Woodbridge, 2011).

29 J. M. Bennett, *History Matters: Patriarchy and the Challenge of Feminism* (Philadelphia, PA, 2006).

30 C. Watkins, *The Undiscovered Country: Journeys among the Dead* (London, 2012).

31 I have benefited from discussing this point with Michael Axworthy.

32 P. Williamson, 'National Days of Prayer: The Churches, the State and Public Worship in Britain, 1899–1957', *English Historical Review*, 128 (2013), p. 363.

33 A. J. Bacevich, *The Limits of Power: The End of American Exceptionalism* (New York, 2008); A. Preston, *Sword of the Spirit, Shield of Faith: Religion in American War and Diplomacy* (New York, 2013).

34 P. Connerton, *How Societies Remember* (Cambridge, 1989).

35 E. Hobsbawm and T. Ranger (eds), *The Invention of Tradition* (Cambridge, 1983); B. Anderson, *Imagined Communities: Reflections on the Origins and Spread of Nationalism* (2nd edn, London, 1991).

36 P. Gillingham, *Cuauhtémoc's Bones: Forging National Identity in Modern Mexico* (Albuquerque, NM, 2011).

37 K. Savage, *Monument Wars: Washington DC, the National Mall, and the Transformation of the Memorial Landscape* (Berkeley, CA, 2009).

38 A. Kallis, 'The "Third Rome" of Fascism: Demolitions and the Search for a New Urban Syntax', *Journal of Modern History*, 84 (2012), p. 55.

39 J.C. Jansen, 'Celebrating the "Nation" in a Colonial Context: "Bastille Day" and the Contested Public Space in Algeria, 1880–1939', *Journal of Modern History*, 85 (2013), pp. 36–68.

40 R .J. Evans, 'The Wonderfulness of Us (the Tory Interpretation of History)', *London Review of Books*, 33, no. 6 (17 March 2011), p. 12. Evans' account of history is clearly left-wing, and can be profitably approached from this perspective. His discussion of conservative viewpoints is less successful.

Chapter Two

1 Originally *Ucideti generalul* (Bucharest, 2011), English edition, p. 1.

2 Address to Budleigh Salterton Literary Festival, of which Mantel is Patron, September 2012.

3 T. Dean, 'How Historians Begin: Openings in Historical Discourse', *History*, 95 (2010), pp. 416–17.

4 H. White, *Metahistory. The Historical Imagination in Nineteenth-Century Europe* (Baltimore, Maryland, 1973) and *The Fiction of the Narrative: Essays on History, Literature, and Theory, 1957–2007* (Baltimore, MD, 2010); S. Berger, L. Eriksonas and A. Mycock (eds), *Narrating the Nation. Representations in History, Media and the Arts* (Oxford, 2008).

5 A. Jones, 'Reporting in Prose: Reconsidering Ways of Writing History', *The European Legacy*, 12 (2007), pp. 311–36, and 'Vivid history: existentialist phenomenology as a new way to understand an old way of writing history, and as a source of renewal for the writing of history', *Storia della Storiografia*, 54 (2008), pp. 212–55.

6 L. Warren, 'History-as-Literature and the Narrative Structure of Henry Fielding', *Clio*, 9 (autumn 1979), pp. 89–109.

7 F. Bouza, *Communication, Knowledge, and Memory in Early Modern Spain* (Philadelphia, PA, 2004).

8 J. de Groot, *Consuming History: Historians and Heritage in Contemporary Popular Culture* (Oxford, 2009).

9 M. Brett, *Approaching African History* (Woodbridge, 2013), p. 313.

10 R. H. Fritze, *Invented Knowledge. False History, Fake Science and Pseudo-religions* (London, 2009), pp. 221–55; M. Macmillan, *The Uses and Abuses of History* (London, 2009), pp. 72–3.

11 C. West, 'Count Hugh of Troyes and the Territorial Principality in Early Twelfth-Century Western Europe', *English Historical Review*, 127 (2012), p. 547.

12 N. Davies, *Vanished Kingdoms: The History of Half-Forgotten Europe* (London, 2011).

13 J. H. Elliott, *History in the Making* (New Haven, CT, 2012).

14 R. Taylor, *Film Propaganda: Soviet Russia and Nazi Germany* (London,

1979); E. Dobrenko, *Stalinist Cinema and the Production of History: Museum of the Revolution* (New Haven, CT, 2008).

15 K. Roth-Ey, *Moscow Prime Time: How the Soviet Union Built the Media Empire That Lost the Cultural Cold War* (Ithaca, NY, 2011).

16 D. Welch, *Propaganda and the German Cinema, 1933–1945* (Oxford, 1983); S. Tegel, *Nazis and the Cinema* (London, 2007).

17 T. Doherty, *Hollywood and Hitler, 1933–1939* (New York, 2013).

18 J. Chapman, *Past and Present: National Identity and the British Historical Film* (London, 2005) and *War and Film* (London, 2008) and *Film and History* (Basingstoke, 2013).

19 M. Glancy, 'The War of Independence in Feature Film: *The Patriot* (2000) and the "Special Relationship" between Hollywood and Britain', *Historical Journal of Film, Radio and Television*, 25 (2005), pp. 523–45.

20 M. Connelly, '*Gallipoli* (1981): a poignant search for national identity', in J. Chapman, M. Glancy and S. Harper (eds), *The New Film History: Sources, Methods, Approaches* (Basingstoke, 2007), pp. 41–53.

21 T. Yoshida, *The Making of the 'Rape of Nanking': History and Memory in Japan, China and the United States* (New York, 2006).

22 R. V. Winkel, 'Hitler's Downfall, a film from Germany (Der Untergang, 2004)', in L. Engelen and Winkel (eds), *Perspectives on European Film and History* (Ghent, 2007), pp. 183–211.

23 E.g. *Daily Mail*, 25 October 2010.

24 J. Chapman, '*Downton Abbey*: Reinventing the British costume drama', in J. Bignell and S. Lacey (eds), *British Television Drama: Past, Present and Future* (2nd edn, Basingstoke, 2014).

25 J. F. Roberts, *The True History of the Black Adder. The unadulterated tale of the creation of a comedy legend* (London, 2013).

26 S. Badsey, 'Blackadder Goes Forth and the "Two Western Fronts" debate', in G. Roberts and P. M. Taylor (eds), *The Historian, Television and Television History* (Luton, 2001), pp. 113–25; S. Heathorn, *Haig and Kitchener in Twentieth-Century Britain. Remembrance, Representation and Appropriation* (Farnham, 2013), pp. 218–19; J. Black, *The Great War and the Making of the Modern World* (London, 2011).

27 R. Hutchinson, *Elizabeth's Spy Master* (London, 2006), p. 9.

28 P. Ashton and H. Kean (eds), *Public History and Heritage Today: People and their Pasts* (Basingstoke, 2012).

29 S. C. Bruggeman, *Here, George Was Born: Memory, Material Culture, and the Public History of a National Monument* (Athens, GA, 2008).

Chapter Three

1 G. Parker, *Global Crisis. War, Climate Change and Catastrophe in the Seventeenth Century* (New Haven, CT, 2013).

2 D. Twitchett, *The Writing of Official History under the T'ang* (Cambridge, 1992); Twitchett and P. J. Smith (eds), *The Cambridge History of China, vol 5, pt 1: The Sung Dynasty and its Precursors, 907–1279* (Cambridge, 2009), pp. 41, 254, 689–92.

3 N. Luraghi (ed.), *The Historian's Craft in the Age of Herodotus* (Oxford, 2007); J. Marincola (ed.), *A Companion to Greek and Roman Historiography* (Oxford, 2007).

4 A. Primo, *La storiografia sui Seleucidi da Megastene a Eusebio di Cesarea* (Pisa, 2009).

5 Xenophon, *Cyropaedia*, translated by W. Miller (London, 1914), pp. 127–9.

6 H. Tanner, *China: A History* I (Indianapolis, IN, 2010), p. 118.

7 E. El-Hibri, *Parable and Politics in Early Islamic History: The Rashidun Caliphs* (New York, 2010).

8 A. Putter, 'Gerald of Wales and the Prophet Merlin', *Anglo-Norman Studies*, 31 (2010), pp. 90–103.

9 T. P. Wiseman, 'Introduction: Classical Historiography', in C. Holdsworth and T. P. Wiseman (eds), *The Inheritance of Historiography 350–900* (Exeter, 1986), p. 2.

10 H. W. Goetz, 'Die Gegenwart der Vergangenheit im früh und hochmittelalterlichen Geschichtsbewuftsein', *Historische Zeitschrift*, 255 (1992), pp. 61–97.

11 M. Oja, 'Fictional History and Historical Fiction: Solzhenitsyn and Kiš as exemplars', *History and Theory*, 27 (1988), p. 122; M. Baár, 'Abraham Viskaski, the patriarch of the Ruritanian nation', *Storia della Storiografia*, 54 (2008), pp. 3–20.

12 Z. S. Schiffman, *The Birth of the Past* (Baltimore, MD, 2012).

13 P. J. Corfield, *Time and the Shape of History* (New Haven, CT, 2007).

14 A. D. Smith, *Chosen Peoples: Sacred Sources of National Identity* (Oxford, 2003).

15 T. Licence, 'History and Historiography in the Late Eleventh Century: the Life and Work of Herman the Archdeacon, Monk of Bury St Edmunds', *English Historical Review*, 124 (2009), pp. 516–44.

16 R. Koopmans, *Wonderful to Relate: Miracle Stories and Miracle Collecting in High Medieval England* (Philadelphia, PA, 2011).

17 A. J. Hingst, *The Written World: Past and Place in the Work of Orderic Vitalis* (Notre Dame, IN, 2009).

18 S. MacLean (ed.), *History and Politics in Late Carolingian and Ottonian Europe: The Chronicle of Regino of Prüm and Adalbert of Magdeburg* (Manchester, 2009); M. Kempshall, *Rhetoric and the Writing of History, 400–1500* (Manchester, 2011).

19 E. Knibbs, *Ansgar, Rimbert and the Forged Foundations of Hamburg-Bremen* (Farnham, 2011); H. Antonsson and I. H. Garipzanov (eds), *Saints and their Lives on the Periphery: Veneration of Saints in Scandinavia and Eastern Europe, c. 1000–1200* (Turhout, 2010).

20 R. Ghosh, '"It disturbs me with a presence": Hindu history and what meaning cannot convey', *Storia della Storiografia*, 55 (2009), p. 98.

21 F. E. Pargiter, *Ancient Indian Historical Tradition* (London, 1922).

22 R. Thapar, 'La quête d'une tradition historique: l'inde ancienne', *Annales*, 53 (1998), pp. 347–59.

23 R. Landes, *Relics, Apocalypse, and the Deceits of History: Ademar of Chabannes, 989–1034* (Cambridge, MA, 1995).

24 J. Gillingham, 'The Historian as Judge: William of Newburgh and Hubert Walter', *English Historical Review*, 119 (2004), pp. 1275–6.

25 C. B. Kendall and F. Wallis (eds), *Bede: 'On the Nature of Things' and 'On Time'* (Liverpool, 2010).

26 C. Wickham, *The Inheritance of Rome: A History of Europe from 400 to 1000* (London, 2009), p. 4.

27 R. McKitterick, *History and Memory in the Carolingian World* (Cambridge, 2004) and *Perceptions of the Past in the Early Middle Ages* (Notre Dame, IN, 2006).

28 C. E. Beneš, *Urban Legends: Civil Identities and the Classical Past in Northern Italy, 1250–1350* (College Park, PA, 2011).

29 C. West, 'Count Hugh of Troyes and the Territorial Principality in Early Twelfth-Century Western Europe', *English Historical Review*, 127 (2012), p. 547.

30 P. W. Knoll and F. Schaer (eds), *Gesta Principum Polonorum: The Deeds of the Princes of the Poles* (Budapest, 2003).

31 R. L. Kagan, *Clio and the Crown: The Politics of History in Medieval and Early Modern Spain* (Baltimore, MD, 2009).

32 P. J. Geary, *The Myth of Nations* (Princeton, NJ, 2002).

33 M. Rady, 'Recollecting Attila: Some Medieval Hungarian Images and their Antecedents', *Central Europe*, 1 (2003), pp. 12–17, and 'Jagello Hungary', in F. Döry, *The Laws of the Medieval Kingdom of Hungary, IV, 1490–1526*, edited by P. Banyó and M. Rady (Apud, 2010), pp. xxix–xxx; L. Veszprémy, 'Mythical Origins of the Hungarian Medieval Legislation', *Parliaments, Estates and Representation*, 15 (1995), pp. 67–89.

34 L. Scales, '*Germen Militiae*: War and German Identity in the Later Middle Ages', *Past and Present*, 180 (August 2003), pp. 80–1.

35 For a sustained argument for pre-modern nationalism, A. Gat, *Nations. The Long History and Deep Roots of Political Ethnicity and Nationalism* (Cambridge, 2013).

36 L. Scales, *The Shaping of German Identity: Authority and Crisis, 1245–1414* (Cambridge, 2012).

37 D. Matthews, *Writing to the King: Nation, Kingship, and Literature in England, 1250–1350* (Cambridge, 2010).

38 A. Butterfield, *The Familiar Enemy: Chaucer, Language and Nation in the Hundred Years War* (Oxford, 2009).

39 M. Clanchy, *From Memory to Written Record: England 1066–1307* (Chichester, 2013).

40 J. Good, *The Cult of St George in Medieval England* (Woodbridge, 2009).

41 G. Parsons, *The Cult of St Catherine of Siena: A Study in Civil Religion* (Aldershot, 2008).

42 S. Boardman, J. R. Davies and E. Williamson (eds), *Saints' Cults in the Celtic World* (Woodbridge, 2009).

43 E. Morrison and A. D. Hedeman (eds), *Imaging the Past in France. History in Manuscript Painting 1250–1500* (Los Angeles, CA, 2010).

44 J. Watts, *The Making of Polities: Europe, 1300–1500* (Cambridge, 2009).

Chapter Four

1 S. MacCormack, *On the Wings of Time: Rome, the Incas, Spain and Peru* (Princeton, New Jersey, 2007).

2 E. Cochrane, *Historians and Historiography in the Italian Renaissance* (Chicago, Illinois, 1981); C. Fasolt, *The Limits of History* (Chicago, IL, 2004).

3 A. Grafton, *What Was History? The Art of History in Early Modern Europe* (Cambridge, 2007).

4 W. Franke, 'Historical writing during the Ming', in F. W. Mote and D. Twitchett (eds), *Cambridge History of China, vol. 7* (Cambridge, 1988), pp. 726–82, esp. 726–33.

5 Z. S. Schiffman, *The Birth of the Past* (Baltimore, MD, 2011).

6 K. Van Liere, S. Ditchfield and H. Louthan (eds), *Sacred History. Uses of the Christian Past in the Renaissance World* (Oxford, 2012).

7 W. Haller, *Foxe's Book of Martyrs and the Elect Nation* (London, 1963); E. Evenden and T. S. Freeman, *Religion and the Book in Early Modern England. The Making of John Foxe's 'Book of Martyrs'* (Cambridge, 2011).

8 A. Walsham, *The Reformation of the Landscape: Religion, Identity, and Memory in Early Modern Britain and Ireland* (Oxford, 2011).

9 V. Chieffo (ed.), *Art, Piety and Destruction in the Christian West, 1500–1700* (Farnham, 2010).

10 A. Kess, *Johann Sleidan and the Protestant Vision of History* (Aldershot, 2008).

11 S. Jeppie (ed.), *Toward New Histories for South Africa: On the Place of the Past in Our Present* (Cape Town, 2004).

12 S. Hanley, 'Identity Politics and Rulership in France; Female Political Place and the Fraudulent Salic Law in Christine de Pizan and Jean de Montreuil', in M. Wolfe (ed.), *Changing Identities in Early Modern France* (Durham, NC, 1997), pp. 79–94.

13 D. R. Kelley, 'Johann Sleidan and the Origins of History as a Profession', *Journal of Modern History*, 52 (1980), pp. 579–72.

14 W. B. Smith, 'Germanic Pagan Antiquity in Lutheran Historical Thought', *Journal of the Historical Society*, 4 (2004), pp. 364, 369.

15 Machiavelli to Francesco Vettori, 10 Dec. 1513, in J. B. Atkinson and D. Sices (eds), *Machiavelli and his Friends: Their Personal Correspondence* (DeKalb, IL, 1996), p. 264.

16 N. Machiavelli, *The Prince* (1513), translated by G. Bull (London, 1999), pp. 48–9.

17 M. J. Cailes, 'Renaissance Ideas of Peace and War, and the Humanist Challenge to the Scholastic Just War: the *Disputatio de Pace et Bello* of 1468; Erasmus and Machiavelli' (PhD, Exeter, 2012), pp. 107–8, 165.

18 N. Russell and H. Visentin (eds), *French Ceremonial Entries in the Sixteenth Century: Event, Image, Text* (Toronto, 2007).

19 M. Bourne, *Francesco II Gonzaga: The Sober Prince as Patron* (Rome, 2008).

20 A. Walsham, *Providence in Early Modern England* (Oxford, 1999), p. 218.

21 C. Dyer and C. Richardson (eds), *William Dugdale, Historian, 1605–1686: His Life, His Writings and His County* (Woodbridge, 2009).

22 I. Djordjevic, *Holinshed's Nation: Ideals, Memory and Practical Policy in the Chronicles* (Farnham, 2010).

23 M. Rady, 'Rethinking Jagiello Hungary', *Central Europe*, 3 (2005), pp. 16–17.

24 P. E. Grieve, *The Eve of Spain: Myths of Origins in the History of Christian, Muslim and Jewish Conflict* (Baltimore, MD, 2009).

25 D. R. Kelley and D. H. Sacks (eds), *The Historical Imagination in Early Modern Britain. History, Rhetoric, and Fiction, 1500–1800* (Cambridge, 1997).

26 D. R. Woolf, *The Social Circulation of the Past: English Historical Culture, 1500–1730* (Oxford, 2003).

Chapter Five

1 G. Parker, *Global Crisis. War, Climate Change and Catastrophe in the Seventeenth Century* (New Haven, CT, 2013).

2 Y. Dai, 'A Disguised Defeat: The Myanmar Campaign of the Qing Dynasty', *Modern Asian Studies*, 38 (2004), pp. 145–88; T. B. Lam, 'Intervention versus Tribute in Sino-Vietnamese Relations, 1788–1790', in J. K. Fairbank (ed.), *The Chinese World Order: Traditional China's Foreign Relations* (Cambridge, MA, 1968), pp. 165–79; S. van Schaik, *Tibet: A History*, (New Haven, CT, 2011), pp. 156–9.

3 R. K. Guy, *The Emperor's Four Treasuries: Scholars and the State in the Late Ch'ien Era* (Cambridge, MA, 1987).

4 P. K. Crossley, *A Translucent Mirror: History and Identity in the Transformations of Qing Imperial Ideology* (Berkeley, CA, 1999).

5   K. Sharpe, *Image Wars: Promoting Kings and Commonwealths in England, 1603–1660* (New Haven, CT, 2010).

6   Anon., *The Conduct of Queen Elisabeth, towards the neighboring nations; and particularly Spain; compared with that of James* [James I, r. 1603–25] (London, 1729); George Lyttelton to Sarah Duchess of Marlborough, no date, BL. Add. 61467 fol. 1; James Hamilton to Philip, 1st Duke of Wharton, describing speech in Commons by John Friend, 18 Febuary 1726, Windsor Castle, Royal Archives, Stuart Papers 90/128; Commons' Debate on Loyal Address, 15 November 1739, Lords Debate on Admiral Haddock's Instructions, 8 December 1740, W. Cobbett (ed.), *Parliamentary History of England* (36 vols., London, 1806–20), XI, 87, 825–30; *Monitor*, 11 August 1759.

7   The Tories were in opposition to the Whig governments of George I and George II.

8   Anon., undated pamphlet, *The Criterion, or certain tests to judge of the designs of private men in censuring public persons and measures*, BL. Add. 61705, p. 34.

9   Anon., *Reasons Against a Standing Army* (London, 1717), p. 30.

10   *Weekly Journal: or the British Gazetteer*, 1 May 1729.

11   The *Craftsman* supported an alignment of Tories with opposition Whigs.

12   Anon., *The Occasional Patriot* (London, 1756), p. 9.

13   Parry to Rawlins, 3 Oct. 1745, Bodleian Library, Oxford, Ms Ballard d 29 fol. 105.

14   Anon., *A Serious Defence of some late Measures of the Administration* (London, 1756), pp. 8–9.

15   See article by Peter Aspden, *Financial Times*, review section, pp. 1–2, 13 July 2013.

16   W. Hudson, *Enlightenment and Modernity: The English Deists and Reform* (London, 2009).

17   K. O'Brien, *Narratives of Enlightenment: Cosmopolitan History from Voltaire to Gibbon* (Cambridge, 1993).

18   W. Johnston, *Revelation Restored: The Apocalypse in later Seventeenth-Century England* (Woodbridge, 2011).

19   M. S. Phillips, *Society and Sentiment. Genres of Historical Writing in Britain 1740–1820* (Princeton, NJ, 2000).

20   H. Trevor-Roper, *History and the Enlightenment* (New Haven, CT, 2010).

21   R. Browning, *Political and Constitutional Ideas of the Court Whigs* (Baton Rouge, LA, 1982).

22   Anon., *Reflections upon the Present State of Affairs* (London, 1755), p. 9.

23   J. Scott, *When the Waves Ruled Britannia: Geography and Political Identities, 1500–1800* (Cambridge, 2011).

24   R. MacKay, *'Lazy Improvident People': Myth and Reality in the Writing of Spanish History* (Ithaca, NY, 2006).

25 R. N. Stromberg, 'History in the Eighteenth Century', *Journal of the History of Ideas*, 12 (1951), p. 298.

26 C. Grell, *L'Histoire entre Érudition et Philosophie: étude sur la connaissance historique à l'âge des Lumières* (Paris, 1993).

27 D. Carrithers, 'Montesquieu's philosophy of history', *Journal of the History of Ideas*, 47 (1986), pp. 61–80.

28 A. Guerra, 'Il "labirinto tenebroso". Appunti per una storia del concetto di Medioevo alla fine del XVIII secolo', *Nuova Rivista Storica*, 93 (2010), pp. 189–204.

29 J. Conniff, 'Reason and History in Early Whig Thought', *Journal of the History of Ideas*, 43 (1982), pp. 397–416.

30 A. Kasekamp, *A History of the Baltic States* (Basingstoke, 2010), p. 61.

Chapter Six

1 M. Shaw, *Time and the French Revolution. The Republican Calendar, 1789– Year XIV* (Woodbridge, 2011).

2 W. Doyle, *Aristocracy and its Enemies in the Age of Revolution* (Oxford, 2009).

3 E. Higgs, 'From medieval erudition to information management: the evolution of the archival profession', *Archivium*, 43 (1997), pp. 136–44.

4 D. A. Bell, *The Cult of the Nation in France: Inventing Nationalism, 1680–1800* (Cambridge, MA, 2001).

5 C. E. Fick, *The Making of Haiti: The Saint-Domingue Revolution from Below* (Knoxville, Tennessee, 1990); P. R. Girard, '*Liberté, Égalité, Esclavage*: French Revolutionary Ideals and the Failure of the Leclerc Expedition to Saint-Domingue', *French Colonial History*, 6 (2005), pp. 55–78.

6 H. Spahn, *Thomas Jefferson, Time, and History* (Charlottesville, VA, 2011).

7 J. Coffey, '"Tremble Britannia!": Fear, Providence and the Abolition of the Slave Trade, 1758–1807', *English Historical Review*, 127 (2012), pp. 844–81.

8 L. Jensen, J. Leerssen and M. Mathijsen (eds), *Free Access to the Past. Romanticism, Cultural Heritage and the Nation* (Leiden, 2010).

Chapter Seven

1 H. Hoock, *Empires of the Imagination: Politics, War, and the Arts in the British World, 1750–1850* (London, 2010); A. Forrest, E. François and K. Hagemann (eds), *War Memories: the Revolutionary and Napoleonic Wars in Modern European Culture* (Basingstoke, 2012).

2 R. Terdiman, *Present Past: Modernity and the Memory Crisis* (Ithaca, NY, 1993).

3 R. A. Vieira, 'Connecting the New Political History with Recent Theories of Temporal Acceleration: Speed, Politics, and the Cultural Imagination in *fin de siècle* Britain', *History and Theory*, 50 (2011), pp. 373–89.

4 C. Hall, *Macaulay and Son. Architects of Imperial Britain* (New Haven, CT, 2012), p. 284.

5 J. Graham, 'Picturing Patriotism: The Image of the Artist-Hero and the Belgian Nation State, 1830–1900', in H. Dunthorne and M. Wintle (eds), *The Historical Imagination in Nineteenth-Century Britain and the Low Countries* (Leiden, 2013), p. 173.

6 D. Johnson, 'The Boadicea principle', *Standpoint*, no. 52 (May 2013), p. 3.

7 J. Parker, *England's Darling. The Victorian Cult of Alfred the Great* (Manchester, 2007).

8 R. Strong, *And When Did You Last See Your Father? The Victorian Painter and British History* (London, 1978); S. Bann, *The Clothing of Clio. A Study of the Representation of History in Nineteenth-Century Britain and France* (Cambridge, 1984).

9 N. Riasanovsky, *The Image of Peter the Great in Russian History and Thought* (Oxford, 1992); K. M. F. Platt, *Terror and Greatness: Ivan and Peter as Russian Myths* (Ithaca, NY, 2011).

10 G. Petkova-Campbell, 'Nineteenth-century Bulgarian private collections', *Journal of the History of Collections*, 22 (2010), pp. 245–55.

11 S. Crane, *Collecting and Historical Consciousness: New Forms of Collective Memory in Early Nineteenth-Century Germany* (Ithaca, NY, 2000); S. Gerson, *The Pride of Place: Local Memories and Political Culture in Nineteenth-Century France* (Ithaca, NY, 2003).

12 M. Yousefzadeh, *City and Nation in the Italian Unification: The National Festivals of Dante Alighieri* (Basingstoke, 2011).

13 C. Jelavich, 'Nationalism as Reflected in the Textbooks of the South Slavs in the Nineteenth Century', *Canadian Review of Studies in Nationalism*, 16 (1989), pp. 15–34; R. J. W. Evans and G. P. Marchal (eds), *The Uses of the Middle Ages in Modern European States: History, Nationhood and the Search for Origins* (Basingstoke, 2011).

14 M. Díaz-Andreu, *A World History of Nineteenth-Century Archaeology: Nationalism, Colonialism, and the Past* (Oxford, 2007), B. Effros, *Uncovering the Germanic Past: Merovingian Archaeology in France, 1830–1914* (Oxford, 2012).

15 E. Weber, 'Gauls versus Franks: Conflict and Nationalism', in R. Tombs (ed.), *Nationhood and Nationalism in France. From Boulangism to the Great War, 1889–1918* (London, 1991), pp. 8–21.

16 J. Kwan, 'Transylvanian Saxon Politics, Hungarian State Building and the Case of the Allgemeiner Deutscher Schulverein (1881–82)', *English Historical Review*, 127 (2012), p. 609.

17 M. Baár, *Historians and Nationalism: East-Central Europe in the Nineteenth Century* (Oxford, 2010).

18 J. de Groot, *Empire and History Writing in Britain, c. 1750–2012* (Manchester, 2013).

19 W. A. Koelsch, *Geography and the Classical World. Unearthing Historical Geography's Forgotten Past* (London, 2013), pp. 141–62.

20 J. Bentham, 'Of the Influence of Time and Place in Matters of Legislation', in J. Bowring (ed.), *The Works of Jeremy Bentham* vol. I (Edinburgh, 1843), p. 191.

21 P. Foncin, *Géographie historique* (Paris, 1888); H. Vast and G. Malleterre, *Atlas historique. Formation des états européens* (Paris, 1900); V. Berdoulay, *La Formation de l'Ecole Française de Géographie, 1870–1914* (2nd edn, Paris, 1995). Pupils learn *histoire-géographie* as a whole. This is one lesson taught by one teacher, and there is only one exam at the *baccalauréat*.

22 D. N. Myers, *Re-inventing the Jewish Past. European Jewish Intellectuals and the Zionist Return to History* (Oxford, 1995).

23 R. Miller (ed.), *Britain, Palestine and Empire: The Mandate Years* (Farnham, 2010).

24 W. Laqueur and G. L. Mosse (eds), *Historians in Politics* (London, 1974).

25 W. Clark, *Academic Charisma and the Origins of the Research University* (Chicago, IL, 2006).

26 I. Hesketh, *The Science of History in Victorian Britain: Making the Past Speak* (London, 2011).

27 P. den Boer, *History as a Profession: the Study of History in France, 1818–1914* (Princeton, NJ, 1998).

28 A. J. Toynbee, *A Study of History*, I (Oxford, 1934), pp. 2–5.

29 M. Bentley, *Modernising England's Past: English Historiography in the Age of Modernism, 1870–1970* (Cambridge, 2005).

30 B. G. Smith, *The Gender of History. Men, Women, and Historical Practice* (Cambridge, MA, 1998).

31 E. Jones, *John Lingard and the Pursuit of Historical Truth* (Brighton, 2001). See also, R. T. Gannett, *Tocqueville Unveiled: The Historian and His Sources for The Old Regime and the Revolution* (Chicago, IL, 2003).

32 L. v. Ranke, *The Theory and Practice of History*, edited by G. G. Iggers (2nd edn, Abingdon, 2010).

33 For a recent instance of this view, W. Mulligan and B. Simms (eds), *The Primacy of Foreign Policy in British History, 1660–2000. How Strategic Concerns Shaped Modern Britain* (Basingstoke, 2011).

34 G. G. Iggers and J. M. Powell (eds), *Leopold von Ranke and the Shaping of the Historical Discipline* (Syracuse, NY, 1990).

35 R. Torstendahl, 'Historical professionalism. A changing product of communities within the discipline', *Storia della Storiografia*, 56 (2009), p. 9.

36 J. A. Thomas, 'High Anxiety: World History as Japanese Self-Discovery', in B. Stuchtey and E. Fuchs (eds), *Writing World History 1800–2000* (Oxford, 2003), p. 316.

37 B. A. Elman, *From Philosophy to Philology: Intellectual and Social Aspects of Change in Late Imperial China* (Cambridge, MA, 1984), *Classicism, Politics, and Kinship: The Chang-chou School of New Text Confucianism in Late*

Imperial China (Berkeley, CA, 1990), and 'The Historicization of Classical Learning in Ming-Ch'ing Times', in Q. E. Wang and G. G. Iggers (eds), *Turning Points in Historiography: A Comparative Perspective* (Rochester, NY, 2002), pp. 101–44.

38 A. Boldt, *Leopold von Ranke und Irland* (Stuttgart, 2012), pp. 64–9. The correspondence of Ranke's Irish wife with her family is used to throw light on his views.

39 J. E. Toews, *Becoming Historical: Cultural Reformation and Public Memory in Early Nineteenth-Century Berlin* (Cambridge, 2004); K. Cramer, *The Thirty Years' War and German Memory in the Nineteenth Century* (Lincoln, NE, 2007).

40 E. Giloi, *Monarchy, Myth and Material Culture in Germany, 1750–1950* (Cambridge, 2012).

41 J. M. Brophy, 'The Rhine Crisis of 1840 and German Nationalism: Chauvinism, Skepticism, and Regional Reception', *Journal of Modern History*, 85 (2013), p. 35; M. Hewitson, *Nationalism in Germany, 1848–1866: Revolutionary Nation* (Basingstoke, 2010).

42 J. Heinzen, 'Transnational Affinities and Invented Traditions: The Napoleonic Wars in British and Hanoverian Memory, 1815–1915', *English Historical Review*, 127 (2012), p. 1433.

43 R. J. Evans, 'History Wars', *Guardian*, 13 July 2013, Review section, pp. 2–4.

44 P. J. Geary, *The Myth of Nations: The Medieval Origins of Europe* (Princeton, NJ, 2002).

45 G. Engelmann, 'Der Physikalische Atlas des Heinrich Berghaus und Alexander Keith Johnston's Physical Atlas', *Petermann's Geographische Mitteilungen*, 18 (1964), pp. 133–49.

46 J. Conlin, 'An Illiberal Descent: Natural and National History in the Work of Charles Kingsley', *History* (2011), pp. 167–87, esp. 186–7.

47 R. Challener, *The French Theory of the Nation in Arms, 1866–1939* (New York, 1952); T. Hippler, *Citizens, Soldiers and National Armies. Military Service in France and Germany, 1789–1830* (London, 2006).

48 L. Riall, 'Martyr Cults in Nineteenth-Century Italy', *Journal of Modern History*, 82 (2010), pp. 255–87.

49 J. Tollebeek, 'Historical Representation and the Nation State in Romantic Belgium, 1830–50', *Journal of the History of Ideas*, 59 (1998), pp. 329–53; A. Liakos, 'The Construction of National Time: The Making of the Modern Greek Historical Imagination', *Mediterranean Historical Review*, 16 (2001), pp. 27–42; O. Zimmer, *A Contested Nation: History, Memory and Nationalism in Switzerland, 1761–1891* (Cambridge, 2003).

50 P. Péporté, S. Kmec, B. Majerus and M. Marque, *Inventing Luxembourg: Representations of the Past, Space and Language from the Nineteenth to the Twenty-First Century* (Leiden, 2010).

51 M. P. Gonzalez, 'Legacies, Ruptures and Inertias. History in the Argentine School System', in T. Taylor and R. Guyver (eds), *History Wars and the Classroom. Global Perspectives* (Charlotte, NC, 2012), p. 2.

52   J.-M. Largeaud, *Napoléon et Waterloo: la défaite glorieuses de 1815 à nos jours* (Paris, 2006); E. Fournier, *La Commune n'est pas morte: les usages politiques du passé de 1871 à nos jours* (Paris, 2013).

53   T. Baycroft, *France: Inventing the Nation* (London, 2008).

54   M. Simpson, 'Taming the Revolution? Legitimists and the Centenary of 1789', *English Historical Review*, 120 (2005), pp. 340–64.

55   V. Caron, 'Catholic Political Mobilisation and Antisemitic Violence in Fin de Siècle France: The Case of the Union Nationale', *Journal of Modern History*, 8 (2009), pp. 315–18.

56   D. Goy-Blanquet (ed.), *Joan of Arc, a Saint for all Seasons: Studies in Myth and Politics* (Aldershot, 2003).

57   J. M. Roberts, *The Mythology of the Secret Societies* (New York, 1972).

58   S. P. Huntington, *Who Are We? The Challenges to America's National Identity* (New York, 2004), pp. 123–8.

59   P. Lorcin, 'Rome and France in Africa: Recovering Colonial Algeria's Latin Past', *French Historical Studies*, 25 (2002), pp. 295–329.

60   M. J. S. Rudwick, *Bursting the Limits of Time: The Reconstruction of Geohistory in the Age of Revolution* (Chicago, IL, 2005) and *Worlds before Adam: The Reconstruction of Geohistory in the Age of Reform* (Chicago, IL, 2008).

Chapter Eight

1   S. Bose, *His Majesty's Opponent. Subhas Chandra Bose and India's Struggle Against Empire* (New Delhi, 2011), pp. 264–5. Written by a nephew who is a Harvard professor, this book is highly partisan. See also R. Hayes, *Subhas Chandra Bose in Nazi Germany. Politics, Intelligence and Propaganda, 1941–43* (London, 2011).

2   J. Chatterji, 'Nationalisms in India, 1857–1947', in J. Breuilly (ed.), *The Oxford Handbook of The History of Nationalism* (Oxford, 2013), p. 259.

3   F. Devji, *The Impossible Indian. Gandhi and the Temptation of Violence* (London, 2012).

4   H. Frendo, *Europe and Empire. Culture, Politics and Identity in Malta and the Mediterranean, 1912–1946* (Venera, 2012), pp. 1–16

5   S. Bazzaz, *Forgotten Saints: History, Power and Politics in the Making of Modern Morocco* (Cambridge, MA, 2010).

6   J. McDougall, *History and the Culture of Nationalism in Algeria* (Cambridge, MA, 2006).

7   A. L. Des Forges, *Defeat Is the Only Bad News: Rwanda under Musinga, 1896–1931* (Madison, WI, 2011).

8   D. Deletant and H. Hanak (eds), *Historians as Nation Builders: Central and South-East Europe* (Basingstoke, 1988); F. Hadler and M. Mesenhöller (eds), *Lost Greatness and Past Oppression in East Central Europe:*

Representations of the Imperial Experience in Historiography since 1918 (Leipzig, 2007).

9   M. Bucur and N. M. Wingfield (eds), *Staging the Past: The Politics of Commemoration in Hapsburg Central Europe, 1848 to the Present* (West Lafayette, IN, 2001).

10   O. Miller, 'The Idea of Stagnation in Korean Historiography: From Fukuda Tokuzó to the New Right', *Korean Histories*, 2 (2010), pp. 3–12.

11   C. P. Hanscom, W. K. Lew and Y. Ryu (eds), *Reclaiming Culture: Selected Essays on Korean History, Literature, and Society from the Japanese Colonial Era* (Honolulu, HI, 2013), pp. xi–xxi, esp. xvii, xx.

12   D. Fitzpatrick, 'Ethnic Cleansing, Ethical Smearing and Irish Historians', *History*, 98 (2013), pp. 135–44.

13   F. McGarry, *The Rising: Ireland, Easter 1916* (Oxford, 2010).

14   Morgan's work underplays the significance of Conservative support in twentieth-century Wales, in part because of his views about Welsh identity.

15   B. I. Schwartz, 'Themes in intellectual history: May Fourth and after', in J. K. Fairbank (ed.), *The Cambridge History of China, vol. 12: Republican China, 1912–1949, Part 1* (Cambridge, 1983), p. 410.

16   P. Duara, *Rescuing History from the Nation: Questioning Narratives of Modern China* (Chicago, IL, 1995).

17   M. Arai, *Turkish Nationalism in the Young Turk Era* (Leiden, 1994).

18   S. Seegel, *Mapping Europe's Borderlands: Russian Cartography in the Age of Empire* (Chicago, IL, 2012).

19   M. Todorova, *Bones of Contention: The Living Archive of Vasil Levski and the Making of Bulgaria's National Hero* (Budapest, 2009).

20   G. Herb, *Under the Map of Germany: Nationalism and Propaganda, 1918–1945* (London, 1997).

21   V. G. Liulevcius, *The German Myth of the East: 1800 to the Present* (Oxford, 2009).

22   A. Confino, 'Why Did the Nazis Burn the Hebrew Bible? Nazi Germany, Representations of the Past and the Holocaust', *Journal of Modern History*, 84 (2012), pp. 376–99.

23   H. Schleier, 'German Historiography under National Socialism: Dreams of a Powerful Nation-State and German *Volkstum* Come True', in S. Berger, M. Donovan and K. Passmore (eds), *Writing National Histories: Western Europe since 1800* (London, 1999), pp. 176–88.

24   D. B. Dennis, *Inhumanities. Nazi Interpretations of Western Culture* (Cambridge, 2012).

25   B. Arnold, 'The Past as Propaganda: Totalitarian Archaeology in Nazi Germany', *Antiquity*, 64 (1990), pp. 464–78; L. Olivier and B. Schnitzer (eds), *L'archéologie nazie en Europe de l'Ouest* (Paris, 2007).

26   J. Wright, *A History of Libya* (2nd edn, London, 2012), pp. 150–1.

27   F. Scriba, 'The sacralisation of the Roman past in Mussolini's Italy. Erudition,

aesthetics, and religion in the exhibition of Augustus' Bimillenary in 1937–38', *Storia della Storiografia*, 30 (1996), pp. 19–29.

28 C. Lazzaro and R. J. Crum (eds), *Donatello among the Blackshirts: History and Modernity in the Visual Culture of Fascist Italy* (Ithaca, NY, 2005).

29 J. Hillgarth, 'Spanish Historiography and Iberian Reality', *History and Theory*, 24 (1985), pp. 23–43.

30 M. R. Menocal, *The Ornament of the World: How Muslims, Jews and Christians Created a Culture of Tolerance in Medieval Spain* (New York, 2003); S. Doubleday and D. Coleman (eds), *In the Light of Medieval Spain: Islam, the West, and the Relevance of the Past* (Basingstoke, 2008).

31 S. G. Payne, *Spain: A Unique History* (Madison, WI, 2011).

32 F. Ribeiro de Meneses, 'Salazar, the Portuguese Army and Great War Commemoration, 1936–45', *Contemporary European History*, 20 (2011), pp. 405–18.

33 J. Connelly and M. Grÿttner (eds), *Universities under Dictatorship* (University Park, PA, 2005).

34 R. Gellately, *Stalin's Curse. Battling for Communism in War and Cold War* (New York, 2013).

35 M. Perrie, *The Cult of Ivan the Terrible in Stalin's Russia* (Basingstoke, 2001); D. Brandenberger, *National Bolshevism. Stalinist Mass Culture and the Formation of Modern Russian National Identity, 1931–1956* (Cambridge, MA, 2002); K. M. F. Platt and D. Brandenberger (eds), *Epic Revisionism: Russian History and Literature as Stalinist Propaganda* (Madison, WI, 2006); N. Davies, *Europe. A History* (Oxford, 1996), p. 36; C. E. Black (ed.), *Rewriting Russian History: Soviet Interpretations of Russia's Past* (New York, 1956); G. M. Enteen, *The Soviet Scholar-Bureaucrat: M.N. Pokrovski and the Society of Marxist Historians* (University Park, PA, 1978).

36 For scepticism, nevertheless, about the effectiveness of Soviet propaganda, K. C. Berkhoff, *Motherland in Danger: Soviet Propaganda during World War II* (Cambridge, MA, 2012).

37 E. J. Perry, *Anyuan: Mining China's Revolution Tradition* (Berkeley, CA, 2012).

38 S. R. Schram, 'Mao Tse-tung's thoughts from 1949 to 1976', in MacFarquhar and Fairbank (eds), *China*, vol. 15, part 2, p. 91.

39 A. F. Galindo, *In Search of an Inca. Identity and Utopia in the Andes*, introduced by C. Aguirre and C. F. Walker (Cambridge, 2010), p. 2.

40 R. Coupland (ed.), *The War Speeches of William Pitt the Younger* (Oxford, 1940).

41 P. Clarke, *Mr Churchill's Profession: Statesman, Orator, Writer* (London, 2012).

42 A. Knight, 'The Myth of the Mexican Revolution', *Past and Present*, 209 (2010), pp. 223–73.

43 D. Reynolds, *In Command of History: Churchill Fighting and Writing the Second World War* (London, 2004).

44 K. D. Qualls, *From Ruins to Reconstruction: Urban Identity in Soviet Sevastopol after World War II* (Ithaca, NY, 2009).

45 P. Burrin, *France under the Germans: Collaboration and Compromise* (1997); H. Stenius, M. Österberg and J. Östling (eds), *Nordic Narratives of the Second World War: National Historiographies Revisted* (Lund, 2011).

46 P. Ahonen, *Death at the Berlin Wall* (Oxford, 2011).

47 C. Morina, *Legacies of Stalingrad: Remembering the Eastern Front in Germany since 1945* (Cambridge, 2011).

48 P. Wagner, 'Imagined Revolutions and Real Executions: Hard-Core Nazis and the Spring of 1945', paper given at the German Historical Institute London, 6 June 2013.

49 M. Spiering and M. Wintle (eds), *European Identity and the Second World War* (Basingstoke, 2011).

50 S. Moyn, 'Intellectuals and Nazism', in D. Stone (ed.), *The Oxford Handbook of Postwar European History* (Oxford, 2012), p. 690.

51 J. S. Eder, 'From Mass Murder to Exhibition: Museum Representations to Transatlantic Comparison', *Bulletin of the German Historical Institute*, 50 (Spring 2012), p. 160.

52 C. Saunders, 'History and the Armed Struggle: From Anti-colonial Propaganda to "Patriotic History"?', in H. Melber (ed.), *Transitions in Namibia: Which Changes for Whom?* (Uppsala, 2007), pp. 13–29; M. Wallace, *A History of Namibia* (London, 2011), pp. 313–14.

53 E. Hanna, 'Dublin's North Inner City, Preservationism, and Irish Modernity in the 1960s', *Historical Journal*, 53 (2010), pp. 1013–35.

54 G. Thum, *Uprooted: How Breslau Became Wroclaw during the Century of Expulsions* (Princeton, NJ, 2011); M. Meng, *Shattered Spaces: Encountering Jewish Ruins in Postwar Germany and Poland* (Cambridge, MA, 2011).

Chapter Nine

1 C. Elkins, *Imperial Reckoning: The Untold Story of Britain's Gulag in Kenya* (London, 2005); D. Anderson, *Histories of the Hanged. The Dirty War in Kenya and the End of Empire* (London, 2005).

2 A. Clayton, *Counter-Insurgency in Kenya: A Study of Military Operations Against Mau Mau* (Nairobi, 1976); D. Branch, *Defeating Mau Mau, Creating Kenya: Counterinsurgency, Civil War, and Decolonisation* (Cambridge, 2009).

3 D. G. Boyce, 'From Assaye to the *Assaye*: reflections on British government, force and moral authority in India', *Journal of Military History*, 63 (1999), pp. 643–68. For an 'imperialist' perspective, N. Lloyd, *The Amritsar Massacre: The Untold Story of one Fateful Day* (London, 2011) and, more subtly, M. Doyle, 'Massacre by the Book: Amritsar and the Rules of Public–Order Policing in Britain and India', *Britain and the World*, 4 (2011), pp. 247–68.

4   *Daily Telegraph*, 5 April 2011.

5   K. Bales, *Disposable People: New Slavery in the Global Economy* (Berkeley, CA, 1999).

6   C. Jaffrelot, 'Nation-building and Nationalism: South Asia, 1947–90', in J. Breuilly (ed.), *The Oxford Handbook of the History of Nationalism* (Oxford, 2013), p. 503.

7   S. Gopal (ed.), *Anatomy of a Confrontation* (New Delhi, 1991); A. G. Noorani, *The Babri Masjid Question: 1528–2003* (New Delhi, 2003); B. D. Graham, *Hindu Nationalism and Indian Politics: The Origins and Development of the Bharatiya Jana Sangh* (Cambridge, 1990).

8   R. J. Reid, *Frontiers of Violence in North-East Africa: Genealogies of Conflict since 1800* (Oxford, 2011); G. Kruijtzer, *Xenophobia in Seventeenth-Century India* (Leiden, 2009).

9   M. J. Wiener, 'The Idea of "Colonial Legacy" and the Historiography of Empire', *Journal of the Historical Society*, 13 (2013), pp. 1–32, esp. 22–32.

10 J. Stapleton, *Sir Arthur Bryant and National History in Twentieth-Century Britain* (London, 2005).

11 M. Ferro, *Resentment in History* (Cambridge, 2010), p. 128.

12 *Times*, 20 July 2007.

13 M. Gove, 'What does it mean to be an educated person', speech delivered on 9 May 2013, quoted from Department of Education website. For a broader account, Gove, 'Please sir, I just want to learn more', *Standpoint*, 55 (Sept. 2013), pp. 28–31.

14 J. Moreau, *Schoolbook Nation: Conflicts over American History Textbooks from the Civil War to the Present* (Ann Arbor, MI, 2003).

15 S. Wineburg et al, 'Common Belief and the Cultural Curriculum. An Intergenerational Study of Historical Consciousness', *American Educational Research Journal*, 44 (2007), pp. 40–76, at p. 71.

16 D. Lindaman and K. Ward, *History Lessons: How Textbooks From Around the World Portray U.S. History* (New York, 2004).

17 R. Carroll, *Commandante: Hugo Chávez's Venezuela* (London, 2013).

18 R. E. Neustadt and E. R. May, *Thinking in Time: The Uses of History for Decision Makers* (New York, 1986).

19 *Civil Service World*, 208, 13 March 2013, pp. 1, 4.

20 J. E. Zelizer, 'Clio's Lost Tribe: Public Policy History Since 1978', *Journal of Policy History*, 12 (2000), pp. 370–82.

21 *Times*, 19 November 2010, pp. 6–7.

22 C. Storer, *The Weimar Republic* (London, 2013), pp. 1–2.

23 M. Cordo and H. James, *The European Crisis in the Context of Previous Financial Crises*, NBER Working Paper 19112, June 2013.

24 Thus, the suggestion in a British newspaper in 2013 that François Hollande was similar to Louis XVI, who was overthrown by the revolutionaries, struck

little resonance: D. Moisi, 'Hollande must heed the lessons of Louis XVI', *Financial Times*, 10 April 2013, p. 11.

25 G. Braunthal, *Right-Wing Extremism in Contemporary Germany* (Basingstoke, 2009); C. Miller-Idriss, *Blood and Culture. Youth, Right-Wing Extremism and National Belonging in Contemporary Germany* (Durham, NC, 2009).

26 For good recent works, K. S. Lal, *The Muslim Slave System in Medieval India* (New Delhi, 1994); E. F. Toledano, *As If Silent and Absent: Bonds of Enslavement in the Islamic Middle East* (New Haven, CT, 2007). Lal is regarded as right-wing by Indian Muslim Marxist scholars.

27 For a useful corrective, R. W. Lotchin, 'Japanese Relocation in World War II and the Illusion of Universal Racism', *Journal of the Historical Society*, 11 (2011), pp. 155–81.

28 *New York Times*, 8 April 2010, p. A23.

29 M. Tyler-McGraw, 'Southern Comfort Levels: Race, Heritage Tourism, and the Civil War in Richmond [Virginia]', in J. O. and L. E. Horton (eds), *Slavery and Public History. The Tough Stuff of American Memory* (New York, 2006), p. 167.

30 *Daily Mail*, 28 March 2008, p. 47.

31 T. Baycroft, *Inventing the Nation. France* (London, 2008).

32 H. Lewis, 'Historians and the Myth of American Conservatism', *Journal of the Historical Society*, 12 (2012), p. 45.

33 For the exposition of schools of thought in foreign policy in terms of historical exemplars, W. R. Mead, *Special Providence: American Foreign Policy and How it Changed the World* (New York, 2001).

34 J. Lepore, *The Whites of Their Eyes: The Tea Party's Revolution and the Battle over American History* (Princeton, NJ, 2010).

35 G. S. Wood, 'No Thanks for the Memories', *New York Review of Books*, 9 Febuary 2011, vol. 58, no. 1, p. 40.

36 B. McConville, *The King's Three Faces. The Rise and Fall of Regal America, 1688–1776* (Chapel Hill, NC, 2006), p. 206.

37 G. S. Wood, 'The American Revolution', in M. Goldie and R. Wokler (eds), *The Cambridge History of Eighteenth Century Political Thought* (Cambridge, 2006), p. 613.

38 B. L. Carp, *Defiance of the Patriots: The Boston Tea Party and the Making of America* (New Haven, CT, 2010), pp. 229–32.

39 J. Nye, *Presidential Leadership and the Creation of the American Era* (Princeton, NJ, 2013).

40 For example, *Americanism. The Fourth Great Western Religion* (New York, 2007), by David Gelernter, a computer science professor.

41 F. Dikötter, *The Age of Openness: China Before Mao* (Berkeley, CA 2008).

42 D. Bell and R. Fan (eds), *A Confucian Constitutional Order: How China's Ancient Past Can Shape Its Political Future* (Princeton, NJ, 2012).

43 A. S. Erickson and L. J. Goldstein, 'China Studies the Rise of Great Powers',

in Erickson, Goldstein and C. Lord (eds), *China Goes to Sea. Maritime Transformation in Comparative Historical Perspective* (Annapolis, MD, 2009), pp. 401–25, esp. 401–2, 418–19.

44 R. Marwick, 'The Great Patriotic War in Soviet and Post-Soviet Collective Memory', in D. Stone (ed.), *The Oxford Handbook of Postwar European History* (Oxford, 2012), pp. 692–3.

45 D. Satter, *It Was a Long Time Ago and It Never Happened Anyway* (New Haven, Connecticut, 2012), pp. 3–4; A. Etkind, *Warped Mourning: Stories of the Undead in the Land of the Unburied* (Palo Alto, CA, 2013).

46 J. Surmann, 'Restitution Policy and the Transformation of Holocaust Memory: The Impact of the American "Crusade for Justice" after 1989', *Bulletin of the German Historical Institute*, 49 (fall 2011), p. 48.

47 D. Stone, *Histories of the Holocaust* (Oxford, 2010).

Chapter Ten

1 P. H. Gries, *China's New Nationalism: Pride, Politics and Diplomacy* (Berkeley, CA, 2004).

2 W. Callahan, *China, The Pessoptimist Nation* (Oxford, 2010).

3 E. S. Rawski, 'Reenvisioning the Qing', and H. Ping-ti, 'In Defense of Sinicization', *Journal of Asian Studies*, 55 (1996), pp. 829–50 and 57 (1998), pp. 123–55.

4 R. Mitter, *China's War with Japan, 1937–1945: The Struggle for Survival* (London, 2013), pp. 384–6.

5 C. Rose, *Interpreting History in Sino-Japanese Relations* (London, 1998) and *Sino-Japanese Relations: Facing the Past, Looking to the Future?* (London, 2004).

6 R. Suny, F. M. Göçek and N. M. Daimark (eds), *A Question of Genocide: Armenians and Turks at the End of the Ottoman Empire* (Oxford, 2011).

7 M. L. Anderson, 'Who Still Talked about the Extermination of the Armenians? Imperial Germany and the Armenian Genocide', *Bulletin of the German Historical Institute* [Washington], 49 (fall 2011), pp. 9–10.

8 D. Bloxham, *The Great Game of Genocide: Imperialism, Nationalism, and the Destruction of the Ottoman Armenians* (Oxford, 2005) and *Genocide, The World Wars and the Unweaving of Europe* (London, 2008), pp. 19–98; T. Akçam, *A Shameful Act: The Armenian Genocide and the Question of Turkish Responsibility* (London, 2007).

9 U. U. Üngör, *The Making of Modern Turkey: Nation and State in Eastern Anatolia, 1913–1950* (Oxford, 2011).

10 G. Martin, *Past Futures: The Impossible Necessity of History* (Toronto, 2004).

11 N. Offenstadt (ed.), *Le Chemin des Dames. De l'événement à la mémoire* (Paris, 2004).

12 M. Burleigh, *Moral Combat: A History of World War II* (London, 2010).

13 See, for example, Boris Johnson's contribution to the Chalke Valley Historical Festival on 29 June 2013.

14 H. Heer et al., *The Discursive Construction of History: Remembering the Wehrmacht's War of Annihilation* (Basingstoke, 2008); (for Berlin), U. Staiger, H. Steiner and A. Webber (eds), *Memory Culture and the Contemporary City. Building Sites* (Basingstoke, 2009); B. Niven and C. Paver (eds), *Memorialization in Germany since 1945* (Basingstoke, 2010); J. Arnold, *The Allied Air War and Urban Memory. The Legacy of Strategic Bombing in Germany* (Cambridge, 2011).

15 D. Chuter, 'Munich, or the Blood of Others', in C. Buffet and B. Heuser (eds), *Haunted by History: Myths in International Relations* (Oxford, 1998), pp. 65–79.

16 C. Ingrao, 'Understanding Ethnic Conflict in Central Europe: An Historical Perspective', *Nationalities Papers*, 27 (1999), p. 292.

17 *The Times*, 8 November 2010.

18 'I don't believe there is accurate short-term history', George W. Bush, interview with *The Times*, 9 November 2010.

19 J. Record, 'The Use and Abuse of History: Munich, Vietnam and Iraq', *Survival*, 49 (2007), pp. 163–80. See, more generally, E. R. May, *'Lessons' of the Past: The Use and Misuse of History in American Foreign Policy* (New York, 1973); Y. F. Khong, *Analogies at War: Korea, Munich, Dien Bien Phu, and the Vietnam Decisions of 1965* (Princeton, NJ, 1992), and, for Iraq, J. Tosh, *Why History Matters* (Basingstoke, 2008), pp. 1–4.

20 The adverse consequences of a situation.

21 *Washington Post*, 19 March 2013, p. A13.

22 P. O. Hundley, *Past Revolutions, Future Transformations: What Can the History of Revolutions in Military Affairs Tell Us about Transforming the U.S. Military?* (Santa Monica, CA, 1999); C. S. Gray, *Strategy for Chaos: Revolutions in Military Affairs and the Evidence of History* (London, 2003).

23 J. L. Gaddis, *Surprise, Security and the American Experience* (Cambridge, MA, 2004), pp. 12–13. For cross-currents, past and present, in the Canadian memorialization of the British capture of Quebec in 1759, J. Mathieu, 'Les rappels mémoriels de la guerre de Sept Ans au Canada', in L. Veyssière and B. Fonck (eds), *La guerre de Sept Ans en Nouvelle-France* (Paris, 2011), pp. 101–19.

24 L. Begley, *Why the Dreyfus Affair Matters* (New Haven, CT, 2009).

25 K. Schultheiss, 'The Dreyfus Affair and History', *Journal of the Historical Society*, 12 (2012), pp. 201–2.

26 N. Crafts and P. Fearon (eds), *The Great Depression of the 1930s* (Oxford, 2013).

27 C. S. Maier, 'Lessons from History? German Economic Experiences and the Crisis of the Euro', *Bulletin of the German Historical Institute*, 50 (spring 2012), p. 83.

28 T. Berger, *War, Guilt, and World Politics after World War II* (Cambridge, 2012).

29 R. Markwick, 'The Great Patriotic War in Soviet and Post-Soviet Collective Memory', in D. Stone (ed.), *The Oxford Handbook of Postwar European History* (Oxford, 2012), p. 692.

30 N. C. Fleming, 'Echoes of Britannia: Television History, Empire and the Critical Public Sphere', *Contemporary British History*, 24 (2010), pp. 1–22.

31 T. Hodges, *Western Sahara. The Roots of a Desert War* (Westport, CT, 1983), pp. 85.

32 R. Aldrich, 'Coming to Terms with the Colonial Past: the French and Others', *Arts*, 28 (2006), pp. 91–116.

33 H. Jones, K. Ostberg and N. Randeraad (eds), *Contemporary History on Trial. Europe since 1989 and the role of the expert historian* (Manchester, 2007).

34 E. Barkan, *The Guilt of Nations. Restitution and Negotiating Historical Injustices* (New York, 2000).

35 J. Thompson, *Taking Responsibility for the Past. Reparation and Historical Justice* (Cambridge, 2002).

Chapter Eleven

1 S. Ehrenpreis, 'New Perspectives on an Old Story: The Early Modern Holy Roman Empire Revisited', *Bulletin of the German Historical Institute in London*, 35 (2013), pp. 39–40.

2 I. Morris, *Why the West Rules – For Now: The Patterns of History and What They Reveal about the Future* (London, 2010) and *The Measure of Civilisation. How Social Development Decides the Fate of Nations* (London, 2013).

3 M. Berg (ed.), *Writing the History of the Global. Challenges for the Twenty-First Century* (Oxford, 2013).

4 D. Stone, 'Memory Wars in the "New Europe"', in Stone (ed.), *The Oxford Handbook of Postwar European History* (Oxford, 2012), p. 730.

5 Brochure for opening of the Museum on 7 June 2013, p. 3.

6 I have benefited from hearing a paper by Claire Eldridge on this subject.

7 R. Bin Wong, *China Transformed: Historical Change and the Limits of European Experience* (Ithaca, NY); J. M. Hobson, *The Eastern Origins of Western Civilisation* (Cambridge, 2004).

8 R. Grew, 'Expanding Worlds of World History', *Journal of Modern History*, 78 (2006), p. 897.

9 K. Naumann, 'Teaching the World: Globalization, Geopolitics, and History Education at U.S. Universities', in T. Adam and U. Luebken (eds), *Beyond the Nation: United States History in Transnational Perspective* (Washington, 2008), pp. 124–6.

10 F. Dikötter, *Mao's Great Famine: The History of China's Most Devastating Catastrophe, 1958–62* (London, 2010). Sold in Hong Kong, but not the rest of China. The iconization of Mao has become an essential substructure for maintaining the power of the Communist Party, establishing a difficult issue for historians.

11 M. J. Maynes and A. Waltner, *The Family: A World History* (New York, 2012), p. 122.

12 C. H. Church and R. C. Head, *A Concise History of Switzerland* (Cambridge, 2013), p. 10 (quote), 302.

13 I. Katznelson, *Fear Itself: The New Deal and the Origins of our Time* (New York, 2013).

14 S. M. Stern, *The Cuban Missile Crisis in American Memory: Myths versus Reality* (Palo Alto, CA, 2012).

15 G. Halsall, *Worlds of Arthur. Factions and Fictions of the Dark Ages* (Oxford, 2013), pp. vii–ix, 135–54.

16 J. M. Headley, *The Europeanisation of the World* (Princeton, NJ, 2008).

17 I have benefited from discussing this point with Martin Wiener.

18 F. Fukuyama, 'The End of History?', *The National Interest*, 16 (1989), pp. 3–18.

19 J. Lukacs, 'Popular and Professional History', in D. A. Yerxa (ed.), *Recent Themes in Historical Thinking* (Columbia, SC, 2008), p. 48.

Chapter Twelve

1 W. James and L. van de Vijver (eds), *After the TRC: Reflections on Truth and Reconciliation in South Africa* (Claremont, 2000).

2 H. Jones, K. Östberg and N. Randeraad (eds), *Contemporary History on Trial. Europe since 1989 and the role of the expert historian* (Manchester, 2007); Y. He, *The Search for Reconciliation: Sino-Japanese and German-Polish Relations since World War II* (Cambridge, 2009).

3 L. M. Danforth and R. Van Boeschoten, *Children of the Greek Civil War: Refugees and the Politics of Memory* (Chicago, IL, 2012).

4 A. Applebaum, review in *New York Review of Books*, 24 November 2010, p. 12.

5 *The Times*, 5 June 2013, p. 13.

6 J. H. Maurer, 'A Rising Naval Challenger in Asia: Lessons from Britain and Japan between the Wars', *Orbis*, 56 (2012), p. 645.

7 W. Murray and R. H. Sinnreich (eds), *The Past as Prologue: The Importance of History to the Military Profession* (Cambridge, 2006).

8 *The Times*, 8 March 2013, p. 42.

9 François de Callières, *The Art of Diplomacy* (London, 1717), H. M. A. Keens-Soper and K. W. Schweizer (eds) (Leicester, 1983), p. 175; H. Tanner,

The Battle for Manchuria and the Fate of China. Siping, 1946 (Bloomington, IN, 2013), p. 221.

10 T. L. Haskell, *Objectivity Is Not Neutrality: Exploratory Schemes in History* (Baltimore, MD, 1998); J. Rüsen, 'Morality and Cognition in Historical Thought: A Western Perspective', *Historically Speaking*, vol. 5, no. 4 (March 2004), pp. 40–2.

11 S. Macdonald, *Memorylands: Heritage and Identity in Europe Today* (Abingdon, 2013).

12 M. Völkel, review of *The Oxford History of Historical Writing. V: Historical Writing since 1945* (Oxford, 2011)', in *English Historical Review*, 128 (2013), p. 491.

13 I. Bondebjerg, 'Images of Europe, European Images; Postwar European Cinema and Television Culture', in D. Stone (ed.), *The Oxford Handbook of Postwar European History* (Oxford, 2012), p. 666.

14 E. Ben-Ze'ev, *Remembering Palestine in 1948: Beyond National Narratives* (Cambridge, 2011).

Chapter Thirteen

1 W. Bagehot, 'The History of the Unreformed Parliament, and its Lessons', in Mrs R. Barrington (ed.), *The Works of and Life of Walter Bagehot* (9 vols, London, 1915), III, 222, 271.

2 R. S. Mantena, *The Origins of Modern Historiography in India: Antiquarianism and Philology, 1780–1880* (Basingstoke, 2012).

3 P. Finney, *Remembering the Road to World War Two: International History, National Identity, Collective Memory* (London, 2011).

4 Visited in April 2013.

5 C. Chazelle, S. Doubleday, F. Lifshitz and A. G. Remensnyder (eds), *Why the Middle Ages Matter: Medieval Light on Modern Injustice* (London, 2012).

6 C. Edel, 'John Quincy Adams and American Foreign Policy in a Revolutionary Era', *Foreign Policy Research Institute E-Notes* (February 2013).

SELECTED
FURTHER READING

The focus is on work published since 1990. Earlier studies can be approached through the bibliographies and footnotes in these books.

Anderson, B., *Imagined Communities: Reflections on the Origins and Spread of Nationalism* (2nd edn, London, 1991).

Appleby, J. L., Hunt, L. and Jacob, M., *Telling the Truth about History* (New York, 1994).

Arnold, J., *History: A Very Short Introduction* (Oxford, 2000).

Arnstein, W. (ed.), *Recent Historians of Great Britain: Essays on the Post–1945 Generation* (Ames, IA, 1990).

Ashton, P. and Kean, H. (eds), *People and their Pasts: Public History Today* (Basingstoke, 2009).

—. (eds), *Public History and Heritage Today: People and their Pasts* (Basingstoke, 2012).

Baár, M., *Historians and Nationalism. East-Central Europe in the Nineteenth Century* (Oxford, 2010).

Bazzaz, S., *Forgotten Saints: History, Power, and Politics in the Making of Modern Morocco* (Cambridge, MA, 2010).

Belgrave, M., *Historical Frictions: Maori Claims and Reinvented Histories* (Auckland, 2005).

Bender, T., Katz, P. M., Palmer, C. and the AHA Committee on Graduate Education, *The Education of Historians for the Twenty-first Century* (Urbana, IL, 2004).

Berg, M. (ed.), *Writing the History of the Global Challenges for the Twenty-First Century* (Oxford, 2013).

—*The Search for Normality: National Identity and Historical Consciousness in Germany since 1800* (Oxford, 1997).

Berger, S., Donovan, M. and Passmore, K. (eds), *Writing National Histories: Western Europe since 1800* (London, 1999).

Berkhoffer, R. F., *Fashioning History: Current Practices and Principles* (New York, 2008).

Black, J., *Using History* (London, 2005).

—*The Curse of History* (London, 2008).

Blouin, F. and Rosenberg, W. G., *Processing the Past. Contesting Authority in History and the Archives* (New York, 2002).

Bosworth, R. J. B., *Exploring Auschwitz and Hiroshima: History Writing and the Second World War, 1945–1990* (London, 1993).

Boyd, K. (ed.), *Encyclopedia of Historians and Historical Writing* (London, 1999).

Brady, C. (ed.), *Interpreting Irish History: The Debate on Historical Revisionism* (Dublin, 1994).

Breisach, E., *Historiography: Ancient, Medieval, and Modern* (2nd edn, Chicago, IL, 1994).

Brett, M., *Approaching African History* (Woodbridge, 2013).

Brown, C. G., *Postmodernism for Historians* (London, 2005).

Burguière, A., *The Annales School: An Intellectual History* (Ithaca, NY, 2009).

Burke, P., *The French Historical Revolution: The 'Annales' School, 1929–1989* (Stanford, CA, 1990).

Burrow, J., *A History of Histories: Epics, Chronicles, Romances and Inquiries from Herodotus and Thucydides to the Twentieth Century* (London, 2007).

Cannadine, D. (ed.), *What is History Now?* (Basingstoke, 2001).

—*Making History Now and Then. Discoveries, Controversies and Explorations* (Basingstoke, 2008).

Cannadine, D., Keating, J. and Sheldon, N., *The Right Kind of History* (2011).

Carr, E. H., *What is History?* (2nd edn, Basingstoke, 2001).

Chakrabarty, D., *Provincialising Europe: Postcolonial Thought and Historical Difference* (Princeton, NJ, 1999).

Clifford, R., *Commemorating the Holocaust. The Dilemmas of Remembrance in France and Italy* (Oxford, 2013).

Cohen, R. I. (ed.), *Visualizing and Exhibiting Jewish Space and History* (Oxford, 2012).

Collini, S., *English Pasts: Essays in History and Culture* (Oxford, 1999).

Costello, P., *World Historians and Their Goals. Twentieth-Century Answers to Modernism* (DeKalb, IL, 1993).

Davies, M. L., *Imprisoned by History: Aspects of Historicized Life* (London, 2010).

De Baets, A., *Censorship of History Thought: A World Guide, 1945–2000* (Westport, Connecticut, 2002).

De Francesco, A., *The Antiquity of the Italian Nation. The Cultural Origins of a Political Myth in Modern Italy, 1796–1943* (Oxford, 2013).

De Groot, J., *Consuming History: Historians and Heritage in Contemporary Popular Culture* (London, 2009).

Dillon, R., *History on British Television: Constructing Nation, Nationality and Collective Memory* (Manchester, 2010).

Dobrenko, E., *Stalinist Cinema and the Production of History: Museum of the Revolution* (New Haven, CT, 2008).

Dummitt, C. and Dawson, M. (eds), *Contesting Clio's Craft: New Directions and Debates in Canadian History* (London, 2009).

Dunthorne, H. and Wintle, M. (eds), *The Historical Imagination in Nineteenth-Century Britain and the Low Countries* (Leiden, 2013).

Echternkamp, J. and Martens, S. (eds), *Experience and Memory. The Second World War in Europe* (Oxford, 2010).

Elton, G. R., *The Practice of History* (London, 1961).

Evans, R. J., *In Defence of History* (2nd edn, London, 2004).

Fasolt, C., *The Limits of History* (2004).

Feldherr, A. and Hardy, G. (eds), *The Oxford History of Historical Writing. I: Beginnings to AD 600* (Oxford, 2011).

Feldner, H. et al (eds), *Writing History. Theory and Practice* (London, 2010).

Ferro, M., *Resentment in History* (Cambridge, 2010).

Foot, S. and Robinson, C. F. (eds), *The Oxford History of Historical Writing. II: 400–1400* (Oxford, 2012).

Friesen, G., *Citizens and Nation: An essay on History, Communication and Canada* (Toronto, 2000).

Frisch, M., *A Shared Authority: Essays on the Craft and Meaning of Oral and Public History* (Albany, NY, 1990).

Fuchs, E. and Stuchtey, B. (eds), *Across Cultural Borders: Historiography in Global Perspective* (Lanham, MD, 2002).

Gaddis, J. L., *The Landscape of History: How Historians Map the Past* (Oxford, 2003).

Gallego, A. (ed.), *Historia de la historiografía española* (Madrid, 1999).

Gorman, J., *Historical Judgement. The Limits of Historiographical Choice* (Stocksfield, 2007).

Grafton, A., *What Was History? The Art of History in Early Modern Europe* (Cambridge, 2007).

Granatstein, J. L., *Who Killed Canadian History?* (Toronto, 1998).

Hazareesingh, S., *In the Shadow of the General. Modern France and the Myth of De Gaulle* (Oxford, 2012).

Hein, L. and Selden, M. (eds), *Censoring History: Citizenship and Memory in Japan, Germany, and the United States* (Armonk, NY, 2000).

Hobsbawm, E., *On History* (London, 2002).

Hoffer, P. C., *The Historians' Paradox: The Study of History in Our Time* (New York, 2008).

Iggers, G. C., *Historiography in the Twentieth Century; From Scientific Objectivity to the Postmodern Challenge* (Middletown, CT, 1997).

Iggers, G. C. and Wang, Q. E., *A Global History of Modern Historiography* (Harlow, 2008).

Isaac, J. and Bell, D., *Uncertain Empire. American History and the Idea of the Cold War* (Oxford, 2012).

Jager, S. M. and Mitter, R. (eds), *Ruptured Histories: War, Memory, and the Post-Cold War in Asia* (Cambridge, MA, 2007).

Jenkins, K., *Re-Thinking History* (London, 1991).

Jeppie, S. (ed.), *Toward New Histories for South Africa: On the Place of the Past in our Present* (Cape Town, 2004).

Jones, H., Östberg, K. and Randeraad, N. (eds), *Contemporary History on Trial. Europe since 1989 and the role of the expert historian* (Manchester, 2007).

Jordanova, L., *History in Practice* (2nd edn, London, 2000).

—*The Look of the Past. Visual and Material Evidence in Historical Practice* (Cambridge, 2012).

Kagan, R. L., *Clio and the Crown: The Politics of History in Medieval and Early Modern Spain* (Baltimore, MD, 2009).

Kewes, P., Archer, I. W. and Heal, F. (eds), *The Oxford Handbook of Holinshed's 'Chronicles'* (Oxford, 2012).

Klejn, L. S., *Soviet Archaeology. Trends, Schools, and History* (Oxford, 2012).

Lambert, P. and Schofield, P. (eds), *Making History: An Introduction to the History and Practices of a Discipline* (London, 2004).

Lamont, W. (ed.), *Historical Controversies and Historians* (London, 1998).

Linenthal, E. T. and Englehardt, T. (eds), *History Wars: The Enola Gay and other Battles for the American Past* (New York, 1996).

Lonetree, A. and Cobb, A. J. (eds), *The National Museum of the American Indian: Critical Conversations* (Lincoln, NE, 2008).

Low, P., Oliver, G. and Rhodes, P. J. (eds), *Cultures of Commemoration. War Memorials, Ancient and Modern* (Oxford, 2012).

Lowenthal, D., *The Past is a Foreign Country* (Cambridge, 1985).

Macintyre, S., Maiguashca, J. and Pók, A. (eds), *The History of Historical Writing. IV: 1800–1945* (Oxford, 2011).

Macintyre, S. and Clark, A., *The History Wars* (Melbourne, 2003).

Macmillan, M., *The Uses and Abuses of History* (London, 2009).

McCullagh, C. B., *The Logic of History. Putting Postmodernism in Perspective* (London, 2004).

Majumdar, R., *Writing Postcolonial History* (London, 2010).

Mandler, P., *History and National Life* (London, 2002).

Meriwether, J. L. and D'Amore, L. M. (eds), *We Are What We Remember. The American Past Through Commemoration* (Newcastle, 2012).

Munslow, A., *The Routledge Companion to Historical Studies* (London, 2000).

Nicholls, J. (ed.), *School History Textbooks across Cultures* (Oxford, 2006).

O'Sullivan, L., *Oakeshott on History* (2003).

Paces, C., *Prague Panoramas: National Memory and Sacred Space in the Twentieth Century* (Pittsburgh, PA, 2009).

Peterson, D. and Macola, G. (eds), *Recasting the Past: History Writing and Political Work in Modern Africa* (Athens, OH, 2009).

Rabasa, J., Satoj, M., Tortarolo, E. and Woolf, D. (eds), *The Oxford History of Historical Writing. III: 1400–1800* (Oxford, 2012).

Rao, V. N., Shulman, D. and Subrahmanyam, S., *Textures of Time: Writing History in South India, 1600–1800* (London, 2003).

Revel, J. and Levi, G. (eds), *Political Uses of the Past: The Recent Mediterranean Experience* (London, 2002).

Rigney, A., *Imperfect Histories. The Elusive Past and the Legacy of Romantic Historicism* (Ithaca, NY, 2001).

Rublack, U. (ed.), *A Concise Companion to History* (Oxford, 2012).

Rüsen, J. (ed.), *Western Historical Thinking: An Intercultural Debate* (Oxford, 2002).

Sahu, B. P., *The Changing Gaze. Regions and the Constructions of Early India* (Oxford, 2013).

Samuel, R., *Theatres of Memory* (London, 1994).

Schivelbiesch, W., *The Culture of Defeat: On National Trauma, Mourning, and Recovery* (London, 2003).

Schneider, A. and Woolf, D. (eds), *The Oxford History of Historical Writing V: Historical Writing Since 1945* (Oxford, 2011).

Scott, J. W., *Gender and the Politics of History* (2nd edn, NY, 1999).

Seixas, P., *Theorising Historical Consciousness* (Buffalo, NY, 2004).

Semple, S., *Perceptions of the Prehistoric in Anglo-Saxon England* (Oxford, 2013).

Seraphim, F., *War Memory and Social Politics in Japan, 1945–2005* (Cambridge, MA, 2006).

Smith, A. D., *The Nation Made Real. Art and National Identity in Western Europe, 1600–1850* (Oxford, 2013).

Spiegel, G. M., *The Past as Text: The Theory and Practice of Medieval Historiography* (Berkeley, 1997).

Stuchtey, B. and Fuchs, E. (eds), *Writing World History 1800–2000* (Oxford, 2003).

Stuchtey B. and Wende, P. (eds), *British and German Historiography 1750–1950* (Oxford, 2000).

Suny, R. G., Gocek, F. M. and Naimark, N. M. (eds), *A Question of Genocide. Armenians and Turks at the End of the Ottoman Empire* (Oxford, 2013).

Taylor, T. and Guyver, R. (eds), *History Wars and the Classroom* (Charlotte, NC, 2012).

Thorstendahl, R. (ed.), *An Assessment of Twentieth-Century Historiography: Professionalism, Methodologies, Writings* (Stockholm, 2000).

Tilmans, K., Vree, F. v. and Winter, J. (eds), *Performing the Past. Memory, History and Identity in Modern Europe* (Amsterdam, 2010).

Todorova, M., *Bones of Contention: The Living Archive of Vasil Levski and the Making of Bulgaria's National Hero* (Budapest, 2009).

Tosh, J. (ed.), *Historians on History* (3rd edn, Harlow, 2000).

—*Why History Matters* (Basingstoke, 2008).

—*The Pursuit of History. Aims, methods and new directions in the study of modern history* (5th edn, Harlow, 2010).

Tyrrell, I., *Historians in Public: The Practice of American History, 1890–1970* (Chicago, IL, 2005).

Unger, J. (ed.), *Using the Past to Serve the Present: Historiography and Politics in Contemporary China* (Armonk, NY, 1993).

Van Liere, K., Ditchfield, S. and Louthan, H. (eds), *Sacred History. Uses of the Christian Past in the Renaissance World* (Oxford, 2012).

Walls, A., *The Cross-Cultural Process in Christian History: Studies in the Transmission and Application of Faith* (London, 2002).

Wang, Q. E. and Fillafer, F. L. (eds), *The Many Faces of Clio: Cross-Cultural Approaches to Historiography* (Oxford, 2006).

White, H., *The Fiction of Narrative: Essays on History, Literature, and Theory, 1957–2007* (Baltimore, MD, 2010).

Wickham, C. (ed.), *Marxist History – Writing for the Twenty-First Century* (London, 2007).

Windschuttle, K., *The Killing of History* (Sydney, 1994).

—*The Fabrication of Aboriginal History* (Sydney, 2002).

Winks, R. (ed.), *Oxford History of the British Empire, Volume 5: Historiography* (Oxford, 2001).

Wintel, M., *The Image of Europe. Visualising Europe in Cartography and Iconography throughout the Ages* (Cambridge, 2009).

Wood, I., *The Modern Origins of the Early Middle Ages* (Oxford, 2013).

Wood, G., *The Purpose of the Past. Reflexions on the Uses of History* (London, 2008).

Woolf, D. R. (ed.), *A Global Encyclopedia of Historical Writing* (London, 1998).

Wormell, D., *Sir John Seeley and the Uses of History* (Cambridge, 1980).

Yoshida, T., *The Making of the 'Rape of Nangking': History and Memory in Japan, China and the United States* (New York, 2006).

Zimmerman, J., *Whose America? Culture Wars in the Public Schools* (Cambridge, MA, 2002).

INDEX